FIND YOUR VOICE

Save Your Life 3

Dearest Reader,
May the
magic of Spirit
always be
with you! ♡
Laura

DIANNA LEEDER

FEATURING

Jen Bates
Tiffany Marie Boerner
Dr. Jessica Chardoulias
Laura Di Franco
Vila Donovan
Melissa Jolly Graves
Jennifer Highmoor
Ashley Hoobler
Maysha
Rev. Pam McDonel
Laura McKinnon
Ashley Moon
Rev. Mary Perry
Lyndi Picard
Mary Raddell
Joy Resor
Shelly Roman
na Maria Snowden
Michele Tatos
Carly Tway
Hayley Verney
Judithann Walz
Sheri Welsh
Atlantis Wolf

Powerful Healers
Spiritual Stories

Find Your Voice, Save Your Life 3: Powerful Healers, Spiritual Stories
Dianna Leeder

© Copyright 2021 Dianna Leeder

Published by Brave Healer Productions

ISBN: 978-1-954047-37-2
eISBN: 978-1-954047-36-5

CRAVE
MORE
>> LIFE

Are you ready to live out loud?

Sign up for

How to Start Finding Your Voice

at

www.cravemorelife.com

Join

Find Your Voice Women

on Facebook

https://www.facebook.com/groups/findyourvoicewomen

Table of Contents

Foreword
by Laura Di Franco
page i

Introduction
page v

A Message to Readers With Their Own Silenced Voices
page ix

Dedication
page xi

CHAPTER 1
Making Space
The Newness of Spirituality
By Dianna Leeder CPCC
page 1

CHAPTER 2
LightenUp!
The Frequency of Angelic Humor and How It Changed My Life
By Jen Bates, Energy Medicine Practitioner
page 8

CHAPTER 3
Not Broken
A Spiritual Journey Through Pain
By Gina Maria Snowden L.Ac. Licensed Acupuncturist, Yoga Teacher
page 15

CHAPTER 4
Loving Every "Mistake"
How to Forgive and Heal Your Heart
By Rev. Mary Perry, Angel Intuitive and Healer
page 24

CHAPTER 5
The Powerful Voices in Your Head
Learning the Language of Your Soul
By Laura Di Franco, MPT, Publisher
page 32

CHAPTER 6
Healing Ancestral Trauma
A Discovery of Our Galactic Family Tree
By Vila Donovan L.Ac. Licensed Acupuncturist, Licensed Herbalist,
Primary Care Physician, Galactic Ambassador
page 41

CHAPTER 7
The Beauty of Impermanence
How I Expanded My Awareness Through the Breath
By Sheri Darya Welsh, MPS, RYT200, RCYT
page 49

CHAPTER 8
Just Shut Up and Step Over the Fucking Line!
The Healing Power of Words
By Rev. Pam McDonel, LMT
page 58

CHAPTER 9
Resisting Surrender
Fighting to Find Myself
By Mary Raddell, Intuitive Bodyworker, Transformational Coach and Healer
page 67

CHAPTER 10
Finding Understanding Through the Akashic Records
How I Stopped Struggling and Started Co-creating My Life
By Ashley Hoobler, Life Coach, Akashic Records Master Practitioner,
NLP and Quantum Healer, Clairvoyant Energy Reader and Healer
page 76

CHAPTER 11
Signs From Spirit
Reminders of Faith, Hope, and Love
By Laura McKinnon, E-RYT
page 85

CHAPTER 12
Immerse Into Stillness
Connecting to Freedom and Peace
By Hayley Verney, ND Human Resource Management,
Certified Life Coach, Yoga Teacher
page 93

CHAPTER 13
Letters to the Future
By Joy Resor, Spiritual Mentor, Minister, Joy-Bringer
page 103

CHAPTER 14
Learning to Trust My Soul's Whisper
In the Midst of Chaos the Soul Speaks the Loudest
By Carly Tway, Certified Sound Therapist
and Vibrational Alignment Specialist
page 114

CHAPTER 15
Listen for the Whispers
Learning to Trust Spirit in a Noisy World
By Shelly Roman
page 123

CHAPTER 16
Music is Truly a Universal Language
And Songwriting is Truly My Earliest, Greatest Gift
By Maysha, Singer/Songwriter, Author, Vlogger, and Joy-bringer
page 132

CHAPTER 17
Embodying Strength, Courage, and Love
Moving Forward by Freeing Yourself From the Past
By Lyndi Picard
page 141

CHAPTER 18
Healing Through Loss
How Our Dreams Guide Us
By Dr. Jessica Chardoulias, PharmD, BCPS
page 149

CHAPTER 19
Decluttering Magick and Empowerment
Letting Go and Getting Free
By Ashley Moon, MA.
page 156

CHAPTER 20
Forging the Phoenix from the Fires of Perfection
By Jennifer Highmoor
page 164

CHAPTER 21
You May Love Differently
Healing Through Trauma
By Tiffany Marie Boerner, Light Channel,
Evidential Medium, Energy Mentor/Teacher
page 173

CHAPTER 22

The Voices in My Head Said I Wasn't Crazy
How They Proved I Was Sane
Melissa Jolly Graves, L.P.N., ORDM, Seer, Priestess, Shaman,
Reiki Master, Documentarian, Philosopher
page 182

CHAPTER 23

Disarm Your Fear
Complete Freedom In One Circular Breath
By Atlantis Wolf
page 191

CHAPTER 24

Stepping Into My Light with Faith, Trust, and Intuition
By Judithann Walz
page 201

CHAPTER 25

Acceptance
Sometimes Our Spirit Has Other Plans
By Michele Tatos
page 209

A Last Message to Readers
What Can You Do With Your Spiritual Gifts?
page 218

My Wholehearted Thanks
page 219

Foreword

by Laura Di Franco

My entire spiritual healing journey was about finding and using my voice and reclaiming the worthiness to do so. When Dianna came to me with the *Find Your Voice, Save Your Life* book idea, I shot back a quick, "I'm in!" It was a full-on Hell Yes!

The profound healing in my life was in moments when, with awareness on point, I spoke up and shared myself authentically, even when the inner critic raged with doubt and fear. My voice was the path for healing. That healing was physical, mental, and spiritual. I move words from my heart to my tongue and hear that vibration as it passes my lips and lands on the ears of my friends, family, colleagues, and sometimes strangers.

In those tiny moments, I heal. My truth is witnessed and acknowledged. I'm guided to stand tall inside my worthiness.

Dianna is a champion for helping women find their voices. With a style that's part kick-ass and part loving compassion, she guides women to their truth, holds your hand while you face it, and then stands closely by on the sidelines to cheer while you shout that truth from the mountaintop.

That voice sounds something like,

"I am here!"

"I matter!"

"I will claim my place in the world and leave my mark!"

And Dianna's voice always creates a magnificent chorus with yours:

"Yes, you are here!"

"Yes, you matter!"

"Yes, you are claiming your place in the world today!"

Dianna knows how it feels to be silenced and discounted. She understands the vulnerability in the stories of her authors. And she preaches the importance of sharing those stories as a path to strength and empowerment.

Partnering with her in this book series made sense from the beginning, bringing a healer and a women's empowerment coach together, trailblazing through the darkness so others may see the light of their truth, heal the wounds, and help give other women permission to do the same. That's what I call badassery.

Warriors practice awareness, persevere on the path, and show up with an indomitable spirit day after day. Dianna is one of those warriors, and being guided by her in this very powerful collaboration of women has been an honor. I know her authors feel the same because I asked them to help me with this foreword, and here's what they said:

"Dianna inspired me to write my stories when I never imagined this was something I could do. She shares her own vulnerability and that makes me feel safe to share mine."

"Dianna makes room for not just the story of struggle but for the story of empowerment. She's curious and compassionate and engenders an aura of trust."

"Dianna has Swan as her power animal (according to what I see in her). It's no surprise. Swan is one of the oldest totem animals, and Dianna is an old soul. I see her 'swanness' in the way she goes with the flow, always a presence of grace and beauty regardless of outside circumstances; un-flusterable. She carries herself centered in her feminine intuition. Her inner beauty shines through her and into every face she meets. She even makes swearing feel feminine and graceful. She's that kind of Earth Mama."

"Dianna exudes kindness and acceptance. She is supportive in a way that is empowering and uplifting."

I will echo all of these beautiful words and add that you're about to read a book full of stories from women just like Dianna, who have a genuine desire to walk their walk and share their powerful stories so that you feel inspired to do the same. Remember, you, amazing reader, are a healer, too. Everyone is. It's a matter of walking through the world with your heart and soul open and taking responsibility for your energy. We can all do that.

When you read this book, understand the heart and soul behind these pages and stories and feel the love and encouragement offered. It's genuine. It's available. This project is for you, amazing reader. And your transformational journey is here!

Introduction

The time is now. Don't wait; the world needs this book right now.

Was that my intuition talking, or was it my ego?

At first, I wasn't sure; I just knew that I couldn't let go of that sense of urgency that filled my body and said to bring this book to life.

With what I'm feeling, it's my intuition for sure.

I fondly refer to myself as a spiritual newbie. Any time in my life that healers have suggested I could use my own healing gifts to support myself, my family, or my clients, I shut it down.

No way do I have such gifts. I don't think I'm connected to Spirit in that way. I could never do the things I've witnessed others do when they're connected.

It's not that I thought it wasn't real. On the contrary, I knew that somehow it was very real. I knew that beyond our worldly experiences, there are beings from other dimensions here to support us and guide us to unconditionally love ourselves to the degree that we can extend that unconditional love to others.

Truthfully, I was in awe of those with spiritual gifts. I have a close friend, a medium, who has been my go-to healer for over 20 years whenever I need some new perspectives or to connect with the love of those who have passed. At first, it was my mother. "Please tell her I love her," I said during a reading. "She can hear you," Frankie replied.

And there it was. Joyful emotion took over my whole body along with an undeniable knowing and acceptance that flowed through my heart space, telling me that there is indeed existence outside of our physical earthly selves. With my eyes overflowing with tears, I could feel my mom's presence around me just like when she was with us, her arms surrounding me in one of her cozy, healing hugs.

She always gave the best hugs.

My heart swelled in my chest, making room for the knowing that had arrived, the knowing that I could trust without any doubt that my mom was with me again. There was no denying what was happening, and in that moment, my belief was solidified.

Since then, I've learned much about my own spiritual gifts. Frankie remains my go-to healer, still helping me hear the messages of not just my mom but now also my dad, grandparents, and other ancestors. Oh yeah, and a woman who was a sorcerer with me in a previous life.

I'm grateful and incredibly honored to have met the authors in this book, all women who are comfortable embracing their spiritual gifts in service of others. As I clicked to end the Zoom interviews with each of them, I was filled with such respect for the wholeness they radiate, the simple acceptance of others, and their dedication and commitment to using their gifts to support other beings to live in pure alignment with themselves. They have gifts that, in turn, become gifts to others.

That's why this book is so important to me. These authors have found their spiritual voices and offer their experiences to you, the reader, with the intention to support you on your spiritual path to wholeness. For those who read that last sentence and assume that your spiritual path is different from your wholeness, as you read through this book you will learn that it needn't be.

All our authors are professional spiritual healers, but most didn't just wake up knowing and embracing their gifts. Some were stopped by being told they were imagining things. Some had their gifts show themselves when they were in times of deep emotional turmoil and spiritual need. Some, like me, denied their ability and kept their gifts silenced. We all have had to understand and accept ourselves and our abilities, acknowledge the power of connecting with Spirit as a healing tool for ourselves and others, and come out of the spiritual closet. Now we all actively help other beings heal through our connection to Spirit.

As you read the story of each healer, you'll see that we don't all offer our magic in the same way. Just as each healer has different gifts, they also offer those gifts differently to support others.

We are yoga instructors, writers, coaches, publishers, songwriters, and even a comic. The common denominator is that we use our spiritual connection to better the world, beginning with ourselves. We are making a difference.

We don't all grow up with the message that our spiritual gifts are okay, real, or valid. Sometimes we're told we're imagining things, that there is no one under the bed, that our gifts are creepy, that there are no beings who keep our children up at night because they know they can be seen by them and they want to play. We're told this means we're kind of crazy, and, "let's go see a doctor." We're told there is no room in our family's religious beliefs for those kinds of things or that we're different. As you will read about, those responses can leave us feeling wrong or like we don't belong, and we suppress or deny our gifts to be accepted and loved.

On the other side of our experiences, some grow up in gifted families who teach their descendants to love and embrace their gifts without fear. With that invitation, we're left feeling accepted for whoever we are, free to embrace our gifts and engage with them in whatever way we choose.

Truthfully, we are all gifted. Do you remember your childhood imaginary friend? We're all born with the ability to connect with Spirit, without the fear or denial that grabs us so tightly later in life. Imagine a world where we have access to more than just what life looked like from our own kitchen table.

This book is not a debate about what is acceptable as a spiritual and/or religious practice. Nor is it a conversation about what is a better practice than something else. This world has enough separation and division to deny anyone their rightful choice of how they relate to Spirit, even if they decide they don't relate at all.

It's about the personal and global freedom that comes from being connected to Spirit, Source, God, the Universe, the Divine, whatever you may want to call it. That freedom looks like unconditional love for ourselves, living from our overflow instead of running ourselves into the ground by refusing to be our own caretakers. It looks like acceptance of others over the judgment that creates limited beliefs in them and us. It looks like peace over all levels of human separation.

In other words, it's about feeling good about being in full alignment with ourselves and allowing that to radiate out around us, with the strength and resilience of knowing that we are whole and we are never alone. We are always supported.

This book is about finding our spiritual voices.

Because when we do, our lives and the lives of those we touch will change.

With gratitude, love, and strong voices,

A Message to Readers With Their Own Silenced Voices

Although incredibly joyous, life can be hard for women. We are natural nurturers, something that needs to be celebrated as powerful and healing. But when our womanly presence gets mixed up with the still common societal messages about what we should and should not be doing, saying, or being, our beliefs about ourselves can take a huge hit.

That's where things stop connecting, we stop connecting, and our inner selves and voices become quiet. It's where the roadblocks show up, where we question our ability to have the life we truly want and chase after things that serve everyone else besides us.

No matter what gets us there, know this:

We always have ourselves to come back to.

This book is meant for you.

Our spiritual voices are easily silenced. Fear and disbelief, the latter sometimes fueled by fear, can determine if and when we decide to respond to any calling to connect with our version of Spirit.

Having and using spiritual gifts is often considered woo or something that lives solely in the imagination, not in real life. While some of the interpretation of what we see, hear, sense, and feel spiritually requires our imagination, there is more to our spiritual gifts than just dismissive terms.

This book is not an indoctrination. It's a place to grow into our voices in one more way. Being sovereign to ourselves, we know all the different parts that we need to keep fed and nourished to show up whole in our lives. Spirituality is one.

Have you had undeniable spiritual experiences?

Most people have; we are all born fully connected. Maybe that's why you picked up this book.

Consider this. The women who wrote on these pages are no different than you or your neighbors. We were born with the gifts we now practice in service to others but had to consciously decide to be true to those gifts and be exactly who we are.

These pages offer an awareness tool that I invite you to embrace as you would any other tool.

Absorb the writers' experiences and decide how each one might help you create more awareness of the path to your best self, in this case, your spiritual voice.

Allow your awareness to be massaged enough to recognize both what you need spiritually in your life, as well as the potential to consider or develop your own spiritual gifts.

Spirituality or soul work is truly just one additional place to connect with and support ourselves. And Spirit is all about being exactly who we are, who we are meant to be. It's part of our purpose to support ourselves to the degree that we can serve the world. It's living life, loving ourselves enough to be true to ourselves. No hesitancy, no drama worth engaging in, no apologies.

Life-changing things can happen for us when we are being true to every part of ourselves, including spiritually. We experience what we need to, when we need to, and all that's left is for us is to give ourselves permission to explore through the eyes of our own awareness.

Do you have spiritual gifts like sensing, hearing, seeing, feeling, or clear intuition?

Maybe picking up this book is the synchronicity that you are on the right path. Go there with joy, self-determination, and wholehearted love for yourself.

I promise you won't be disappointed.

Please join my Facebook group, **Find Your Voice Women**. The authors of this book are there, along with all the authors of the *Find Your Voice, Save Your Life* book series, to share more about their experiences and help you find your spiritual voice.

Joy is our birthright, and strong voices get us there.

Find your voice, save your life.

Dedication

To all the spiritual healers who have made a difference in my life over the past two decades: You taught me what we humans can see, hear, sense, smell, and feel when we're open to Spirit that isn't obvious to everyone. You offered me guidance I never knew existed.

To our brave, amazing authors: You've opened up a part of your life that in some circles is considered simply out there, crazy or weird. Yet you showed up fully embracing who you are in service to others. You are here to show others that they, too, can unlock their own spiritual connection. You're offering them the opportunity to find their own spiritual voices and live incredible, whole lives.

Thank you for bringing the vision of this book alive and for furthering my own awareness that much more.

I am grateful.

CHAPTER 1

Making Space
The Newness of Spirituality

By Dianna Leeder CPCC

"We all have wings,
But some of us don't know why…"

NEVER TEAR US APART, INXS

Awesome, *the Emergency Department isn't busy!*
That's a good thing. In and out with a prescription is a good thing.
As I awkwardly walked through the snow and cold at 10 pm on a Sunday night through the front door of the E.D., I knew that my thinking could change in a heartbeat.

Sure enough, after going through the routine questions and screenings that one always wonders the necessity of, I watched the wide doors begin to swing open with regularity, bringing in people whose medical emergencies were kept as private as possible, without much success.

How do they pull that off, anyway? This E.D. space is so small, and medical workers need to be in the moment to react to save or repair a life, not worry about who can hear what.

Sitting on a hard table covered in white sheets that smelled like bleach, I was flooded with feeling somewhat unworthy to be there. *Who was I to take up space that someone else may need more than me?*

My emergency was not life or death, not at that point anyway, but it happened after regular doctor and clinic hours, so I had no choice but to be there for urgent care. Even knowing that medical professionals were well versed in triage didn't stop the thoughts. This was still tough for me. I've worked hard to gain the clarity that my life is about using my voice to get my needs met, not despite someone else, but in acceptance of them. Being in the E.D.

took me back to old mindset patterns that said I should be okay putting everyone before me.

Put that shit-thinking away, Dianna. You know it's not one or the other. It's both.

It didn't help any that we were in the second wave of COVID. The fear of being exposed was big for me, especially being in a place with ill people hanging out and after being isolated for several months in the safe comfort of my home. *Omg...doorknobs, sink faucets, and toilet handles!* I waffled between the fear of being exposed and feeling claustrophobic wearing a mask for far too long.

Earlier that evening, I recognized the all too familiar feeling associated with a UTI; it had happened so many times before. The extended lower abdomen, the recognizable frequent need to pee, the painful spastic urgency of always feeling like there was more, the bleeding that I always associated with the peeling away of the walls of my urinary tract.

I knew the symptoms well, and I also knew that they wouldn't go away without the aid of an antibiotic. I disliked that part immensely. Prescription drugs have not been part of my health plan for some time, opting instead for a healthy lifestyle and natural supplements that kept infection and illness at bay. Yet here I was during the dark hours of the night, waiting my turn to be seen by a doc amid the bright lights, smells of strong disinfectant, and busy but hushed voices.

Alone with my thoughts and with a close-to-dead phone battery needing to be preserved to send a message to my husband, who sat patiently in the car so as not to offend COVID restrictions, I searched my brain for things to occupy my time.

Sleep would be nice, but that's not happening.

By then, I was three hours into what was a five-hour wait. Then it came to me.

Use your healing hands.

When I tried to dismiss that thought, a stronger one came.

Trust your ability.

Since I was sure by then that I couldn't have much bladder left after so many trips to the bathroom, I answered back, "Why not? What do I have to lose?"

I started by breathing deeply into myself and releasing the

doubt that lingered in my head as I exhaled. *In, and out. In, and out.* I asked my mom, dad, grandparents on both sides, guides, angels, all my other ancestors, and my friend Annabelle, with who I shared a past life as a sorcerer, to please help me heal this UTI.

I rubbed my hands gently but intentionally together, feeling the friction and the heat. Gently pulling my hands apart, I acknowledged the presence of a ball of energy between them while still a little skeptical that the ball could truly have any effect on my spasming bladder. The skepticism was quickly replaced with an intuitive reassurance to simply trust. I placed my hands on my lower abdomen area, accepting that reassurance to mean that I indeed have healing hands as well as the support to use them.

I felt the energy from my hands on my belly and visualized what was happening. I saw the healing energy, the heat sinking and absorbing into me, seeking out the infection and ridding me of it, not unlike a surf-worthy wave of healing strength. I felt the power of all those I had asked to help me. I left my hands where I had placed them and thanked my backup team. Within 90 minutes, my symptoms were gone. The need to pee was close to normal, and the bleeding had stopped.

Did that actually just happen?

"I'm Dr so-and-so, and I understand you're here for a UTI. Tell me your symptoms," said the guy in green scrubs entering the room at hour five of my E.D. visit. As I told him the symptoms I came in with, the good girl in me wanted to be honest about them no longer being there, but the more experienced woman in me knew that sharing that fact and how it came about would not land well. He had a matter-of-fact look on his face as he handed me the prescription. I shoved it in the pocket of my jeans and left with it, but I didn't use it.

I have been told many times that I have healing gifts. Healers would say, "Your hands are healing hands." "You vibrate at a different frequency with magical colors." "Your gifts are limitless." But I brushed off those and every other suggestion like one brushes off fallen crumbs.

And yet, I knew there was something different about me, something different than my family and friends.

I would base who to sit beside at a meeting or social event on what I called their vibe. *I'm just not good with bitchy people.*

My empathic nature made my heart physically ache when I saw something or someone being hurt. *I'm just a lover, not a fighter.*

My intuition has always made it easy to identify the blocks my clients and others carry to being themselves. *I'm just good at what I do.*

It turns out all those things are divine gifts. Gifts that we are all born with but not all understand and embrace, like I didn't.

While I ignored my own gifts as being real, I didn't ignore my belief in the existence and the healing power of Spirit.

I spoke regularly to my loved ones who had passed and felt their presence comfort me.

"All energies must leave the room now; these kids need to sleep!" I would say loudly to clear our bedrooms each night, removing energies that kept them awake or frightened.

A lover of real estate, I could recognize by the familiar tingling in my body when Spirit was present in a property and if that Spirit was light or dark.

Even though Spirit was part of my life in those ways, I never accepted that I could be a conduit of healing energy and love. My belief that Spirit was real was strong; accepting my own spiritual voice was not.

"There's a woman living in your house, and she's pissed that you're ripping up her kitchen." *Okay, I'll talk to her. (Thanks, Maria, we're good to get back to the renovations now.)*

"Did you know you have a blue dragon flying around you?" *No, I didn't know that but, cool!*

"You teach women how to use their voices; it's time for you to use yours more." *Boom. There's no ignoring that spiritual wake-up call.*

When I look back, it all makes sense. I allowed my voice to be shut down for a long time because of my own limiting beliefs and lack of awareness. Then there I was, being nudged by Spirit to use my voice in one more way. The funny thing is that learning to use our voices, spiritually or otherwise, follows the same path.

That path is about three things, based on my newbie research.

First, there is taking responsibility for ourselves and our experiences. We can't do that if we remain in negative mindsets or behaviors based on fear or blame others for our circumstances. All that takes us away from who we really are.

Next, we have knowing exactly who we are authentically. This isn't just knowing whether we're right-handed or left. It's an awareness of who we are at our deepest core. It's what will lead us to the path of least resistance to get as close as we can to our highest self.

And lastly, we must hold ourselves to honoring and being our own truth, being that highest self. This one is always a battle for most women at some point in their lives, if not throughout, as it has been for me. We know what we should do, but we don't do it. There are other things and other people who get dubbed more important than us. There are always times when we don't get it right, but we're not here to betray ourselves by ignoring parts that the Universe is nudging us to let out, spiritually or otherwise. And she will nudge us, without a doubt. Sometimes more obviously than others, but always as a way to remind us of what we're missing by not being in integrity with our true selves. When we pretend to be anything other than who and what we came here to be, we hold ourselves back. We hold our soul's essence back.

My E.D. experience and knowing how our lives can change when we start living our truth were my spiritual turning points. I was ready for whatever more was in store for me. If I could heal myself from a UTI, I was ready to step into accessing any of the gifts I was intended to have whenever I was intended to have them.

"Holy shit!" My head was spinning.

Is this really happening?

What do I do now?

Will things just happen, or is there something I'm supposed to do?

Will I be able to see and hear Spirit, adding to my knowing and feeling?

Will I have the guts to put my gifts out there so I can help my clients even more?

Will I tell people who know me now and are likely disbelievers?

Calm down and hold all the questions! None of this can be rushed, but its newness can be enjoyed.

That newness is one of the most exciting things I have ever experienced. Here is this thing that's so much more than a thing, that's already changed my life by spiritually nudging me to set the bar higher to be myself, and to offer my magic in service to others.

What isn't exciting about that?

I'm like a child who walks into a whole new world full of

amazing things that I have never seen, heard, or considered before. And depending on divine desires and how connected I allow myself to be, all of those amazing things are open to me. Quite honestly, the grin on that child's face may never come off. I feel blessed and am also incredibly grateful.

Allowing myself to accept my spiritual gifts was a process. I began by accepting that there are no coincidences in the world; nothing is random. I've often pondered decisions just to come across articles or messages shortly after that telling me why I should decide one way or the other. I've had different animals show up in places they don't frequent, then learn that they represent a specific message that encourages me to keep on the path I'm following or follow a new one. I've met people I felt destined to meet and then learned crucial lessons from them that I needed. Our timing is divinely chosen to guide us at just the right point to grow into our highest self, fully aligned with our true self. I don't expect things to all happen at once; life and Spirit are too fluid for that. But I do expect to come across things along my journey that confirm where I'm headed or give me things to consider, awareness to grow from. Once I allowed myself to be open to that, more magic began to show up.

Coaching women has been my thing for over ten years. I often find myself finishing a session with, "Man, I love this work!" Most of that's because I'm able to connect another human being to how she can have a life that can be so much happier than she thinks possible. I'm so excited about adding more skills to my toolbox, my spiritual skills.

I've based my practice on what I have learned about women over those ten years and from the decades before working with women in different social development roles. Self-alignment, knowing our true selves, and using our voices to get our needs met have always been an integral part of my practice. I've developed a specific model that I teach women for how to be themselves in every aspect of their lives and how to use their own voices to express it.

As I opened myself up to learning how to connect with Spirit, I realized that what Spirit calls us to do isn't much different from what I call my clients to do in my coaching practice.

Coincidence or synchronicity? Experienced coach or divinely guided coach? I believe the latter of both those comparisons.

I watch, wonder, and watch some more, and I allow myself to celebrate the personal benefits of having a strong spiritual connection. My purpose is clearer as the creator of my own reality. My tolerance for negativity is decreasing. I'm prioritizing my own ongoing healing in a whole new way for me, my clients, and my community.

I'm embracing all that is happening for me spiritually and have created a practice of regular meditation and stillness to help me connect. I know that the more open I am to my gifts and the more I'm connected to myself, the faster they will arrive.

I have added Intuitive Coaching to my website. Instead of being tied to their limiting thoughts, beliefs, and emotions, I'm using my intuition to understand the support my clients need and the path that will help them practice the truth of who they are. I love sharing with them when Spirit gives me that familiar feeling of tingles on my legs or whole body. I have come to understand those tingles to mean that I'm on the right track, that healing has taken place, that truth has been spoken, and sometimes that I am in complete joy as I belt out tunes during my morning kitchen dance parties.

Dear reader, I want to leave you with some questions.

What is our spiritual voice? Is it defined by the act of embracing our spiritual gifts to heal others? Or is it really the process of embracing our gifts to heal ourselves? I'm thinking it's both.

Either way, what do you have to lose?

 **Dianna Leeder** is a Canadian author, podcaster, and owner of Crave More Life Coaching. She is a Certified Professional Co-Active Coach and an American Confidence Institute Certified Confidence Coach.

She has dedicated the last four decades to helping women find and use their voices. A self-professed life-hack, Dianna uses her spiritual intuition to help women understand blocks to being their highest selves and how to actually become her in all their relationships, including the one with themselves. She is currently on her own path of spiritual ascension.

More on Dianna's work and programs can be found at the back of the book.

CHAPTER 2

Lighten Up!

The Frequency of Angelic Humor and How It Changed My Life

By Jen Bates, Energy Medicine Practitioner

Matters of the heart don't ever make sense. The comedy is on us when we try to take our extraordinary life experiences and fit them neatly into some kind of compartment so others can feel comfortable. When we try to manipulate the incredible beings of light that we are into numbed out consumers—whose only purpose is to fit in—we're committing true blasphemy. These times now call on us to dig deeper into the truth of who we are. The resonance of that truth is too bright and too messy for many people. Regardless, the truth remains. We can choose to stay rigid and confined by our fears, or we can let go and open up to a world filled with so many more possibilities—all held within and coming from our own miraculous, imaginative, and creative souls. Picasso said, "Every act of creation is first an act of destruction." What must we allow to be destroyed now in order to create a better world for all tomorrow?

I've only met two angels in my life. These were legit angels, not the "extraordinarily generous" or "exceptionally kind" people who may sometimes bump into our experiences. The first did not have any wings, but he did have a red-and-white-striped-Cat-in-the-Hat-looking-hat on his head, a wide engaging grin, deep brown eyes, and a warm touch when he reached for my hand. I would never have thought he was an angel if it wasn't for the extenuating circumstances and the fact that he basically vanished from plain sight when the nurse returned to my room.

There was no special light or sound, and I was not on any kind of medication that might have induced this experience. At the time, I was lying on a stretcher and had just been shoved into a hospital room while the medical team raced out to assist the several souls involved in a horrendous car accident, leaving me alone, completely panicked, my head and shoulders immobile, strapped down to a board on a cot, convinced that I was now permanently paralyzed. An hour or so before, I had launched myself over the handlebars of my new mountain bike (a gift from my new boyfriend, Frank) and face planted into a jagged, protruding tree root. The root stretched up out of the dirt and curved back into the rich soil, hinting that there was, perhaps, far more beneath the surface of life's experiences—even this one. I ripped my bottom front teeth through my lip from how hard I was biting it, caved in my upper front teeth, and caused my body to basically crumple on top of my head. In an instant, I was knocked out of my body and into the trees. Looking down at the hapless heap that was physically me, I thought, *where is Frank?* And then, *wait, where am I?*

I looked left and right and saw that I was indeed in the treetops. I had a sense that if I turned around, I would witness something that might make me want to leave the physical world, and I also had absolute certainty that I did not want to leave my body. And so, I stared with an intensity so electric I could probably have created lightning and incinerated myself right there. With this precise focus on my physical body, I refused to allow any sensation or curiosity to cause me to look away. And there were many. I felt a strong pull behind me, filled with a sense of love and familiarity. *Were my ancestors behind me?* I felt embraced and adored.

Desperately, with longing and an inertia of intention, I looked through the green leaves and winding branches for this guy I'd followed into the depths of the woods and whom I was now entrusting my precarious life to.

Please get back to me there—that me over there. Now, Frank! What is taking you so long?! Get down there to my body! Don't you see I'm not moving!

These were the thoughts racing through my consciousness. I didn't see him, not from my bird's eye view perched amongst the branches. I did hear him, though, when I quieted my own inner (outer?) voice. Frank was calling for Misha, his dog (Yes, his dog. I was maybe dying, and he was worried about his dog). The sound was distorted; it was more like a frequency I could feel, like sound through water, muffled and vibratory. And I thought, *Frank! You are worried about the dog while my body is there in a heap? Get over there, pronto, buddy!*

I laugh when I think about it now so many years later—at my insistent demanding—even when out of the body. Fortunately for me, Frank and I've been together now for 20-plus years, same as it ever was.

Eventually, after tethering Misha's collar to a tree with his bandana and belt tied in some kind of sailor's knot, no doubt Frank did make it to my body, carefully lifting me up and putting my legs back where they belonged. The minute he touched my shoulders, I was instantly reunited with the physical world. The pain was immense, and the blood was never-ending. Once we'd gotten our bearings, Frank had me ride piggyback as he scrambled up a steep slope matted in poison ivy to a guardrail by the interstate, intent on finding help. There we sat, perched on the barricade, Frank holding me up while trying to flag down a passing motorist. And we wondered why no one stopped. I'm sure they were thinking, *look, there are two people who just climbed out of the woods without any sign of a vehicle, and her Peter Gabriel t-shirt is covered and dripping with blood! Let's stop and see what they need!*

The cars whizzed by in an endless barrage of colors and growling engines. With God's immense grace, a tow truck driver finally pulled over and radioed for help, and a nurse stopped to make sure we were okay. As I was rushed to the hospital in an ambulance, Frank stayed back to collect our bikes and sweet pup before catching up with me at the ER.

It was there, in the whitewashed room of the hospital, while staring up at the square tiles in the ceiling, that the red and white stripes slowly slid into my periphery. Unable to turn my head to investigate further, I said, "What is that? A hat? Who are you?"

My mind raced along with my heartbeat as I felt the warm radiance and loving, attentive eyes that I suppose only an angel can offer. Leaning in so I could see his face fully, he spoke softly with a funny accent that I could not place, telling me he was a friend of a friend from the theater department at the college I was attending and that he had heard about my accident.

"Not to worry, Jen. You are going to be just fine," he said as he gently took my right hand in his. Light, magnetic pulses that felt like a delicate breeze enveloped my arm. "Keep smiling, my friend. All is well. I'll see you again soon." Then he squeezed my hand, winked at me, and disappeared as I heard the door open and the nurse come in. I asked her, "Where did he go? The guy in the tall red and white hat? He was just here! You had to see him? Where is he?" She crossed to the other side of the bed, looking concerned. "No, sweetie," she said. "I'm sorry we had to leave you alone for a bit. There was a huge car accident. The doctor will be in soon."

The second angel came in early 2020. I was doing stand-up comedy for about three years and scored a win during the Write Club Atlanta competition for my seven-minute diatribe, too timely we would soon discover, on fear. The next day the world would shut down into a paralyzing reality gripped by the unknown. The television shared stories that the world was about to experience the spread of a deadly virus that would leave us all completely wrecked if we did not go into quarantine. And so, in America, we all did our duty and tried as best we could to keep ourselves sane as nearly 100,000 small businesses were forced to close, parents struggled to work double duty at home, and children stared at computer screens in some sorry semblance of an education. In the isolation, the world felt like it was imploding in on itself, reaching a deadening vibration that was unrecognizable. It was such a crazy and somewhat debilitating time. In the beginning of the lockdown, I was immediately flooded with a tsunami of fear and panic running through my mind and keeping me glued to the news for any information that would ease the incessant questions. All I could think over and over was that in less than a year's time, my parents, many family members, and friends would probably be dead, my entire city would be a wrecked wasteland and all from a virus so tiny it couldn't be isolated from the many other corona-type viruses. Nothing made sense, but I know now it's because this was about something much deeper.

During this time, in the stillness of the days, I discovered a deep resonance within me, a vibrational pull that felt familiar and comforting. I found myself easily rising—almost floating out of bed—in the early morning darkness before Frank or the kids began to stir. I would go to my meditation space and light a candle for compassion, hope, and peace. It's important to note that up until this time, the life I created was filled with loud and fun late nights in boozy bars trying to get a laugh out of folks. Before 2020, my mornings were mostly committed to pushing myself up and having some semblance of quality time with my kids. Or just sleeping because my body screamed that I had no choice. But in the time of lockdown, I found the morning stillness was offering something new, a solace and a remembrance that beckoned me to listen and receive.

On August 8, 2020, I was awakened in the middle of the night to the familiar touch and warmth of an angel's hand. He was standing on the right side of the bed, smiling down at me, with huge white wings framing his face and a goatee'd smile. I thought two things almost simultaneously. First, I hoped he wouldn't wake Frank, and then, *Woah. Who knew Angels had facial hair?!* His eyes were light sky blue, and as he lovingly embraced me with a gaze of assurance and peace, I could understand what he was communicating, though we did not speak.

You will help humanity using light healing for their bodies. You will be guided in how to best assist. Keep listening and receiving. Your guidance will teach you more.

And I said, "Um. Nope. Absolutely not. Excuse me, but you've got the wrong person. I'm a comedian and an actor. I've got kids and a life. Save that woo-woo for the psychic-smokey-incense ladies in the flowy purple pants who listen to too much Fleetwood Mac and have too many cats. Nope. Thanks for coming, but time for you to go. Bye!"

The angel did leave. And I fell right back to sleep. But the next morning, I couldn't shake what happened. *Was it a dream?* I asked Frank if he'd noticed me making any strange noises in my sleep? No, he'd slept soundly through it all.

The presence and proclamation of what the angel symbolized and spoke of stayed with me for the days and months that followed. Every attempt I made to distract or numb out from what happened that night led me right back to knowing I had no choice but to surrender. And once I finally gave in to this reality, my daily meditative experiences ramped up to full throttle warp speed. First, I began to receive daily messages from my guides about how I could assist humanity's healing. Yep, I had officially launched myself into the world of the weird and woo woo. Second, I decided that the Fleetwood Mac incense lovers were actually pretty cool, and I was the one who had been super lame. Even though this time the shifts occurring felt so personal and exclusive, I knew the information and support I was receiving were available to everyone. These were skills all human beings had; we had just forgotten and were now being given the opportunity to remember.

I've learned most through this journey that it's easy to dismiss the things we don't understand. And that just because we don't understand something doesn't make that thing wrong or bad or even untrue. We hear the stories and experiences of other people, and if it isn't our truth, we often attempt to control or negate them because of our fear. But the truth doesn't go away just because other people can't hold space for it. Life is way too expansive for that. My life has been a long journey toward this moment now, stepping into the fullness of who I am—all the roles I get to be. My skill with light perception and clairvoyance allows me to talk to angels, aliens, dead people, and unicorns. Perhaps most importantly, I now get to (in full consciousness) work with light and help others do so, too.

I know now that it's completely within our capacity to heal ourselves, and the greatest role I get to play is helping people remember that.

When we choose to let go of fear, we align with the infinite and become unstoppable. In essence, we Lighten Up!

Jen Bates is a light medicine intuitive and Reiki Master skilled in clairvoyance, clairaudience, light body attunement, and mediumship communication. Founder and creator of Lighten Up with Jen Bates, Jen offers one-on-one high-resonance sessions to ignite your light body and transform stagnant energy with curiosity, compassion, and joy. Jen holds a BA in Theater Arts & Performance from The University of Georgia, and prior to launching LightenUp, performed stand-up comedy at many local and regional clubs. Jen serves on the Board of PushPush Arts, plays numerous roles as a Standardized Patient with Emory University, and consults for the Clean Beauty movement with Beautycounter. Most days, she can be found cracking up with her family, dancing with her dog, and immersing herself in the wonders of Quantum Consciousness and the Electromagnetic Biosphere of human potential. She looks forward to connecting with you to Lighten Up together!
www.lightenup.lol

CHAPTER 3

Not Broken

A Spiritual Journey Through Pain

By Gina Maria Snowden L.Ac.
Licensed Acupuncturist, Yoga Teacher

Over the years, I wrestled with the term "healer." I felt uncomfortable with that title. It felt too big, too all-knowing. I just wanted to help people. I felt the same about the label, teacher. Prior to becoming an acupuncturist, I was a personal trainer and group fitness instructor for over 20 years and a yoga teacher for over 15. When my students gave me praise, I'd brush it off with, "I'm just your fitness facilitator." Or, "I've just read a few more books than you." But it did feel good to think, *I must be doing something right.*

When I began teaching yoga, things started getting weird. Many times during a class, I'd come out of the session slightly discombobulated as if waking from a dream. There were times I tried to describe this phenomenon to others with, "I felt as if I was being guided," or, "It feels like I'm channeling some ancient yogi." One friend reminded me of the concept of universal knowledge, and perhaps I had tapped into a stream of this universal information and infused it into my session. There were times I couldn't even remember the sequence I used but remembered each person I touched for adjustments or reassurance. It was bizarre. Here I was teaching in a military gym, in a weirdly shaped squash court, with zero ambiance, and I regularly had these experiences. Until I became a bodyworker, I only experienced this profound level of being while teaching yoga. Over time, I accepted the term more readily as I had an external source to pass on the credit. However, it was a long journey into my healing to find my way around the term healer.

To look at me, one could be forgiven for not recognizing me as a member of the 1%. It's not universally known that to arrive at the position of Chief Master Sergeant in the United States Air Force, one must compete with the best of the best to arrive at the top 1% of the enlisted force. The journey is not without peril, hardship, and sacrifice. It was fraught with bumps, bruises, and trauma to my mind, body, and spirit. While my entire story began long before I wore a uniform, my uniformed service formed the majority of this tale.

During my formative years, the three most memorable attributes bequeathed to me from my parents were, "You're too smart for your own good," "You're like a bull in a China shop," and "You're so damn hard-headed." Over my life, I morphed these jibes into new phrases like, "You're so smart!" "You're so strong!" "You're so determined." These transformed nuggets nourished every layer of my being, and they helped sustain me during my career.

For the majority of the time, I was in a very physical job requiring those attributes while working under the high tempo of aviation operations during the Cold War to the Gulf Wars. That job and the people in it helped hone those aspects of my layers to both my detriment and eventual success. I leaned into my Strength Trio often. There were times I left my body and continued pressing forward with the sheer power of will. That meant I exceeded my body's limitations as often as I survived something or found success. It was normal to brag about the knee, back, and neck pain and injuries sustained on the job in my field. Bragging rights to 'Who Fell Off the Highest Aircraft' or 'Who Carried the Most Parachutes' were chased like achievement medals.

While I'm not certain about the origins of the phrase, "Just rub some dirt on it," I wouldn't be surprised to find it came from a military person. During my time, there was an adage that if you did ten years in the field without injury, you weren't working hard enough. Well, I worked hard. The end result was head-to-toe injuries sustained over almost three decades. Not all of my injuries were physical. Many were mental, emotional, and spiritual. In hindsight, I recall feeling a visceral tug from my solar plexus or my gut when I was faced with a particular situation or choice. It was as if my spirit was protesting. That is when I swallowed. I swallowed down the insults, back-stabbing, gaslighting, and the pain. I swallowed down the warnings of my intuition and inner guidance with the mantra, *I'm smart, I'm strong. I'm determined.* I just kept pressing forward and upward with an axiom that served me well. *Success is the best form of revenge. If you can't beat 'em, outrank 'em.*

One day, not far off from the pinnacle of my career, I ran a 5K. About a kilometer to the finish, I felt something not right. Then a sharp *twang* ran from my back and down my right leg. The pain was enough to take away my breath and almost bring me to my knees. I limped-ran to the finish. The next morning I could not push up from the bed. I couldn't sit up or roll over. I couldn't walk. I painfully slithered my body down the foot of the bed to the floor. Then in an excruciating maneuver that wrenched out a scream, I flopped to my stomach and combat-crawled to the bathroom, dragging my legs and trying to not think about paralysis or using a cane the rest of my life. I just needed to get dressed and get to work, and everything would be fine. After some time, I was able to get to my knees then pull myself to the sink and lever myself to the toilet. Eventually, I was able to stand and make my way through a hot shower. As my body warmed, the tightness and restrictions lessened until I could get dressed and off to work. I did not go to sick call. I did not see a doctor for weeks. I feared being relieved of my duty and position, of which I was the first woman to hold. So I powered through, hiding my condition from those who would see me fail. I leaned heavily on yoga, core exercises, and massages during this time. Eventually, common sense prevailed. An MRI revealed the spine of an elderly person, according to one doctor. I was 39. Steroid injections soon followed along with physical therapy and pain medication. Six years before my own finish line, I was officially broken.

Through medical and divine interventions, I prevailed and self-actualized as part of the 1% with another first a couple of years later. I became the first female Chief Master Sergeant in my career field. I'm proud to have served my country in a manner that supported the people and the mission. I earned my place and all the goodies, but at what cost? It was with trepidation that I decided to stop hiding how broken I truly was. Now, the fear of being removed from my job and being kicked out for failing to meet standards no longer rode me. I was now in a position requiring more brain than brawn. I decided to give in to a doctor's repeated recommendations to visit this new military clinic trying something "different," called Pain Psychology.

As my psychologist would later say, I was a "tough nut to crack." I was plagued with so many voices telling me, *who am I broken? How can I support my family like this? I'm just so tired I can't stand it! Why is she trying to get me to tell her about my childhood? The military broke me, not my childhood.* Eventually, my shell softened, and I became more open to therapy. That was when I finally admitted to the terrible nightmares wrecking my already broken sleep and to suicidal ideations.

Through our sessions, I was diagnosed with Complex PTSD, and we spent a lot of time working on self-regulation. Unfortunately, I was also becoming more dependent on opioids and still in incredible pain and badly broken. The pills seemed to hold me together at times when I couldn't do that myself. Over the next few years, anti-depressants would be added to the anti-inflammatories and pain meds. My stomach lining and digestion were also broken. Physical dysfunctions multiplied into chronic neck pain, sciatica, and migraines. More medication, more physical therapy, and more feelings of being broken followed each new diagnosis. Mentally shutting down and compartmentalization were coping mechanisms that got me through many situations but made talk therapy more difficult. Spiritually I was disconnected except for Sangha gatherings and yoga. They provided a tenuous tether.

Flowing into retirement, I remained a fixture in the clinic that evolved from Pain Psychology. In the Interdisciplinary Pain Management Clinic, along with some out-of-the-box thinking M.D.s, the clinic boasted experts from psychology, pharmacology, nursing, physical therapy, massage, chiropractic, and acupuncture. This was a model clinic that would eventually be replicated around the military. Together, they made it their life's work to help us manage our pain. Here, I was introduced to acupuncture. Oh, and by the way, I was terribly afraid of needles! After having so many steroid injections, nerve blocks, and nerve ablations, I just couldn't. The thought of having one more needle in me was too much. I did finally acquiesce, and my life started to change in a new direction. During that time, my acupuncturist would say how receptive I was to treatment and how much it would benefit me to become an acupuncturist. Every visit, she would talk about how the process of learning acupuncture could help me heal. Her messages weren't totally in vain. I began to think, *I love massage, and it has been so helpful. I may not be able to stick needles in people, but I want to help others like I've been helped. I can touch them and help them through the magic of massage therapy.* Those thoughts flowed right into a connection with a massage teacher who was starting up a school.

The teacher, fellow students, the school location on a bountiful plot of land filled with nature, a rescued Doberman Pinscher, and a host of semi-feral cats were such a blessing. I learned so much about myself and working with others suffering from pain, but this time from a practitioner's point of view. This helped me start coming out of my self-abuse when I began to think, *how can I empathize with my clients if I'm bashing myself?* This was just one of the lessons that would form the foundation for my development in the healing arts.

One day, toward the end of the training, I became very ill during class. Still battling many ailments, which now included fibromyalgia, IBS, migraines, and Hashimoto's thyroiditis, my body just crashed. My teacher and classmates gave me space. I tried to incorporate self-regulation and pranayama to break the flare. That's how I found myself lying on my yoga mat under a mango tree, feeling a light breeze on my face, knees bent, and trying to breathe without whimpering. I'm not sure how long I lay there before I noticed a presence at my side. It was the huge dog lying next to me. Then, another presence took a spot on my other side. It was the big-boss cat that led the tribe of felines. I also felt a presence above and below me that I assumed was more cats, but to this day am not certain. I just felt safe.

Without a concept of time, things occurred in no memorable order. At some point, the resident acupuncturist gave me a treatment. There were a few points in my abdomen and head, as I recall. I remember starting to feel more than the breeze on my face. I began to feel more than the sharp pain in my gut and penetrating pain in my skull. I felt something deep inside begin to rise to the surface. It was as if another part or another layer of me was coming into being. As a visualization, I perceived a body shaped of golden light lying supine and being raised on a bed of light, with cables of light that rose through empty space. This light body came up through my back body and traveled toward my front body before settling somewhere in the middle. I felt as if I was released from something greater than just the physical pain and that a gateway opened. It was confusing and disconcerting but beautiful. I perceived soft crying, and I was not certain if it was me or someone else from a long distance away. While I felt uncertainty, something real shifted. As if in time-lapse, a thought blossomed, *I am a healer, and I can be whatever I want.*

The fall after earning my massage therapy license, I enrolled in Chinese Medicine school. I was still a repeat customer in the IPMC and dependent upon opioids. Learning a new way to live through this ancient medicine gave me a burst of enthusiasm and excitement I thought was long gone from my life. By the spring term, I weaned myself off of the pain meds. It was not pretty, but I received weekly acupuncture and herbal remedies to help get me through, along with medical guidance.

By summer's term, I worked in the same pain management clinic that changed my life, teaching yoga to military patients. It was a blessing for me to be able to help them in a manner that demonstrated, "I see you. I hear you." Their comments about being broken and thrown away resonated with me. Through them, I began to see how far I'd come. As I witnessed their pain and feelings of no-longer-worthy I also saw the potential of all of this amazing talent entering the civilian world to share their gifts. Through my lens, I saw a world of possibilities for them. Each had an opportunity to live a full and abundant life. Once I was able to take "selfies" with that same lens, I began to see how not broken I was. Through this yoga assignment, I began to have new thoughts like, *a work in progress is not broken. It's always evolving.* It became my mission to help as many people as possible recognize the same in themselves.

My relationship with the IPMC continued throughout Chinese Medicine school as an acupuncture intern until I eventually flowed into my first acupuncture job at the IPMC. Prior to starting the job, I began to have nightmares and flashbacks, along with thoughts of suicide. The louder voices returned with, *who do you think you are? How can YOU be an acupuncturist? Why don't you go sit your ass down somewhere?* Self-worth issues and imposter syndrome kept cropping up along with more physical pain due to the stress of completing a master's program and studying for national boards. The stress, the feelings, and even the voices were nothing new to me, but this time I had help. I listened to my inner healer, who said, *I will serve my future patients better if I shore up my mental health.* I self-referred to the Veterans Administration for mental health and returned to therapy. It was one of the best things I could have done for myself and, by extension, my patients. It was self-care that enhanced patient care.

Serving in the IPMC, I shared what I learned as a patient and as a professional about self-care. In the clinic, the word "fix" was an "F-word," which strengthened the idea of being broken. Self-care was the goal for each patient. Often words used frequently begin to lose emphasis. For me, self-care took on new meanings and eventually a new life. When I was a patient, self-care was for survival. I learned to pace, manage expectations, and dial life way back to benefit from any modality. As a professional, it was an extension of medical care. Chronic pain patients who do the homework do better overall than those who depend solely on passive care. As a teacher and healer, self-care has come to embody the idea of placing my oxygen mask on first before helping others with theirs. When I am well-rested, nourished, and mindful, I have so much more to give. I can attest that giving, with depleted resources, leads to burnout physically, mentally, and spiritually. With substantial resources, an environment of healing can be sustained. Practicing balance and allowing boundaries help provide the means to serve and be the healer that I am.

Now, I practice allowing my intuition to have a say and not

swallowing down my truths. Sometimes, I struggle, but the evolution continues even now as I place these words and free my voice. This is a love letter to all beings who aided this journey. I thought I could never be a healer because I was such a wounded, broken thing with a recurrent recording of, *how can I be a healer when I can't heal myself?* Until that day under the mango tree, I honestly didn't get the idea of the healer within. On that beautiful day, something shifted, and I arose from that experience knowing I found the healer within. Worn-out recordings and pain still exist, but I rule. I earned my place through education, dedication, and skill. I deserve to be here. I am worthy. I am whole. I am smart enough to do this. I am strong enough to carry the healer within to others. I am determined enough to share my story in the hopes that even just one person can relate and say for themselves, "I am not broken."

 **Gina Maria Snowden** is a 28-year veteran of the United States Air Force. Today, she holds a Masters of Science in Oriental Medicine and is licensed in acupuncture and massage. Certified as a personal trainer, group fitness instructor, and yoga teacher during her military career, one of her greatest joys is to have introduced generations of active duty and military family members to yoga. As a life-long learner and perennial student, education is a great passion. She carries a wealth of experience into each encounter.

Integrating modalities for pain management and teaching self-care are two of Gina's specialties. With bodywork, acupuncture, yoga, and fitness training in her tool shed, multiple patient needs can be addressed. Gina believes that people are multifaceted. Therefore, self-care and professional sessions need to be multifaceted. Self-care addresses the facets a person can "polish" on a daily basis. Regular professional encounters such as acupuncture, massage, and yoga classes can help with the facets that require some guidance or facilitation toward healing.

Working with the healer within is an evolution in Gina's own healing journey. She intends to create a safe space for the patient to meet or recover the healer within and eventually incorporate that ancient wisdom into their own self-care. The meeting of the practitioner's healer and the patient's own healer is a wonder!

Gina concludes that her ancestral heritage must have been no-madic as she happily lives between Oahu, Hawaii, and Portland, Oregon, with her partner Joseph. She is the proud Tiger Mom of Courtney and Camille, and Nana to Keegan.

Engage with Gina at <u>HealingRootsIM@gmail.com</u>.

Veterans in crisis call 1-800-273-8255 and Press 1, Text 838255 or Chat online at <u>https://www.veteranscrisisline.net</u>

CHAPTER 4

Loving Every "Mistake"

How to Forgive and Heal Your Heart

By Rev. Mary Perry, Angel Intuitive and Healer

I grew up in a Catholic family with strict parents, the only child for 11 years, and the first grandchild on my Mother's side. I was precocious, loving, and entertained the adults around me and talked a great deal (still do). I was happy and creative. My parents and grandparents cherished me, but I did not feel loved.

What? How can that be? I know now that was my perception of myself. As I began to heal the hurts, forgive others, and most of all myself, I learned to love myself. My healing journey brought this wisdom to light, and I am still opening to healing more pieces of my life events.

I am telling this story now for all of us who have had less than perfect upbringings or other traumas happen in our lives. The process of shutting down our voices leaves us feeling like we don't matter or are not worthy. This is a story of my resilience, and how through each trauma, I decided to step forward in new ways to survive. I call myself a survivor, and yet, for every "mistake," I find gratitude flowing through my heart and soul for all my experiences. As you read this story, please do not find pity for me, as I would not change one minute of my life and experiences. I was exactly where I needed to be to learn what I needed to learn, and I am in a place of being happy, peaceful, and finding miracles all the time.

In 1971, I had a boyfriend with who I was deeply in love. I got pregnant intentionally and thought my parents would allow me to marry this young man. *I wanted out of the house.* I remember the day that we told them about the pregnancy, both of us shaking in our boots, and after telling them the news with abundant tears, they asked my boyfriend to leave. Imprinted in my brain are these words from my dad as my mom went upstairs to take her nerve pills, "Go after her and make sure she does not take too many." Those words at the time just made me feel so guilty and ashamed, and I carried that for years.

Of course, they went to the priest the next day to see how they could handle this situation. When they came home, we discussed what to do, or rather they told me what would happen. My parents decided that I would never see my boyfriend again and that I would go to a Catholic unwed mother's home in Philadelphia for five months until the baby came. In May of 1972, I gave birth to a beautiful baby girl. Knowing the love her father and I had for each other had created this spark of joy, I loved every minute of being pregnant. I loved her moving in my belly. I loved singing, talking to her, and writing poems. It was shameful in the eyes of my family that anyone would acknowledge this spark of love I was nurturing to life. Giving this child up for adoption was the hardest thing I ever did.

Back then, I thought I always knew what was best for me and what I wanted. I wanted *out of that house*. The alcohol use and my father's sexual and verbal abuse were hard, and yet, I thought it was perfectly normal in many ways. He took me to the court hearing where I would sign papers giving up my parental rights to my child. As we sat, waiting for the court proceeding to begin, I had a moment of strength and great clarity. I looked at my dad and said, "You know, I don't have to sign these papers." The silence was threatening, followed by dark rage that seemed to bubble up from every cell in his body as he glared at me. "Yes, you do!" he said. But my courage to talk back to him bubbled in me too. "This is my choice; I don't have to sign. However, I believe it's the best thing for my daughter." This was the beginning of a new relationship between my dad and me.

After my daughter's arrival, sadness was so deep in my soul that I thought it would never leave. I returned home to my family, and it was as though it had never happened—as if I had never experienced the trauma of giving up my child. No one asked, *"How am I?" " Do you need to talk?"* When doctors asked me, "Have you had any pregnancies?" my answer was always, "No." Message received; my voice was quiet.

I graduated high school in 1973 feeling miserable and not knowing where I belonged. I spent many years trying to find my way and adapt to a world that did not feel welcoming. I felt ashamed and self-conscious everywhere I went. I put on a happy face because I was a "good" girl, being responsible, getting a job, and doing all that my family thought I *should* do. I walked down the street or in a mall, looking at every little girl that passed by, wondering if it was my daughter.

In 1974, I met my husband on a blind date. He was very charismatic, and I fell under his spell quickly. We married in 1975, and I moved to Maryland. I was twenty-one, very naïve, and I believed that my marriage would help me find happiness. *Boy, was I wrong about that one.* In my thirties, in counseling, as my depression had gotten worse, I discovered the term alcoholic. Imagine my surprise when I discovered I was married to an alcoholic and drug-addicted man. As I searched inside for answers, I discovered I had grown up in a very dysfunctional alcoholic family. I struggled with life and my marriage. I thought the alcohol and drug use would lessen over time. *He would grow out of it.*

Instead, it became worse. I was a very good co-dependent, and I used food and shopping to soothe myself. During counseling in the '80s, I started reading self-help books and working on myself. I began taking college classes to work toward my accounting degree and non-credit classes to learn how to paint, make macramé, ceramics, and jewelry. One night my husband asked me, "Can't you just be?" I answered, "No, learning stops only when you die, not before. I want to be the best I can be always." We kept drifting apart; however, it took another ten years until we divorced. I still have love for him; he was a wonderful man but could not leave the alcohol and drugs behind. I was never first in his life. *I deserve to be first.*

During all of this, my life went on. Even during my lows, I did not turn to my religious upbringing and God, and I had not yet turned to the spiritual life I now lead. My voice kept getting smaller and smaller. I never wanted to go into large groups of people, and if I did, I was a wallflower. I worked in corporate finance during my 37-year career and was proud of my growth and advancements. I ended up at the American Cancer Society for 16 years and moved into Human Resources in payroll. It was the best move of my corporate career as I started to understand that people liked and trusted me and had no trouble talking to me about issues that they were having. My supervisor was so special, and she nurtured and encouraged me in ways previously unknown to me. I grew, and at one time, although shaking in my shoes, I even presented to 750 staff at a conference. I didn't understand myself fully yet but knew I had a gift to connect and help others.

During counseling, when I was in my 30's my voice started opening, but not until I was 40 did the deep healing begin, and with it, my voice becoming louder.

My dad died of lung cancer when I was 40. During the last month of his life, I moved home to help my mom, who did not drive and was not handling his illness well. I was back in the family dynamics now in a much different way. I was there to help with everything that needed to happen during my dad's transition. My dad was on morphine for the pain and still drinking. I was not going to fight him about drinking as I realized his time was short. The morphine drops had a bitter taste, and he hated taking them. So one night, thinking I was clever, I put the drops in his Crown Royal shot. As soon as he drank the shot, he said, "Don't you ever ruin my Crown Royal again!"

I had many deep talks with my dad over that month, and while not all of them were healing for me, one of my treasures was with tears in his eyes, "I am so proud of you." He talked to me about taking care of my mom; his concern for her was foremost, as she was not used to taking care of the bills or the house other than cleaning and cooking. A few years prior, I gave her driving lessons, and she got her license, but she had not driven the Chrysler New Yorker. "It's way too big to drive, and your father will shoot me if I hurt it."

In the year following Dad's death in April, I made many trips to Pennsylvania to teach her things like how to balance her checkbook and how to pay the bills that were due. I sold my Dad's car, purchased a Ford Escort for her, and took her driving to get comfortable. I helped her purchase a condo, sell the family home, and even start working a part-time job. It was quite a busy year. The house was awaiting settlement, the dining room set in the house was awaiting pick up, and Mom had moved to her new place. It was a year to the day of Dad's passing, I was in Maryland at work, and I called her to see how she was coping. What happened next was the start of my healing journey and the opening of my voice.

The phone rang and rang, it was early and *Where could she be?* I wondered. The answering machine picked up, and the voice on the machine was my dad's, which we had erased and replaced a year prior. *I could not have heard that right,* I thought through my tears. Calming myself, I called back and received the same message. I became hysterical, and everyone in my office came running to see if I was okay. "I am okay, but what does this mean?" is all I kept asking.

I knew this was a message from the beyond. I was not spiritually where I am now as far as trusting messages from beyond the veil. I was just opening to the idea that there was more than we could see in the physical. Healing started with that voice mail message and I am so grateful for the journey that followed.

I had my first reading at that point, and I was skeptical and excited to see what transpired. As I walked in the door at the reader's home, she said, "Your dad is right behind you." I had not told her of my dad's passing or the voicemail message. The message that he wanted me to know was that there were papers in the dining room set that he knew were important to me. Mom overlooked them and was going to put them in the trash. I went to the house a few days after the reading. After finding the papers, as I walked across the kitchen, glancing into the living room, my dad was sitting on the sofa, like he did, smoking a cigarette, drinking a beer, and watching TV. The vision was quick, but I knew what I saw.

This began my search for answers that were not mainstream. I had unusual occurrences start happening in my life, such as finding many feathers in unusual locations. I needed to start the healing I desperately wanted.

I started a search for my daughter through the Catholic Social

Services. I knew the adoption had changed me so much that my heart needed to heal from the sadness of giving her up. I met her in June of 1996, and that day was the happiest of my entire life. I cannot express the emotions of seeing this beautiful soul who was such a part of me, and yet, even though 24 years had passed, it was as if my heart healed instantly when we hugged and talked through our tears. This brought a treasure I will never forget, and I can still feel this joy today.

During this time, I continued to get readings from different readers around the United States, and every one of them told me that I could do readings. I bought Tarot cards, but they did not feel right for me. After finding an angel reader in my town, I felt as though the heavens had opened down upon me. In the last days of my dad being here physically, he would talk to the angels that surrounded him and tried to get himself lifted up to go with them. I did not see them at the time but heard him talking to them.

Angels helped me heal my life from the traumas that I experienced. As I meditated with them, setting intentions for help and healing, it happened; as I read more and more about the angels, my excitement and passion to learn more kept growing. I started journaling to let go of the traumas that had happened and embrace the joyful experiences I had. I learned that the angels would help with anything as long as you ask for their help. All day, every day, I asked for help and healing. I journaled about the challenging circumstances of my life, and I began to ask for forgiveness for myself and for those who hurt me. My Gemini self talked about my experiences to all who would listen. Yes, my voice was open once again.

After my Dad passed and I started healing the trauma of giving my daughter up for adoption, I thought that when I had healed that, my life would be stellar. Yes, I am smiling as I write this because I am still healing that instance and many others in my life. Embracing healing is to begin a sacred journey to remember who you are.

We come here innocent and loving. We accumulate conditionings along the way from families, society, and religions. If we can look inside deep enough in the right way for us, we can begin to discern our truth. I call myself an angel intuitive and healer, and I connect deeply to the angels and my spiritual path. As I flow inward to my deepest wisdom to find my truths and listen carefully to the whispers that ask me to follow the guidance, I find my life lit with beautiful light, and I am excited to feel the connection.

My words of wisdom to the reader are to follow your inner wisdom and if you do not feel connected to it, follow the breadcrumbs that may lead you to someone who can help you connect. There is no one way to do this. It is different for all of us, but finding your voice and wisdom is a journey that inspires us to be the best we can be. I was just an ordinary girl with some rather big hurts in my energy fields. As I chose not to go under when the traumas arrived, I always found a way forward by following where my heart led me.

Listen to your heart.

Meditate. Journal.

Forgive.

I forgive myself, and I set myself free!

Ask what love would do.

Trust your inner wisdom.

Remember, this sacred journey is worth taking!

Rev. Mary Perry is an Angel Intuitive and Healer. After opening to the angels in 1996, she has spent 25 years learning and growing her passion by connecting to the angelic world. Her biggest desire is to help others connect with the angels and witness the transformation of their vibrational frequency. In her business, Wings Unfurled, she holds sacred space for her clients as she offers Angel Readings, Healing Sessions, Soul Readings, and Sound Healing Sessions. Rev. Mary teaches Seraphim Blueprint and Integrated Energy Therapy healing as well. As she works with her clients, she hopes they feel the beautiful angelic love that is there for them. In all she does, angels are at the center of her work. She has taken many workshops over the years to shift her energy and bring new angel energies to the world.

Rev. Mary lives northeast of Baltimore, Maryland, on the water and loves connecting with the nature that surrounds her. She loves sharing her space with her heart partner and cat.

Let's talk. A complimentary Angelic Care Call is a great way to discuss your needs and desires.

Email: Angel@Wings-Unfurled.com

Website: https://www.Wings-Unfurled.com

Facebook: https://www.facebook.com/WingsUnfurled/

CHAPTER 5

The Powerful Voices in Your Head

Learning the Language of Your Soul

By Laura Di Franco, MPT, Publisher

Bring your laptop so you can write your chapter while you're enjoying the Caribbean breezes.

I've learned to listen to my inner warrior and voice of joy and truth. She lets me know what to do. There were many years she didn't show up as loudly as she does now. I had to discern between my conditioned thinking and her. Let's call her Sierra. She's my wise goddess voice.

I named my inner critic voice (Martha) a few years ago after attending a writing retreat with my mentor, Laura Munson. Giving that voice a name allows me to call out the limiting beliefs (as an awareness tool) when I need to. Martha has a way of keeping me afraid and feeling not-good-enough. Naming her was a game-changer. Accepting, befriending, and having conversations with her not only changed my life, but it also turned me into a powerful manifesting beast who makes her dreams come true. More on that later.

"The goddess voice deserves a name, too." A group of us in my writing class just finished our journaling exercise and talked about the awareness practice and how to use writing as both an awareness and healing tool. I now know there's an answer inside me for every single thing I have a question for. I learned that the clarity I crave in life (about *anything*) is always there in my hut (heart and gut).

I never outed my goddess voice name until today. Sierra is a name that's been with me for a while. I grew up in California near the Sierra Mountains and great redwood trees. Sierra is like those trees, solid, gorgeous, and ancient. She stands in community with the power of the souls around her. A tree gets its strength and protection from the storm from the others next to it. She stands tall in her worthiness. The community has her back.

Laura, you were always connected like this.

Sierra is helping me write today.

You were always good at feeling. And feeling, sensing, and noticing is the language of your soul. You've spoken that language for a long time, she reminds me.

She's a badass. Sierra, I'm so glad I'm finally truly listening now.

She's right about me being a great feeler. Kurt and I were lab partners and secret lovers in grad school, out to earn our physical therapy degrees. "Ooh, I can feel this right here," I rolled the tip of my thumb into the knot in his right upper trapezius.

"How can you feel that?" He said, impressed with my palpation skills. "I don't know; It's easy for me."

Those couple of years might have been the first time I understood the body as a portal to the language of my soul. I just didn't fully understand its power and certainly didn't call it channeling then. But, I was channeling my intuitive and higher power through my ability to feel (under my hands but also notice in my mind and body in other ways). I also channeled treatment ideas, solutions, and words I used to educate my physical therapy clients.

Amazing reader, it's your turn. I'm an anatomy geek, so I love to help people understand their bodies. Take a deep breath, and as you exhale, relax all your muscles, including those at the top of your shoulders—you know the ones jacked up into your ears with worry, doubt, and fear? Yeah, those. Allow them to drop away from your ears with each exhale as you continue to breathe deeply into your pelvic bowl.

Oh, and here's a little trivia you can use at your next cocktail party. Did you know there's an intimate connection between the neck, shoulders, and jaw and your butt and pelvic floor? So, it turns out, if you're clenching your lower abdominals, hips, or buttock muscles, you're probably also clenching your jaw, and vice versa.

Stop that. Breathe. Relax.

I have a feeling some of us have been sucking it in and clenching for decades, all in the name of that flat belly. Newsflash: We were not meant to clench for a lifetime. Let it go.

Laura, tell them about when you first knew you were a channel for your words.

Thanks, Sierra, you're talking about the Quantum Leap story. I love that story! It was the moment I knew I could channel my words and that they were coming from a much bigger source than just me. In 2014, I attended the Quantum Leap John F. Barnes Myofascial Release course in Sedona, Arizona. It was also when I learned the connection to my inner warrior was much more powerful than I realized. It was also the weekend I became a poet.

Awesome reader, if you haven't read or heard my spoken word poetry, I'd be honored for you to take a peek. Please find lots of it on my poetry page on Facebook: <u>https://www.Facebook.com/WarriorLove/</u>

Quantum Leap is an advanced course in the John F. Barnes Myofascial Release curriculum available to those of us who complete the multiple prerequisites. When the excited feelings landed in my gut after calendaring the course, I mentioned it to a friend, "The course starts the day you sign up. Crazy things are already happening!"

When there's an energy of intention as you purposefully choose aligned actions, the Universe understands that energy. It begins putting things into motion the second you emit the frequency of that intention and energy and move into action. I was feeling it after signing up for the course, even though I wasn't sure what exactly I was feeling. It was a cross between excited and nervous, gut and heart pangs.

Then, the day I left for the airport, the cab was early; the flight, on time. I boarded the plane for Sedona and headed for the rear. I find the seat number above and realize it's a completely empty row.

Whoa, a whole row to myself, thanks, Universe!

Midway through the flight, I reach down for my purse sitting under the seat in front of me, unzip it, and pull out my journal and pen. The motions feel like someone else is making them. I watch it all happen with awe. I write a several-page journal entry which I title *God on the Plane*. The writing moves through the pen uncensored and continuous from the first word until the last. I close the journal, place it back in my purse with the pen, shove my purse under the seat, and push it a little further under with my foot.

That wasn't just for you; you need to read that out loud.

The message starts and then continues repeatedly until I arrive at the class ballroom in Sedona the next day.

The buzz of energy in the room is palpable. I walk to the very middle seat of the 220 in the room. *OMG, what are you doing? You hate the middle seats!* My usual M.O. is to sit on the end near the door, just in case I need to pee or escape. The wooden chairs sit lined up in rows touching each other. We're meant to (purposefully) be out of our comfort zone in these classes. I'm already feeling it. I enjoy my personal space; a born introvert.

"See you at the break," I say to Ronda. Ronda and I found each other on the online myofascial release chat and arranged to room together for the course. The ride to Sedona from the Phoenix airport proved that the Universe arranged an interesting few days for me. The journaling incident wasn't enough, I guess. I felt like we were long-lost sisters. The conversation is easy. *We have so much in common,* I think. Healers, divorced, Taekwondo black belts, two kids, and a myofascial release specialty. Oh, and I never room with anyone for courses. So why did I decide to say yes to it this time? Thanks, Universe.

The class begins, and our instructor addresses the group: "Welcome to Quantum Leap, everyone. Does anyone have any questions?"

That wasn't just for you; you need to read it out loud.

I spend the entire morning noticing everyone else raise their hands to ask questions or make comments about being there. I'm too afraid to raise my hand and read my journal. My heart is pounding a dent into my front ribs.

I hear again, *that wasn't just for you; you need to read it out loud!*

Thanks, but I heard you the first time.

Sierra did not have a name back then.

It was time for our break. I see John go to sit at the table on the side of the room, and the usual barrage of students approach him for a photo. He leans back in his folding chair, arms crossed high over his chest, usual neutral face peeking from behind his white beard. My heart beats harder as I approach the table. In the dozen or more courses I attended before this day, I never approached him at the table for anything.

"Hi, John. I wrote something I'd like to share with the class. Would that be okay?"

"How long is it," he says without any other greeting.

"Just a couple of minutes."

"Okay," he says.

I walk away and can feel my heart starting its escape plan. I feel it bumping up against my chest, and now I feel my legs weakening.

John walks on stage after the break and speaks into the tiny black microphone pinned to his lapel. "Someone wanted to share something?"

I stood up from my center seat in the ballroom. "This is called God On the Plane," I start.

I have my journal ready and open it to the dog-eared page. I read the cursive words from start to finish, without missing a word, without being asked to speak up, like many of the morning's question-askers were. The students seated next to me hold space as they watch my journal shaking in my hands. But my voice does not quiver.

Finishing the last few words, I immediately sit back down and look at the floor while the entire room erupts in applause. I look up with the sound, still shaking. I don't expect applause. And what I truly don't expect is what happens next. Jude, a fellow healer, catches up to me at the next break tapping me on the shoulder as I lazer-beam for the door. I turn around and smile.

"Laura, thank you so much for sharing your poem with us!"

Poem?

That was the day I became a poet. I still love telling that story and am so grateful to Jude. After that day, 48 more poems came pouring out of me, followed by five self-published poetry books. Everything changed when I gave myself permission to open the channel, receive the words, and then share them with the world. When I listened to and trusted the voice, moved through the purpose-driven fear, and spoke the words out loud, I created the crack in my armor where my soul's purpose could move through. I haven't looked back since. I know my words are channeled through from something much bigger than me. I know how to connect to it. I dropped the boring armor and fear of not-good-enough and use awareness and joy as a daily guide and compass.

Now, to you, amazing reader:

What kind of armor do you wear?

Do you know you're a channel too?

Can you feel purpose-driven fear in your body? What is the sensation?

Can you discern it from normal, survival fear?

Do you honor joy in your life and say yes to it every day?

Do you get that what's in the way of the connection to your soul's purpose, and just about everything you could ever want in life, is your thoughts and conditioned beliefs?

Good news: You get to take responsibility for all of this.

Dear reader, if you grab a notebook and pen right now, we can practice together. Take a moment to feel your feet on the ground, clear your mind, and breathe deeply into your pelvic bowl for a few minutes. With each exhale, let go a little more and relax your body. With each exhale, clear your mind of your to-do list and revel in the present moment sensations anchoring you to the magic of life. It's right here in the next breath (and your ability to feel it) that lies the door to the channel. Without censoring yourself, fill in the blank: I feel _____. Write as fast as you can for at least five minutes. Move the words, thoughts, and messages out from the inside of you to the paper.

"Awareness is everything. It's the key to a magical, purposeful, extraordinary life. Couple it with detaching from the outcome and not adding meaning to your moments, and you have a very powerful practice that'll serve you for the rest of your life." I'm speaking to a group of healers about awareness, again. It's my favorite topic because I know it's how I landed in the amazing life I'm living right now.

Laura, don't forget to mention the unapologetic choice of what brings joy and how listening to that made you a master manifestor.

Thanks, Sierra. Yes, the joy-o-meter. It's my continual challenge to myself to see how high that needle can go.

So you guys, right now, I'm sitting on the balcony of my suite at Zoetry, a five-diamond, all-inclusive resort in Isla Mujeres, Mexico. Espresso roast is brewing in the coffee maker in our room, and I hear the waterfall in the pool below competing with the rhythmic waves on the beach just beyond that. I just plopped a dollop of fresh whipped cream in that espresso, and the milk in the container was warmed before being served.

"Gracias," I say, for the thousandth time to the young gentleman in the white uniform joining me on my balcony with a genuine smile.

"It's a pleasure," he replies, for the thousandth time that week.

I'm watching three colors of Caribbean blues in the water past the palm trees and the morning sailboats float across my view. The special gentleman sitting next to me at the round wooden table is aware, kind, and hella-sexy, and I couldn't want for a better companion, especially for travel. Laughter and music fill our room and lives every day. The joy is real.

I could choose to tell you the story of tragedies we've endured in the last year and use these pages to help you resonate with how I got where I am today and the healing work I've had to do to get here. But why would I waste my precious word count on lower vibes keeping *me* from more joy? That's the practice. It's my choice.

I choose, in every single moment, to wrap my mind and arms around joy. I know how to honor the feelings and process and release the pain fully. A three-decade career in holistic healing was the playground, every moment chosen for me; every struggle, obstacle, and pain an opportunity to find more joy. It was always up to me to choose what parts I placed my intention and focus on.

There was a time when I was stuck in suffering, unaware of my power. We're all good at the suffering. We've been trained to practice it, notice it, talk about it, and analyze it, sometimes to the point of exhaustion. But how good can we get at the joy? That's the question I ask myself every day now.

The spiritual journey brought me here. It's the spiritual path and practice that's given me the ability to experience some of the most joyful moments of my life after moving through some of the most painful. It's why I use the word "magical" and "awe" a lot now.

"What will you do with your one wild and precious life?"

– MARY OLIVER

Find joy, Mary—find more joy!

And with, on average, 20,000 breaths a day, there are a lot of opportunities to pause, clear your mind, and feel gratitude, joy, or love.

You have all the secrets, Laura. All you have to do is remember.

Thanks, Sierra.

And I wonder now, amazing reader, are you remembering, too?

All the answers lie inside you.

All your power is there.

Every moment is a sweet opportunity.

Everything is happening for you.

The spiritual work is to notice when you resist, and the clench builds in your body again. Let it go. Awareness is the key and life-long practice. You will always have a choice, as long as you notice.

So, what do you notice right now? And what are you choosing?

I hope you choose joy.

Laura Di Franco is CEO of Brave Healer Productions, where they publish world-changing wellness books. With thirty years of practice in holistic physical therapy, a third-degree black belt in Taekwondo, and 20 books and counting, she offers powerful expertise and energy that'll help you leave a legacy with your brave words. She's the author of *How to Have Fun With Your Fear*, which is full of practical awareness exercises, journaling tools, mindset mastery techniques, and affirmations. You'll find it on Amazon, along with several of her other books!

When Laura chills out, you'll find her with a mojito at a poetry event with friends, driving her Mustang, bouncing to the beat at a rave, or on a beach in Mexico with something made of dark chocolate in her mouth. Joy is the way she healed herself. Ask her about that sometime. Are you ready to contribute a chapter to one of our collaborative books? Or maybe lead your own project? I can't wait to hear from you!

Website: BraveHealer.com

Facebook: https://www.Facebook.com/BraveHealerbyLaura

Free Facebook group for healers: Brave Badass Healers, a Community for World Changers

Instagram: https://www.Instagram.com/ BraveHealerProductions

LinkedIn: https://www.linkedin.com/in/laura-di-franco-mpt-1b037a5/

Twitter: https://www.Twitter.com/Brave_Healer/

CHAPTER 6

Healing Ancestral Trauma
A Discovery of Our Galactic Family Tree

By Vila Donovan L.Ac. Licensed Acupuncturist,
Licensed Herbalist, Primary Care Physician,
Galactic Ambassador

I can still smell the scent of the seaweed as it floats on the surface of the water as our little boat glides through the kelp beds. My father, a Santa Monica lifeguard and stunt man, likes to take me out on the water in his little rowboat for his daily workout.

My parents were beatniks. I like to say I came out of the womb knowing every word to the Beatles White album. Born in 1971, I grew up in the wake of the Kennedy and Martin Luther King assassinations, Vietnam, Watergate, Monterey Pop Festival, Woodstock, and the sudden deaths of Jimi Hendrix, Janice Joplin, and Jim Morrison.

Los Angeles seemed to be the center of the world back then, and to some extent, still does today. A third-generation Los Angelino and Irish American on my paternal side, I was raised on stories of the little people and the water fey. Mermaids and selkies were our ancestors, and I was named after the fairies that live in the rivers and streams.

My mother's family were immigrants from Russia and Poland who fled extreme poverty and anti-Semitism during the first world war. In Russia, under the rule of Czar Nikolai Romanov, poor Jewish boys were conscripted into the army as "disposable soldiers" and sent off to fight at ages as young as thirteen. At the age of fifteen, my great grandfather, knowing his conscription papers were coming, fled Russia on foot during the night, telling no one he was leaving. He found his way south to Belgium where he met my great grandmother, who made sandwiches at a lunch counter. My great-grandmother worked full-time as a housemaid since the age of eight after her father was executed for theft when she was six.

It was 1917; he was 18, and she was 17, and they married. And since the Czars government wanted my great grandfather for escaping conscription, my great grandparents boarded a ship in Antwerp, Belgium, and sailed—not for the United States, but Mexico.

They joined a small community of Jewish immigrants who settled in the Chihuahua region of central Mexico. My grandmother was born shortly after they arrived, and her two brothers, my uncles, would follow. They sold lace on the streets of Mexico and saved up until, after fifteen years, they immigrated to the United States. They settled in East Los Angeles and built a successful business. Their journey from the sketels and ghettos of Europe to coastal California was the epitome of the American dream. However, the scars of hundreds of years of racism, anti-Semitism, and extreme poverty would send ripples through our family for generations.

My mother's family was intensely critical and disapproving, mean-spirited, and at times, cruel. One had to be perfect, better than perfect; the smallest flaw would validate the stereotype thrust upon us by those who were prejudiced against us.

Now don't get me wrong, there were many things I appreciated about my mother's family. It is some of my biggest sadness that our family was not a happier one. Rich in culture and history. I was taught to value education, democracy, civil rights, and reproductive rights. Though I would not consider my family particularly religious or even spiritual, our history as Jews was always taught. From the stories of the Old Testament to our migration to Mexico, ours was a story of survival.

My mother's family did not approve of my father, nor did they approve of my mother, and consequently, I was considered "less than." On any particular evening, my grandmother would lean over and whisper cruel things to me when we were together. "You're so smart; it's such a shame you will never amount to anything," she would say casually. "You have so much potential; it's so sad," she would whisper in my ear.

I've come to realize the things said to me are the very things racism and prejudice say to their victims. One is never good enough because of their skin color, race, religion, or sexual orientation. How many generations of families have heard these things from their governments, institutions, neighbors, and communities? Generations living these realities until finally; it becomes so systemic and internalized that mothers project these beliefs onto their daughters and granddaughters and onto themselves.

There was never a question of if I would go to college, but to what college I would go. So after some time off, following the Grateful Dead, it was time to go to college. My grandparents expected me to be a doctor or a lawyer, so when I chose acupuncture and to follow a holistic medical career, needless to say, they were not pleased. They did, however, pay for me to go to acupuncture school. At the time, I did not know that by studying eastern philosophy, I was being handed the education and the tools I needed to heal the very wounds my family created.

So, to acupuncture school I went. A heathen, a wild child, an Aries, brave but unsure, I began my education. There were two voices in my head: *You're a magical child* (my father's family and my mother's input), and *you're a damaged person* (my mother's family's input). Both voices spun around within me day to day. But, what happened next was a journey into self-discovery.

Chinese medicine made sense to me. I found it easy to comprehend, and I seemed to absorb the information and remember it without much effort. I could see the acupuncture points on the body in light, and I could sense congestion and stagnation along the meridians. The herbs spoke to me with pictures in my mind. I saw images of ancient sages in caves wandering the forests experimenting with the plants. *Are these my memories from other lifetimes, or the plant's memories, or both?*

I would sit in class, open my mind, and imagine the lectures downloading into my long-term memory through my third eye. My exams were successful, and I began to get approval and encouragement from my teachers and my classmates.

On one pivotal day in case studies class, the teacher asked students to answer with treatment and diagnosis. I answered in my head and watched as hand after hand went up around the room, and the teacher called on them shaking his head no. Eventually, I raised my hand, answered, and the teacher laughed out loud, "Yes," he exclaimed. Eventually, in the weeks to come, the teacher, who was well known for being tough, would ask the class to answer and say, "Not Vila!" Then he'd have me answer when no one else got it right. A light switch went on in my head. I was not the loser my family told me I was.

My confidence grew, and one night, sitting next to my grandmother in an upscale restaurant in Venice, my grandmother in her usual stylish attire, leather pants, crisp white blouse, and silver and turquoise jewelry, leaned over to me and said, "What is the most important thing to you?"

I knew she expected to hear me say, "Boys!" Or, "Clothes!" Or, "Sex!" What I did say to her was, "God." My grandmother seemed shocked; she leaned back into the leather booth and asked me to explain to her what I meant. I told her how I had just read *The Mists of Avalon* and that all the Gods were one God and all the Goddesses were one Goddess and that religions of the world held one piece of truth but believed they held all the truth. We spent the rest of dinner talking about spirituality and religion, my grandmother eager to hear all I had to say. Before my eyes, my grandmother changed from the tyrant I knew her to be to a small curious child. She was never again cruel to me or unkind. In fact, our entire relationship changed. A few weeks later, she gave me a gift of the book, *The Chalice and the Blade,* and shared with me that she had read it and believed Britain's ancient druids and priestesses were related to the Hebrews and that druidic magic was sourced from the Kabbalah. Years later, I would have the opportunity to meet and get to know the author of *The Chalice And The Blade,* something my grandmother never would know. For what none of us knew then was that my grandmother would die suddenly from heart complications only two years later.

A year later, I graduated, my grandmother was gone, and I struggled to build an acupuncture practice from scratch. On one particularly frustrating day, in true Aries fashion, I marched home and pulled out the phone book and called every acupuncturist in

Monterey County. "Hello, my name is Vila Donovan; I just graduated. I feel unprepared to take on the responsibility in the clinic alone, and I'm wondering if you need any help at your office?" I called about twelve offices. Of the three who got back to me, Dr. Wha Ja Kim needed my help. She was ready to retire and wanted someone to train in her style and leave her practice to. *Viola!*

Wha Ja believed in me. She told me the most important thing was heart, that from my heart, I was a healer like her. I had my struggles in the early days, but as I became more relaxed, the magic happened. I began not only to see the acupuncture points but to hear my patient's spirit guides and guardian angels. Acupuncture points, vitamin supplements, and herbal formulas would appear in my mind. Success after success taught me to trust the visions. Each patient was a new meeting, my guides, their guides; each person arrived with a set of their own guides eager to help me help them.

I spent twelve years in practice in Monterey, but in 2012 my life changed again. The love of my life had an unwanted career change. We had six weeks to move for his work. There was one job in the country available for what he did, and that job was in Hawaii. You might think that sounds amazing but, my relationship with Hawaii falls under the category of "it's complicated." Putting our hesitations behind us, we moved, and what I found was my relationship with Hawaii would continue to be complicated. Under no circumstances was the state of Hawaii licensing board letting me use my California license to work as an acupuncturist in Hawaii. No reciprocity!

For eight years, I petitioned the state of Hawaii to let me work, one odd job after another until, eventually, they gave me a five-year academic license. The only catch was I had to be in an academic clinic or a teaching institution. I quickly found a position at a very busy clinic. I was thrilled, but not for long. I found myself in a highly stressful office environment and inter-office dynamics completely out of alignment with me and how I worked. A dark night of the soul descended upon me. I needed perspective; I craved mountains, big endless mountains, and wide rivers. I wanted to smell the pine trees and sagebrush, and I wanted to get lost out in the wild.

My partner and I agreed I should explore new places for us to move, and so I went to McCall, Idaho. I had never been to Idaho but knew I needed to go; it called to me. So, Hi-Ho, Hi-Ho, to Idaho I go. I arrived late at night, accompanied by a good friend from California, and I settled into my hotel room. I laid in my bed in the dark and reached my mind out to the ancestors of the Native Americans who lived in the area, and I asked permission to be there. (Anyone who has lived in Hawaii knows the importance of asking the ancestors for permission). When I asked permission to be there, a very large being answered—an intense giant of a being. The presence was so tangible it startled me. In my mind, I showed the being my belly like a puppy does with a bigger dog. I focused on my heart chakra. As soon as I did, the being retreated to the far end of the room and became soft and gentle. I told the being I was lost in my life and in need of guidance, and I had come to the mountains in search of my power and my path. Compassion flood-ed the room. The being showed itself to me as a medicine man and a being of light. He told me he was many things and that he existed in many dimensions. He told me he would help me, and I was wel-come to be here, in these sacred mountains.

Idaho was hot and dry and did not seem like a place for us to live. The lake, however, captured my heart. I watched the moon set over the water and disappear behind the mountains. I saw memo-ries of Native Americans from long ago, lighting fires, dancing, and celebrating beside the lake. I felt safe here and far away from my troubles. From the mountains to the moon, I was at peace.

The night I arrived back in Hawaii, scrolling Netflix, I watched a documentary on the old west. I chose an episode randomly and sat stunned as it centered on the stories of the Nez Perce Native Americans that lived in Idaho. Pictures of the Nez Perce danced on the screen, reminding me of the being who came to me the night I arrived in Idaho. The chanting of Native American songs brought me back to the lake, and I knew that I had met my spirit guide and was being guided on a new path.

I returned to the clinic, sometimes seeing over forty people a week. I was drained, exhausted, and miserable. All I could do each day was say, *how can I serve? How can I serve?* Eventually, the situation at the clinic went from bad to worse; my body hurt, my health declined, and then, BAM! Covid hit. I had spent the last few years running around like a chicken with my head cut off, stressed out, over-caffeinated, and now the world had gone quiet. The lockdown ensued, and I reached my mind out to my new spirit guide and found myself guided into a wholly new world.

I was introduced to a new group of folks who channeled beings existing in other dimensions. With each connection, I found myself having experience after experience of contact. I had download after download of galactic history and ancient civilizations from Lemuria to Atlantis, Egypt and Sumer, and times before even Lemuria and before this Earth. In my silence, I found a new voice.

It was time to finally begin writing the novel I always wanted to write. Now I knew what I would write about. Amid a pandemic, watching the world turn in so many ways, I decided it was time to tell the world the greatest story ever told, the history of life in our galaxy, and introduce the world to the story of our extra-dimensional selves. How our struggles here in this world now—like racism, prejudice, war, and pollution—are all issues passed down to us from our galactic ancestors. And how we are here now to heal these things, once and for all.

From Yggdrasil, the Norse tree of life and its nine worlds, to The Mayan World Tree, Sumerian, Hebrew, Hindu, and Islamic traditions, the knowledge of the tree of life has been preserved for us. Now we have the tools to understand it. It is our galactic lineage.

The wounds passed down to me from my family reflect wounds passed down to our species as a whole. Perhaps this world is a melting pot for galactic issues, and as each of us heals ourselves, we heal not just the ancestral traumas of our own families but of our galactic ancestors as well. Perhaps that is our purpose as a species.

As I sit here now telling you my story, my family and I are moving back to California. My novel is nearly finished, and I have a wonderful new clinic in California that is in alignment with how I work. I do believe there is a bigger plan we don't always see. I needed to heal my relationship with Hawaii, and through this novel, tell the story of Lemuria, the ones who come from the sea. I understand and am grateful for how it all unfolded.

As I reflect on my journey and the concept of finding one's voice, I believe that finding your voice is an ongoing discovery. Once found, things can change, but if you ask the angels and the universe for help, you will find your voice again, and that voice may be bigger and brighter than ever before.

 **Vila** has over 20 years of experience as an acupuncturist and herbalist and over 30 years of experience as a Tarot reader and psychic. She received her Masters degree in Chinese Medicine in 2000 from Five Branches University, in Santa Cruz, California. Her treatments include a combination of gentle acupuncture, acutonics (sound healing using tuning forks instead of needles), Internal Medicine, and Angel and spirit guide work. Her acupuncture specialties include women's health and hormone balancing for women of all ages, gut health, balancing of the emotional body, and deep relaxation treatments.

Her psychic services include Tarot readings, and angel, spirit guide, and fairy readings. Galactic services include galactic history sessions, galactic lineage sessions, and galactic healings for ancestral trauma.

You can find all the details for her acupuncture and psychic services or to make an appointment at:

Website: www.viladonovan.com

Email: viladonovan@yahoo.com

Facebook: You can follow her @ladyofthemountaincenterforgalacticconsciousness on Facebook and see Vila's free weekly updates and tarot readings.

Acupuncture services are available in Ojai, California.

Psychic services are available everywhere, remotely.

Visit us at www.viladonovan.com for the release date of her novel, *The Vila*. The story of Lemuria and those who come from the sea.

CHAPTER 7

The Beauty of Impermanence
How I Expanded My Awareness Through the Breath

By Sheri Darya Welsh, MPS, RYT200, RCYT

Life is a series of cycles, and of those cycles, breath is the most persistent and accessible one. When we breathe deeply, we expand our awareness. When we step outside our comfort zone, we live a fuller life.

Although the breathing process is cyclical, each breath is fleeting and impermanent. This impermanence reminds us that nothing in life lasts and to savor *this moment*, right here and now. Greeting our memories with an open heart helps us better accept and appreciate the now and prepares us to face whatever comes next.

As I sit and write in a quaint Airbnb in Reno, Nevada, the world around me continues to reel from the COVID-19 pandemic. The US has abruptly withdrawn from Afghanistan, capping a 20-year war with chaos and despair. Hurricane after hurricane pummels the Caribbean, Gulf, and Atlantic coasts. Haiti recovers from another devastating earthquake. And wildfires tear across the Sierra Nevadas, forcing people out of their homes, some even losing everything. Mother Nature is enacting cycles and reminding us of impermanence in the most deranged way. I sit in stillness.

My husband, our three-year-old daughter, and I recently returned from a few days in wine country, where we fled, escaping the wildfire smoke in Lake Tahoe and hoping for a little fresh air. We moved here last year from the Washington, DC area for a change of pace. I was prepared for the massive amount of snowfall in the winter. I was prepared for the influx of tourists in the summer. I was not prepared for the August wildfire season and the uncertainty that came with it.

This past year has been filled with ups and downs with the pandemic, from deciding whether or not to pull our daughter out of preschool, to calling it quits on the east coast and driving 5,000-plus miles across the country to start anew. Somehow, none of that prepared me for the uncertainty of whether or not we will be able to return to our home nestled in the mountains of Lake Tahoe.

I wasn't prepared to gasp for air every time I left the house, scrambling to get my daughter and I into our air-purified home with fans running around the clock as if to simulate the cool mountain air to which we have become so accustomed. Normally I'd step outside and take a few deep breaths to help me think more clearly. Instead, my mind is in a fog, and my only real sanctuary is the yoga studio where I teach on the far side of the lake.

I find myself in a state of flux, keeping a positive mindset by assuring myself that we will be home in one week and that life will return to normal. Even though there's that voice inside me saying that our home will be destroyed, somehow, I am also at peace with that possibility. The difference between the old me and the new me is that the new me can say these things out loud and know that everything will be okay.

The impermanence of this moment is both terrifying and comforting. Terrifying because I so desperately want to hold on. Comforting because I know change is cyclical, and something better is around the corner.

It was a frosty January evening in Bethesda, Maryland. Our west-facing eighth-floor condominium captured the fading amber sunlight and dimmed street lights merging at sunset. I was preparing an early supper for my 13-month old daughter, who sat contently in her high chair with bits of food scattered on her face, tray, and floor, fingers opening and clasping for more.

My phone buzzed, and I glanced over. Lindy was calling. That's odd, I thought. She rarely calls. I freed up a hand to answer.

"Hey, Lindy!" I answered in my usual chipper telephone voice.

A brief pause followed. I immediately knew something was not right.

"Sheri," she said faintly, "Candace died."

The spatula hit the floor with a crash, and the lump in my throat went with it. The lights suddenly burned my eyes, and the room spun around me as I sank down, eyes wide and stomach churning. I struggled to inhale each breath. "No, no, no," I kept repeating in my head, or maybe I said it out loud. I spent the next five minutes in denial as I begged her to tell me this wasn't true.

I looked up at my daughter from the cold kitchen floor as my tears hit the tiles. She looked back at me with that nonchalant, nearly toothless face toddlers make, completely oblivious to my state of shock.

It seemed we had just seen Candace, my friend Krista's daughter, two weeks prior to exchange Christmas gifts. Krista and I met in college, and our friendship grew strong over the years. She was always a planner, putting others first and encouraging us to celebrate big milestones. She and I became even closer once she had her two children, and I had my one.

Candace was diagnosed with leukemia on Christmas Day but was on a seemingly steady road to recovery. She was scheduled to go home the next day. She was supposed to turn four in four months. I was now informed that this would not be the case.

My head continued to spin as I forced myself to stand up, scooped my daughter off the messy high chair, and held her tight as I wept.

Much of my journey towards expanding awareness and finding my spiritual voice stems from my upbringing. My parents never discussed religion or spirituality with my younger brother or me. Born and raised in Iran, a country ruled by religion, they both found their own paths. My father proclaimed himself an atheist, and my mother, a secular Muslim. Faith, religion, and spirituality were not a part of our family's life. I seldom asked them questions about these topics because most of the answers seemed canned and mechanical or hopelessly idealistic.

Many young people find their identity and sense of self through participation in physical exercise and sports. I dabbled in soccer and swimming but never got all that serious about either. We weren't an athletic family; we thrived on music and the arts. My weekly classical piano lessons kept me disciplined and developed my strong sense of independence and self.

I had very little tolerance for change in my younger years. Whenever a plan changed or got canceled, my reaction could make you think a loved one had just died. As a teenager, whenever someone did not reciprocate romantic feelings, I would immediately write at least one dozen poems in my journal. I even went on to publish a few of my pieces in coffee table books.

Come high school, I fell into the recreational drug trap, snuck out of my house a few times, and chased fleeting, fiery situations because they made me feel good for a little while.

I didn't realize it at the time, but something was missing. As I floated through my youth, I somehow knew it would all come together, even when I felt like I was stumbling toward rock bottom. My awareness was like a small flashlight in a large tunnel of endless possibilities.

Something shifted at the end of my first semester of undergrad. I was sitting in a final math exam when the answer bubbles suddenly scattered before my very eyes. I tried to blink it away, but then the sounds in the room felt like a drill inside of my skull—pencils scratching paper, my classmates' breathing, then an alarming cough. I was short of breath, and the lights became unbearably bright, leading me to shade my eyes with one hand. *Am I having a heart attack?*

I jumped up and, with blurred vision, somehow asked my professor if I could take a quick bathroom break. Without thinking, I took some deep breaths outside and let the rustling of the trees bring me back to earth. *Why is this happening to me, and how do I get out of here, pronto? Something is not right.* I returned to my seat in a numb haze and quickly filled in all the "C" bubbles, then submitted my ticket out of there. In hindsight, the repetition of filling in the line of bubbles felt meditative.

One of the distinguishing qualities of my panic attacks was the need—no, the sheer desperation—to escape the present moment. I started sitting closest to the exit door in school, weddings, and other occasions, putting a mental plan in place in the event my head spun, my heart pounded out of my chest, my lungs seized, and microbeads of sweat rolled down my clammy skin. My already-existing anxiety was made worse tenfold from my recreational drug use, and the voice inside told me I could not continue this way.

My doctor encouraged me to open up to my parents about my drug use. After their initial shock faded, my parents set me up with a therapist who introduced me to hypnotism and *meditation* to cope with my anxiety. Initially, having someone to talk to was comforting, but his focus on using *medication* as a key component of my treatment frightened me. I stopped going.

Fast forward a few years; I signed up for a 5K charity run with some coworkers. I didn't have a clue about running, but for shits and giggles, I signed up anyway. An epiphany unfolded. Running exposed me to the physiological and mental benefits of breathing evenly and rhythmically.

One year after the 5K, I joined a running group and trained for my first marathon. This health-centric, fun-loving community in which I had immersed myself was just what I needed. For the first time in my life, I genuinely felt good about myself. Physically, I noticed tightness in my knees, hips, and feet. When sports doctors and foam rollers didn't seem to cut it, I signed up for my first in-studio yoga class. The physical relief I felt and the healing that took place were secondary to the mental and emotional benefits from moving and breathing mindfully.

Meanwhile, I was one year deep in an emotionally abusive relationship. A relationship that filled my soul with sporadic bursts of excitement yet had me questioning my self-esteem and worthiness. Running and yoga provided immediate relief, but the impermanence of their benefits bothered me. I craved more control, and that led me down a self-destructive path. I found myself in all-consuming and emotionally draining altercations, barricading the door in one instance and physically overpowering his small stature.

I found myself crying after finding out he could not make it to the finish line of a major race because he relapsed on cocaine the night before.

I found myself on the shower floor experimenting with what it felt like to slice my skin with a razor. *Maybe this will get his attention.* Only to eventually end up handcuffed in a cop car and then the emergency room for a psych evaluation.

Throughout these terrifying experiences, I can easily admit my awareness and inner voice were sorely suppressed.

Once I moved on from the clutches of this relationship that did not serve my highest purpose, clarity seeped in. *Why do I keep returning to someone that hurts me time and time again?* I deserved better than this. Even couples therapy could not salvage what was already lost. I couldn't help but think, *instead of trying to control someone else's actions and feelings, what if I only tried to control this breath, in this moment right here? What if this breath is the only thing I could (should) control?* It was time to get back to myself.

My breath became my connection to the voice within. Looking back on my journey, practicing yoga was the anchor that led me to expand my awareness in understanding that nothing is permanent and the silver lining isn't always crystal clear.

One fateful day several years later, I was put to the test once again. I made a comfortable living working as a marketing professional at a security and defense agency. My now-husband and I had been on a few fantastic dates. Life was good. Out of the blue, my boss called me into her office. There, the Director of HR apprehensively sat at the round table, fingers visibly clasped. My chest tightened, and, for a moment, my breath was suspended.

"We are making company-wide cuts," she said with the same deadpan expression she made the first day we met and every day after. "I am sorry to say we have to let you go."

I returned to my desk and robotically gathered my belongings. A cardboard box in hand, I said my goodbyes and walked out emotionless. I sighed a big sigh in my car. *What do I do now?*

Instead of over-analyzing and jumping into the job search, the voice inside told me to try something different. Something out of the norm. Something that scared me. One week later, I found myself on an airplane from DC to San Diego, journaling the entire way.

California was always my dream, and I was determined to make it come true. I stayed with my best friend for a week while scoping out various yoga studios that offered 200-hour teacher training. In my mind, I was simply continuing my education. Never in a million years did I imagine I'd become a teacher! Upon registration, I flew home to get my life in order and hugged family and friends goodbye. Now *this* change? This change revived me.

As incredible as my experiences were during teacher training, the memories that really stuck with me had nothing to do with the training itself. It was about my quickly expanding awareness and the beautiful souls with which I was fortunate enough to connect.

I explored a new part of the country that was breathtaking beyond words and even befriended a willow tree at a local park that I often sat, studied, and meditated under.

I had a major falling out with my best friend, who essentially told me to go screw myself and never spoke to me again without remorse.

I lived in a hotel for a week, paint peeling and party-goers partying next door before a generous classmate offered me a room for the rest of my stay.

I confessed to my now-husband that I loved him over the phone while walking past a dingy strip mall, feeling lost and found all at once.

I was encouraged to get past my stage fright, call myself a teacher, and share with others the very same tools that helped me.

Once I returned home from California, I signed up with a local yoga studio, and my practice progressed. My world settled, and I became more peaceful. Through pranayama and meditation, yoga poses that previously seemed unattainable were now second nature. I went on to marry the love of my life, traveled up and down the north and central American continents and the Caribbean, and gave birth to my daughter on the evening of a winter's first snow. Postpartum anxiety led me to leave my career and focus on myself and my family. Still, Candace's death was ultimately the catalyst for the real change that began to take place.

I attended yoga retreats, solstice celebrations, women's circles and met with metaphysical leaders more regularly. I participated in numerous healing sessions and felt my guardian angels around me. Any time I saw a rare animal, I would immediately research its spiritual significance. I sought to understand life beyond death. I came into alignment with the moon and her cycles. I collected crystals and educated myself on their powers and purpose. I was gentler with myself. I meditated and journaled. I noticed the subtle energies around me.

My curiosity led me into questioning my very being, like *why on earth am I even here? Why are some taken away too soon, and what were they here to teach us?*

While soaking in all of this knowledge, my beloved french bulldog suddenly passed away, and my grief took me to a place of further expanded awareness. I realized that all my experiences thus far were pointing me to a deeper understanding of what it meant to *exist* versus what it meant to *live*.

Soon thereafter, my inner teacher burst forth, and I pursued yoga gigs. At first, I mimicked a lot of what other teachers have said and done. My authentic voice, while still a work in progress, is my spiritual voice. It's the voice that whispers to me during deep meditation. It's the voice that stems from my heart and guides students to move and be still in their bodies. It's the voice that comes through when I am comforting my daughter. Looking back on the poetry I wrote all those years ago, *that* was my voice too. I just didn't know it yet.

Our experiences are building blocks to the paradise still under construction today. While our experiences don't define us, we can find real happiness in the process and in hindsight.

With my voice, I hope to help others connect with themselves through mindful breathing and movement. Through awareness of life's cycles, we can find beauty in impermanence. While this is a lifelong process for many, we can come closer to paradise if we surround ourselves with love and lead the way with an open heart.

Sheri was born in Tehran, Iran, just a couple of years after the revolution. Her parents left the country and found themselves in the outskirts of New York to raise their two children. She began practicing yoga in 2007, and six years later, she became a certified yoga teacher from Pilgrimage of the Heart yoga studio in San Diego. After having her daughter in 2017, she wanted to find ways to better connect with her. So she left her 15+ year marketing career to focus on motherhood and her overall well-being, even learning infant massage! She began her children's yoga journey in 2019 and is now a Registered Children's Yoga Teacher.

Having grown up in Philadelphia, PA, and Washington, DC, Sheri studied classical piano at the prestigious Levine School of Music. After high school, she graduated with a Bachelor's degree in English from the University of Maryland, Baltimore County. After graduation and five years of working as a technical writer, she enrolled in Georgetown University's School of Continuing Studies' Public Relations and Corporate Communications (PRCC) program. She studied part-time while working full-time, even traveling a semester to London to work closely with big name marketing firms, resulting in her Master's of Professional Studies (MPS).

In 2020, Sheri and her little family of three moved their lives from DC and traveled across the country, settling in beautiful Lake Tahoe. She currently teaches adults and children in Kings Beach, CA and Incline Village, NV, and resides in Zephyr Cove, NV, just a mile up the road from the lake. You'll find her outside daily for a run, bike, hike, snowboard, swim, loving on other people's dogs, or riding her SUP on the lake.

Learn more about Sheri's offerings at www.fierceheronyoga.com and her travel blog at www.welshsvoyagewest.com.

CHAPTER 8

Just Shut Up and Step Over the Fucking Line!

The Healing Power of Words

By Rev. Pam McDonel, LMT

*A*re you sure you want to lead with this? That conservative, proper southern country girl voice asked loud and clear—my PSSS (Play Small Stay Safe) voice. *It's gonna sound offensive to some. They may not read your chapter, and they sure ain't gonna think it's spiritual!*

Well, this is what continues to come to me each time I try to decide the "most defining moment" that brought me to who I am now. So, yes, I do. My badass Warrior Goddess/High Priestess voice answered, the one that has been silenced far too long and is now determined to show up with courage and stop playing small!

I shouldn't have to feel ashamed about writing what's in my heart.

Now don't get me wrong. PSSS saved my bacon more than once, so I honor her as much as I now revel in my newfound Warrior Goddess. I am in a more sacred place to not only listen to the wisdom and guidance of both, but make bolder, trusted decisions.

Sister Lightworker! Remember who you are.

This year I am discovering more about my spirituality, my High Priestess healer self, and business acumen. I want all three to work together to create and provide the best possible outcome for my clients.

I'm part of a year-long business study for writers. The founder encourages connection with others to share information, gather ideas, and learn new strategies. I chose this because I want to learn how to compose well-written, meaningful text and documents to share strategies and motivate my clients—information that will help them understand, shift, and promote their journey of healing.

I received the title of this chapter during one of those connection conversations.

With a bit of trepidation, I sought out one of the instructors, Donnie Boivin, known for his rather rugged, no-nonsense ability to help others see through and past their business stumbling blocks. This was a brave step for PSSS, who wasn't sure we were ready for such direct influence, so Warrior Goddess stepped out.

"Tell me a little about yourself. What brought you to this place in life?" He asked as we were getting to know one another.

"Well," and I began. I took Donnie for a short walk through what I view as my somewhat normal childhood. I shared snippets of my adult life and the memories of taking care of my mom, who developed Alzheimer's. I paused briefly as this one vital moment flashed in my mind. The one I experienced time and again on each visit:

Will she know me today? And as quickly as that thought would cross my mind, I would say: "Hi Mama." Her head would lift, tilt toward the sound of my voice, and her lips form the semblance of a smile. Although she couldn't speak and didn't have much movement, the energy and the love of that body held captive by this debilitating disease would come alive as if a bright and brilliant light had just shot into the room out of nowhere.

As I continued to outline what I do now, he interrupted to ask: "Okay. Wait a minute. What just happened?"

"What do you mean?" I answered, totally unaware why he asked this question.

He explained that after a stirring explanation of the journey of love and care I had given my mom, I suddenly deflated as soon as I began to share what I did now.

A brief discussion ensued, and I continued at his urging.

"Go on." Shortly into my story, he stopped me and affirmed with a sharp tone: "You just did it again! What's going on? Your energy just bottomed out." Then, a little softer, "What is that all about?"

As we examined it further, I responded: "I don't know. It's like I'm not supposed to go there. Like there's this line I'm not supposed to cross."

PSSS suddenly showed up to remind me about the imposter syndrome. *You can tell people about the work you do, but you can't claim to be a healer! Only God can heal. So stay in your lane, girlie.*

His questions broke her little tirade: "What does it look like? Where is it? Does it have a color?"

Wait a minute, I thought, *this sounds familiar. I use this with my clients.*

"It's like this wide," my hands expand to show the width to be about ten to twelve inches, "and it's right in front of me. It's on the ground. Like a line in the sand. I can walk up to it, but I can't step over it."

"That's interesting," he mused. "So, I'm going to say this with all the love and encouragement I can because I know you're sensitive." And with a bold, direct, and yet tender manner, he boomed at me:

"Just step over the fucking line, Pam!"

And to my surprise, my immediate response was: "I can do that?"

"Of course you can!" he replied with a bit of humor mixed with a giggle.

Now at one time, hearing these words said with that force would have completely shut me down. But that day, those words brought new meaning to my life—a moment of complete understanding. Embracing the mighty High Priestess Healer. I am gives me a unique and creative vision for the work I came here to do— the Lightworker who raises and holds the vibration for others to achieve personal healing and full potential.

Why does my "humanness" keep getting in the way? I know my "spirituality" is and has always been there. I've had a lifetime of nudges, the gut feelings, the knowing, the intuition knocking at my door.

Reader: You have them too! We all do.

For as long as I can remember, I've always been connected and had conversation with Source. As a little girl, I knew the Divine as God. I've come to realize there is much more to the Divine Source than I learned from the Baptist pulpit. There is a greater connection to the whole of consciousness—one that defines my spirituality. My humanness is the physical feelings, emotions, and experiences of this earth.

Oh boy, this is where you're gonna lose family and friends! Warns PSSS. *How are you gonna justify precisely what that means to you?* And my Warrior Goddess/High Priestess answers: *I don't need to. I know my faith is strong. They either accept me, or they don't. It's none of my business what they think about me.* And, of course, I shudder at this reality because a part of me does care. My human aspect wants to be accepted, loved, and honored for who I am and what I believe, not what's comfortable for others and who they want me to be. There's also that tiny thing of conviction by some. The belief I need to be saved because I don't believe what and how they believe. I don't need to be saved. I'm satisfied and strong in my faith in who the Creator is.

The beginning of my remembering who I am came in the next few years after my mama's death in 2002. Physically, emotionally, mentally, and financially exhausted and depleted, I knew I needed help to restore.

In those first few years after my mama died, I was introduced to my highly sensitive and intuitive side by Monica. She was my hairstylist, esthetician, good friend, and mentor. Monica shared, and I listened. She guided, encouraged me, and I found my way back to my inner knowing. I explored, studied, and "tested" the waters, so to speak, as I grew to understand being a highly sensitive person and empath. Many things began to make more sense.

For the first time in my fifty-plus years, I recognized my inner guidance system and identified my gifts, skills, and talents. I asked myself: *how can I begin to use them intentionally rather than by default?* Like a curious child, I began to study all I could about those things outside the tiny world I had built around myself to stay safe.

Some years later, home from the courthouse after my third divorce, one of my most defining moments appeared. I found myself on my couch, alone, rocking back and forth with knees pulled tightly to my chest. I looked up and quietly asked what I had been asking all my life:

"Who am I, and why am I here?"

There was no one there to answer. Then with more force, I pleaded:

"Why am I in this same place once again? Things never seem to change! What is it I'm supposed to learn from all this?"

At that moment, I suddenly saw myself, outside of my body, on the floor in front of the couch as if someone or something unseen forcefully pulled me there. On hands and knees, I was sobbing uncontrollably and asking again, this time with much more intensity:

"Who. Am. I. Why the hell am I here? What is it I'm supposed to be doing in this life?"

Memories of my past flashed through my mind of the hundreds of times a little voice shouted out a warning for me. As my mind flipped through the pages of my history, a jolt shook my whole body, and I heard a voice ask:

"Who do you want to be? What do you want to do with the rest of your life?" Startled, I looked up through teary eyes to find no one else in the room. After all, I was alone, *wasn't I?* I now understand that voice is my Warrior Goddess/High Priestess.

This wasn't the first time I received such counseling. Before, the guidance always came as an intuitive knowing or understanding, but this was the first time the words seemed to be spoken loud enough for me to physically hear them, although I knew they were only being felt somewhere deep inside me.

My mind drifted through numerous situations when my intuition was issuing warnings. Sometimes I ignored them because the alternative suggested just seemed too scary. I just couldn't cross over that line. Every time I chose *not* to act in cooperation with my intuition, I learned to play small.

A nudge I have learned to listen to: when something shows up three times, I better listen up and do it. So when writing a chapter in my first collaborative book rolled around for the third time in a few weeks, I stepped up to the challenge. I never desired to be published in a book, but I'm glad I did. That led me to the business study, where I realized how small I'd learned to play.

Thank you, Lord, for your nudges and your safekeeping, even when my humanness didn't respond with lightning speed!

I digress.

Get up off this floor, I told myself, *and figure it out. It ain't the first time you've started over, and it probably won't be the last!*

"Let me see," I said out loud as I saw myself dragged back upon the couch. I relaxed a bit and curled my legs up under a blanket to ponder those words, the questions I'd asked, and the answers I clearly heard.

"I'm damned near 62. This is not what I expected at my retirement age! Whatever happened to grow up, get married, have kids, and live happily ever after. What a lie that's turned out to be!"

I sat still with my eyes closed and allowed that quiet, calm, peaceful wave of confidence, love, and all-knowing to wash over me—a time of contemplation and understanding. As a younger version of this woman, a time like this would simply include falling asleep to escape the drudgery of life's events and decisions to be made. Today was different. It was time to get to work! I was ready to move forward into the new awakened authentic me.

I decided to be a massage therapist. I studied, received my certification, and began practicing out of my home studio on evenings and weekends while working my full-time corporate job. I also studied Reiki and became a Reiki Master. I became skillful in cranial sacral therapy, essential oils, and several energy techniques. The technique I most love to work with is tapping. I researched several versions and decided to study Emotional Freedom Technique through EFTUniverse. Today I combine these techniques and therapies in one manner or another based on my individual client's needs.

I spent a lifetime in what I call a chameleon role—taking care of everyone else, doing or being what I thought everyone else needed me to be or do, never recognizing there was also a "me" that needed my attention. Those years and subsequent years later brought me to a new place to explore my spiritual knowing.

My journey, experiences, training, and roles I played have given me the knowledge and skill to do what I do today—the ability to listen to my clients. I empathize yet stay focused and guide them in a direction that best suits their healing. I am that safe and sacred place. They know their most profound shares will be honored and protected with confidence.

I'm a vessel through which healing energy flows from the Divine. This is my gift. My skill. My talent. I chose to come to this place, this time, to open and hold sacred space for others' healing, to raise and maintain the vibration of this place so that others may come into it at their own pace. I'm here to bring harmony and light, together with others, and shine so brightly, this world will emerge victorious from the darkness.

Words. Are. Powerful!

As I struggled with whether our readers would be offended by my title and whether I should use it, I remember the book by Don Miguel Ruiz, *The Four Agreements*. You may wish to read it.

Be Impeccable With Your Word.
Don't Take Anything Personally.
Don't Make Assumptions.
Always Do Your Best.

"The word is the most powerful tool you have as a human; it's the tool of magic. But like a sword with two edges, your word can create the most beautiful dream, or your word can destroy everything around you." *The Four Agreements.*

I'm human. I'm not always impeccable with my word, and sometimes I make assumptions or take things personally. But I always intend to do my best. I choose to give myself permission with ease and grace as I work with the other three.

How will you use your word, your voice? Which edge of the sword will you choose? Will you stuff your feelings deep inside and choke on them day after day? How often do you defer to your critical voice–the one that holds you down? I encourage you to find and use your warrior voice to move further into your spirituality, your highest path, and whatever it is you came here to do.

And please, remember to give yourself permission with ease and grace.

No one's path is quite the same as someone else's. Neither is the delivery and receipt of the spoken word. When invited to write about the most defining moment that brought me to who I am now, the title of this chapter was the words that shook me to the core.

For me, there isn't just one defining moment. It's like life. It's a journey. Each life experience brought me one step closer to looking deeper into that journey of my soul and the spirituality of becoming who I am.

Playing Small to Stay Safe can no longer hold me captive in a world that is anything less than complete abundance, love, and gratitude. I'll step over that fucking line and into the light as many times as it takes. This is who I came here to be—a light working with the Great Light to help others find their light.

As we come to the end of this chapter in my life, one last nugget from a friend pops into my head, "No one else is supposed to understand your calling; it wasn't a conference call."

So whoever or whatever holds you hostage and keeps you from your innermost longings, I encourage you to find a way to step over that line! Now is your time to know and become you.

This chapter is dedicated to all my family, friends, and acquaintances that have propelled me along in my spiritual journey. The ones who push, pull, and sometimes drag me kicking and screaming across that fucking line! Thank you!

 **Rev. Pam McDonel, LMT,** owns Sandbox Enterprises LLC and co-owns Sacred Space Restorative Bodywork LLC. She is a gifted healing artist, empath, Lightworker, best-selling author, ordained minister, beach walker, and happy napper.

Depleted from adrenal fatigue and other stress-related issues, Pam's journey of self-discovery and healing stirred her long-shushed intuitive skills. It led her to share these skills with others who have a deep desire for personal healing of the body-mind-spirit connection.

Pam's expertise in the sacred movement of energy skillfully guides and empowers others to recognize, navigate, shift, and transmute challenging emotional and behavioral patterns. She blends traditional and alternative energy and spiritual healing modalities with her natural intuitive skills and gentle touch. Some have termed her work as "a little bit of WuWu Heaven."

Pam believes finding the tools that work for you and being

intentional about your healing can allow your body to respond in miraculous ways to heal itself. Blending modalities of Energy Tapping to release blocked emotions and trauma, Reiki for balance and harmony, or Therapeutic Massage for relaxation and stress relief, she designs a plan for your well-being.

Pam will partner with you to help you embrace your authenticity, connect with your inner healing wisdom, and honor your truth. She can help you release the stress, the tension, and the decades of blocked energies that could be holding you hostage.

You can find out more about Pam or connect with her at:

Website: sacred-space.biz

Business Facebook: SacredSpaceOK

Instagram: https://www.instagram.com/sacredspaceok/

LinkedIn: https://www.linkedin.com/in/pam-mcdonel-81971b12

Personal Facebook: https://www.facebook.com/pam.mcdonel

Wellness Universe World-Changer:

https://www.thewellnessuniverse.com/world-changers/pammcdonel/

Amazon Readers Short link:
https://www.amazon.com/-/e/B08WB4L8W4

Crave More Life Roadshow Podcast:
https://cravemorelife.com/with-pam-mcdonel/

CHAPTER 9

Resisting Surrender
Fighting to Find Myself

By Mary Raddell, Intuitive Bodyworker,
Transformational Coach and Healer

t all started in a desperate moment of surrender. I had no other
choice but to lower myself face-down onto the ground. The only
person with me was three feet away, unconscious and completely
unaware of what was happening. He didn't even see them coming.
I threw my tattered, heavy purse off to the side, hoping they would
take it and run. Instead, I felt the barrel of the gun pressed firmly
into the back of my skull. I could feel how perfectly cylindrical it
was, the weight of the metal as it kissed the back of my head, the
pressure at which they held it to reassure me that if I tried to get
up and run, they would kill me. The ground was wet, somehow
warm and cold at the same time as the snow had begun to melt on
an unseasonably warm day in December. My jeans were damp and
itchy; my peacoat hiked up to my neck, choking me; I could barely
breathe. My mind was racing. *Is this really happening?*

As one man held the shotgun to the back of my head, the other
began to search my pockets; each pocket searched individually.
I could feel the outline of his firm hand graze against my body,
each move more violating than the next, from my coat pocket to
my pants pocket. I had nothing in them, yet here I was with a
stranger searching me, purposefully, intensely, as if there were
more he was seeking than my money. I later realized it was in this
moment that they stole my sense of identity along with any sense
of safety and stability.

The weeks and months following the attack were debilitating. As I tended bar, I listened to the neighborhood speak of the

robbery and how they would've done things differently, not realizing it was me it had happened to. I felt the only way I could process it was to talk about it as it replayed in my head like a broken record. *Maybe if I keep talking about it, it will go away.*

But it didn't. I had friends tell me they couldn't listen to me talk about what happened anymore. Everyone around me was frustrated and continuously told me to get over it, not knowing the terror I continued to feel deeply in my body. Night terrors kept me from sleeping, and paranoia kept me from living a normal day. I constantly looked over my shoulder, never feeling safe, counting doorways and escapes everywhere I went. I couldn't even have my back to a door or be exposed in an open room. Agitation and exhaustion plagued me, along with frequent mental breakdowns, panic attacks, and bursts of anger. I didn't feel as if I could trust myself. My only perception of safety was trying to control everything around me.

Who was this person? This wasn't me.

I used to be confident and carefree, and suddenly I was a shut-in in my own body. I didn't have the sense of confidence or security to save me, and no one knew how to help, so instead, I pretended I was okay. I would put on a fake smile to get through my day, but often I would isolate myself, crying alone incessantly, never telling anyone what I was truly feeling. Or when I would come out, I would drink heavily in hopes of not remembering and tried to tell myself that tomorrow would be a better day. I went from a thriving 27-year-old in the process of getting licensed as a Physical Therapist Assistant to broken and mentally unstable, plagued with PTSD. I felt like I was losing everything.

With one semester left, getting my degree and license were the only things motivating me. As time went on, suicidal ideations began to take over. I was grasping for any reason to live as my life literally became a day-to-day struggle. Most of my friends abandoned me. I was already disconnected from most of my family, and I felt no one could help me. I kept hearing this voice in the back of my head: *If you stay in Cleveland, you will die.* I felt it in every cell of my body. I wished for death daily, welcomed it, and it didn't seem to be coming. As time went on, I knew the only thing

I could do was start my life over; my only option was to leave. I passed my board exams and became a PTA, but that was just the beginning.

For years I fought myself. The need to control everything around me consumed my mind and body. Nothing worked cohesively. Everything was in constant chaos.

There has to be a better way to live; this can't be it. Something has to give.

I begged and pleaded for someone to save me. The help wasn't coming.

I give up; I don't know what to do, I threw my hands up in surrender, and that was it.

Next thing I knew, I was being offered a contract job in Cincinnati. I quit the bar that day, packed up my car, and left two days later. I didn't even tell anyone I was leaving. Just as I was getting comfortable, the contract job was ripped away, and six weeks later, I was back in Cleveland unemployed, lonely, and without any direction or anything to look forward to. I sat there in defeat, no purpose, no motivation, not even a dream of what I could be doing. I didn't know what was next. I clung to my last ounces of hope, and within a couple of weeks, my new chapter would begin. I finally got out of Cleveland and moved to Maryland. I went somewhere no one knew me or my story. I was free! Unfortunately, that was temporary. With this new beginning, I also carried my past. I skillfully tried to hide it underneath a new identity, but it came back, raging. Thus, I began therapy.

I was broke in a new city, no friends, new career, a new beginning, and just when I thought everything should be getting better, it began to fall apart. So I began searching for any piece of me that made sense. That's when I found Elena.

Elena was a clinical counselor, but there was something special about her. I couldn't place it at the time, but she knew how to read me and tap into me, unlike anyone I had ever met before. I had seen therapists before, but it was always the same bullshit, and I felt they couldn't help me. I'd tell them what they wanted to hear, then on my way I would go. But Elena was different. She called me on my shit. She tapped into my tendency to run and be avoidant and wouldn't let me play games. She looked me dead in the eye and said to me, "Mary, one day something is going to come up in one of our sessions, and you're going to want to run. All I ask is when that day comes, you come back for one more session, and we discuss it."

Eventually, that day did come, and I avoided Elena for months. During that time, I began to recognize who I was becoming. I began to see what was happening; my intuitive abilities were expanding. I could feel energy coursing through my hands when I touched someone. Messages would come to me, things I could've never known without someone telling me. I began channeling, and my clients were healing more rapidly. There was a stillness in my body and quiet in my head, and for the first time, my life was beginning to make sense. It scared the shit out of me. Remembering Elena's request from months before, I knew I had to go back.

As I began to connect with Elena and her intuitive healing abilities, she helped me peel back the layers of my being. We dove into everything; inner child healing, EFT, energy healing, ancestral trauma, sexual, mental, physical, and emotional abuse, boundaries, and consent. But, most of all, she helped me find my ability to speak up for myself strongly, confidently, and unapologetically. I got licensed as a massage therapist during that time, and Elena guided me to open my own private healing practice. I was then led to work with my first Embodiment Coach and eventually found Tantra and working in the Akashic Records, all of which have forever changed me.

It took five years with Elena to begin to remember who I was, and I fought her almost every step of the way. As I sat in my resistance, making every excuse I could as to why I couldn't move forward, I was often paralyzed by my fear. Still, over time, I began remembering my intuitive abilities and sensitivities. As a child, my sensitivity and empathy would cause me frequent mental breakdowns and severe exhaustion because I didn't know yet how to differentiate my energy from others or how to ground and clear it out of my body. I remembered seeing angels and spirits as young as six and into my early 20s, but developing PTSD created fear around my clairvoyance, and I shut everything down around me. I remember fighting my parents as a teen as they couldn't see what I saw happening within the family, how we were breaking, and they weren't doing anything to help. Apparently, I've always had access to my "clair-abilities," and now I was in a time of remembering how to come back to them after years of trauma and stress had hidden them from me.

I learned I could see and feel energy intensely, yet all the while, I had no clue what I was doing. Elena began to teach me how to work with energy and enhance and tune into my abilities. Three years into our sessions, she revealed to me her gift was helping emerging intuitives come back to themselves, and for me, that took healing through trauma and family wounding. Ironically this is now part of what I do with my clients. I assist them in their breakthroughs and bring them back to trusting their intuition by reconnecting the mind and the body. The last two years of our sessions focused on shifting my awareness and refining how to access my intuition and abilities. She gave me the tools to process energy physically in the body, mentally, emotionally, and spiritually. Over time I connected my ability to help others process and heal their trauma using my words, hands, energy, and the tantric tools I was learning along the way.

Our last session was in June of 2020. As I sat in my car in between clients on a video session, I noticed Elena was no longer giving me the answers to the questions I asked.

"Elena, why don't you give me the answers anymore? You used to tell me what to do."

"Let me think about that for a minute," she replied.

I watched Elena sit there and listen to Spirit, which I now recognize spoke through her during our sessions. She replied, "It's about your sovereignty, you have the answers within you. I no longer have to answer your questions for you."

In that moment, I realized I was done. That was it. No more therapy for me. I had all the tools I needed. I could trust myself, my intuition, my mind and body, and it was time for me to continue my journey. Yet, there was a piece of me I was still fighting, and something was still missing.

In 2019 I started working privately with embodiment and

empowerment coaches, began my training in the Akashic Records, and started to study Tantra. In the beginning, my resistance showed up full force. It overpowered me as tears and frustration consumed me with doubt and uncertainty of what I was capable of. I was terrified to tell people what it was I could do. Was I really a powerful healer and intuitive? I didn't even know what that could mean for me. I could hear my inner guidance telling me: Go deeper, lean into it, there's more coming. I would have no choice but to lean into the discomfort. The more I tried to fight it, the worse it got, and I would sit there in tears, fighting with my coaches, each of whom would tell me, "Surrender, quit fighting it, you can do this, Mary."

But I wasn't ready.

I didn't know what they wanted from me.

Surrender felt like death to me, like I was giving up. My chest would tighten, I'd break down crying. I was defeated and drained, and I felt I had nothing left in me.

"You just don't understand it's not that easy. I'm trying; I'm surrendering! How do I surrender more deeply?" I would exclaim.

It didn't make sense to me. *What was I missing?*

I began to realize what was happening. I would connect into my confidence and my power, but as soon as I would catch any momentum, my resistance would rise from deep within, breaking my stride, breaking me right back down to where I began. Consumed with anger and frustration in what felt like a constant defeat, something kept telling me to keep going, "go deeper, Mary, soften, be patient; it's coming."

"Soften." That word seemed to resonate deeply within me, and it didn't feel as harsh or finite as "surrender." I noticed my body began to let go, my heart began to open, and with that, I began to relinquish control. I learned to access the power of vulnerability, let people in, and use my voice to reach them. As relief set in, I began to own the truth of who I am. My life began to change rapidly, and somehow in the chaos, it got easy. Suddenly I had an entirely new community of people who supported me and understood where my life was going.

This eventually led me to Cabo for a weeklong immersive trip called "Tantra, the Art of Falling in Love with Yourself." This was the place where my heart fully cracked open. I found the missing pieces I was looking for. I gained access to my sexual energy and femininity in a new and powerful way, and with it come clarity and greater access to who I am, to my divinity. Finally, I could step fully into my power with trust and ease, and all I had to do was stop fighting and lean into it.

Instantaneously, the Akashic healing and bodywork sessions were taken to new levels. I came home and felt my calling more deeply to embodiment, empowerment, and transformation through teaching, healing, and coaching, giving others greater access to their own hearts, vulnerability, and their power to create the life they truly want to live—coming back to center and wholeness. Living in magic and wonder is how I want to see us all live. This is my calling, to bring you back to yourself, to remember who you are and what you came here to do.

When I got home from Cabo, my life began to transform magically before my eyes. Money began to flow, any remaining pain and PTSD began to slip away, new opportunities began to show, and when I would ask my bodywork clients what they wanted to address, they would directly say to me, "Mary, heal me. Do whatever you have to do."

It was in those moments I realized I could take my clients wherever they needed to go and deeper than they had ever gone before. We use things like inner child healing, past life regressions, healing trauma, removing pain and blocks and realigning the energetic system, to activate and enhance one's intuitive abilities and align them with their soul's purpose to transform their entire being in new and beautiful ways. The breakthroughs have been amazing. And just like that, I knew this is what I was here to do. I began to notice the healers, the teachers, the seers and knowers, and everyone inbetween coming to see me, each began reporting "Mary, since working with you, doors have been opening, my life is transforming... I've been looking for you and I can't believe I found you. I didn't even know you were what I needed."

I've come to name these sessions my Soul Journey Healing Sessions. An intention is set, and Spirit brings through whatever it is your soul is ready to address. In this space, we connect to your purpose and greatest desires and anchor them into this reality. You must be ready, you must be trusting, and you must be willing to go deeper than you've ever gone before. Authentic healing can be messy and uncomfortable, so you must be ready to go on a journey, ready to surrender, ready to face every aspect of yourself, and lean into the discomfort to find and bring through the beauty and joy in the transformation that you desire.

So, let me ask you, are you done fighting, resisting, and avoiding your calling? Are you ready to take a journey and connect to that which your soul truly seeks? Are you ready to open your heart fully, bringing more joy, love, pleasure, and purpose to your world? Then come join me for Transformational Coaching and Soul Journey Healing Sessions and let the truth of knowing who you are come forward. Take a deep breath. Connect. And when you are ready, let's set up your first session.

 **Mary Raddell** is a Transformational Healer, Coach, and Soul Journey guide, who brings her magic through the Akashic Records. She uses her loving, playful, nurturing energy to create lasting shifts into your life to bring more joy, pleasure, and curiosity into your world. Mary is a licensed PTA, LMT, and Certified Reiki and Akashic Practitioner. She has spent the last decade touching the lives of 1000s of people, helping them to find their confidence by moving them through their emotional and mental blocks, and bringing them back into a state of balance and harmony by reconnecting them to their divinity and their body. She weaves various forms of healing into her sessions from her background in Tantra, physical therapy, integrative bodywork modalities, and various forms of energy healing, including her own creation of Soul Journey Healing Sessions through the Akashic Records. Mary uses her intuitive wisdom to help her clients return to their fullest selves. She guides them to facilitate their own healing and connect mind, body, and spirit so they can show up

for themselves in full authenticity no matter where they are on their journey.

Mary thrives on personal development. With each training, she gains new tools to teach her clients how to connect into and shift their own energy. She gives them the skills they need to continue their journey. In her free time, Mary loves traveling, writing, and being in nature. Keep your eyes open because this is just the beginning; there's more magic coming.

Book a session with Mary online at PerceptiveTouchHealing.com

Connect on Facebook at www.facebook.com/mary.raddell or email her at perceptivetouchhealing@gmail.com

CHAPTER 10

Finding Understanding Through the Akashic Records

How I Stopped Struggling and Started Co-creating My Life

By Ashley Hoobler, Life Coach, Akashic Records Master Practitioner, NLP and Quantum Healer, Clairvoyant Energy Reader and Healer

L ife is like a giant puzzle, but often we're just putting the pieces wherever we think they'll fit because we can't see the bigger picture it's meant to become when it's complete.

Have you ever seen those amazing picture murals, the ones with tiny pictures that make up the big picture? You can see how all those tiny frozen moments create this amazing larger picture when you step back. I can't think of a better way to describe this journey of life. Your early childhood and formative memories create the border of the picture, and the moments leading up to you reading this fall into place on top of that foundation, creating the bigger picture unconsciously.

There are those moments in life where suddenly everything clicks, where you see the complete picture and know exactly how all the pieces come together. So often, we ignore those moments, not wanting to acknowledge the image starting to form. Sometimes though, we take notice.

There was one significant moment for me, where suddenly I saw the picture, crystal clear, down to the smallest little detail, and fully understood how all the pieces came together. I saw how my past, present, and potential futures would play out to form that picture. I saw how every relationship I ever had—every struggle, sacrifice, and interaction—was playing into that larger picture. The bright moments from childhood, and even the harder ones, all had a place at the bottom of the puzzle. My rebellious adolescent years formed towards the bottom, starting to take a larger shape. My early adulthood memories were there, too, from joining the Army to when I told the drill instructor in Basic to go back to kindergarten and learn to count properly. There were the many moments spent in stress, grief, fear, and exhaustion in Afghanistan, to the moment I met my former husband. And there was the joy and uncertainty when I found out I was pregnant to the moment my daughter came into the world. All the emotional moments locked into place to create the glorious bigger picture and the woman I would soon become.

It was a journey to get there. Throughout my life, I always considered myself unlucky. You know the adage "when it rains, it pours?" Well, I always seemed to attract a hurricane. One thing after another, it felt like anytime I set my mind to something, I would hit a wall. But, being the stubborn and driven person I am, I would find a way through the wall with determination.

But the moment when the pieces of that puzzle became clear, I finally realized I didn't have to bust through that wall like a raging bull. All I had to do was make a different choice and simply walk around the wall to keep going. At that moment, I realized that I had created the wall. I wasn't consciously aware of it at the time; honestly, I was oblivious. But when that last puzzle piece dropped in, I could clearly see that through my choices and actions, I was getting in my own way.

A series of events led to this aha moment. Some of the unfolding came from things that weren't so obvious. Sometimes they were the unexplainable situations in life that opened my mind to possibilities. There were also a lot of hard moments and battles fought. I felt like the world as I knew it was crashing around me, but there were also these new deep, soul-driven urges telling me to look in a different direction. That, my friend, is what I call serendipity.

I have always been spiritual, but not in the modern, religious way. I had what people would call gifts. I tried to ignore them, pretending I didn't "see things" or "sense things" or "know things." I had many premonitions in high school. After they played out before my eyes time and time again, I knew I had to trust what I was seeing, and I knew to pay attention to those random curious urges.

From then on, I began to use my intuition frequently. I joined the Army and enlisted as an Intelligence Analyst; my job was to predict enemy actions. Fitting, isn't it? Upon enlisting, I always intuitively knew that I wouldn't make it to the twenty-year retirement, and I wasn't going to become a senior Non-Commissioned Officer. That decision was also a moment of serendipity.

It was common for leaders to ask soldiers why they joined in the wake of 9-11. My honest answer was always that it was a moment of serendipity.

In my teens, I was a rebellious, outspoken girl that blended into several different crowds, not really having one specific clique to stick to. In junior year, the high schools had all the students take a military aptitude test, and then they unleashed the relentless recruiters on us come senior year. There was one recruiter who was hot on my heels. He would not go away no matter what I tried. I scored well in all subject matters, and this was about the time that the surge of forces was happening in both Iraq and Afghanistan. One day, exhausted from the constant calls, texts, and face-to-face interceptions at the high school, I finally agreed to go into the recruiting office.

"If I agree and come in and let you give your schpeal, will you just leave me alone and delete my contact information?!"

"Yes, of course! Can you come in this afternoon?" the eager recruiter responded.

An hour later, I pulled up and parked right in front of the recruiting station in the next town over. I took a deep breath before getting out of my car. *What am I even doing here? I am not the type to join the military. I can't keep my mouth shut. Ugh!*

I stepped out of the car and started to take the few steps forward to the door. As I stepped inside, a sudden wave of clarity washed over me. It was like I was living in the dark without realizing it, and someone had just turned on the lights.

In that moment, of simply walking through the door, I *knew* it was exactly where I was supposed to be and what I was supposed to do. There were no words to describe this sudden revelation. Nothing was said; nothing was shown. It was just this viscerally deep knowing, and time froze for a millisecond to allow me to truly take in that moment of reckoning. After that, I walked to the recruiter's desk and spent the next hour turning pages and scanning the books that described the jobs the military had to offer. Intelligence Analyst: they predict enemy movements, anticipate their actions, and track them. *Hmm. Since I can't be on the front lines, this might be a good way to help people and have a big impact.*

I created my list and went through the paperwork. Two weeks later, I was on a plane to Basic Training, much to my entire family's surprise. While serving in the Army, I had many moments of intuitive knowing that helped form my analysis of what was to come and used it to help guide me through the struggles and moments of uncertainty.

When I turned 28, the universe stepped in and forced me to take another path. I wasn't paying attention to my serendipitous moments. It started gently, as a thought in my mind that I kept puzzling over, then started to escalate until it was a full-force hurricane and there was no getting past it.

While overseas on a deployment, away from my daughter, I kept wondering if I needed to get out of the Army or if I should try to stick it out. My back and hips were starting to slowly stop functioning while I was there, but it was manageable. I should mention I was also fighting an assignment to a new unit. The big Army wanted me to leave my deployment to go to a new unit down the street, an assignment that wouldn't benefit my career at all. The Army ordered my unit to send me home, but I was filling two important roles at the time, and they couldn't afford to lose me, so I stayed on with them. After getting back, I traveled to a new country with people I had never met before for a month-long training mission. I had to choose to keep my daughter with my parents until I was finally settled back in, prolonging our separation.

About six months later, I was selected for promotion, and I knew deep down that it wasn't meant for me. Being a Senior

Non-commissioned Officer never felt right or meant for me. I missed that sign.

A few months after that, I was put on orders to become a Drill Sergeant. But the required training would have taken me away from my five-year-old daughter again, and I couldn't continue to let her endure a constant whirlwind of ever-changing living arrangements.

She just moved back in with me three months ago! What am I supposed to do? If I don't go, they will kick me out of the Army. If I do go, she'll have to live with my parents again. I don't know anyone here. Ugh. What am I supposed to do with her when I am working all the long hours afterward!

I was stuck. From that point, things only escalated.

I walk into my commander's office. "Ma'am, do you have a moment?"

"Yes, come in; what's going on?"

"Ma'am, I can't do drill sergeant. I don't have any other options either. I have no one here that can watch her for the three months I'd be in training, and she just moved back with me three months ago! She's struggling in school and acting out; if I move her, it'll just make it worse."

I bit the bullet and asked my commander to start the paperwork to get me out of the Army. I didn't see another option. As word spread amongst my co-workers, I started getting approached by many of my seniors.

"Staff Sergeant Hoobler, you need to fight this! The Army needs more leaders like you! We always lose the good ones. We need to keep people like you."

After many conversations like that, I decided to appeal the decision. Oh, boy, did that open my eyes. I watched people I knew well testify before a panel, "I used to praise her, but now I'm disappointed. I heard she told people that she got away with it." The rumors were flying. People that had encouraged me to fight to stay in were starting to show their true colors. I barely scraped by. The so-called win only left me more stuck.

Meanwhile, as I was waiting for that administrative hearing date, my hips decided to really start acting up. "Hey, can you grab my hip when you pass by? I think I left it back there!" I would joke during morning physical training when my hip would drop from under me as I was doing warm-up drills.

Fast forward a year, just before the pandemic hitting the United States, I'm seeing my fourth surgeon, hoping this one will be able to help after several had declined to treat me. He tells me, "You need hip replacements, but you're too young to be a candidate. The best we can do is address some of the issues and hope that it doesn't aggravate your condition any further. If you proceed with surgery, you won't be fit to continue your military service. What do you want to do? I can't promise this is going to make it better or worse for you." So, I was damned if I did, damned if I didn't. I couldn't win. It felt like I was being shoved out of the Army again after only a few months since being given a second chance at staying.

When it rains, it pours; I get the hurricane.

Even with my intuition activated and acknowledged, life still wasn't flowing with ease for me. There was more to the puzzle that I couldn't see. I was on medical leave from work at the onset of the pandemic in 2020 when I suddenly had the strong, unexplainable urge to research the Akashic Records. I learned through the years not to ignore these obsessive urges.

I finally found a teacher who was perfect for me after searching; I just knew. Once I completed the training and passed the certification, I finally had the opportunity to look at my own Akashic Record.

Things started to fall into place as I accessed my record and started pulling information about my karmic patterns. It all made sense! The bombardment of struggles I was facing seemed serendipitous now.

I uncovered that I had a vow of obedience: *You are both rebellious but begrudgingly obedient, like, "Fine! I don't want to, but I'll do it!"* Ugh! I have a Negative Soul Mate contract: *You equate romantic relationships to having to overcome struggle after struggle or are very co-dependent.* And I have an Etheric Implant, *an installed coping mechanism at a soul level,* that upheld the energy of humility at my throat chakra. It all fit!

It explained why I kept attracting the same type of partner

repeatedly. It explained my rebellious attitude but deep-seated need to comply with orders, rules, and regulations. It explained my inability to take a compliment (even though I earned that credit, I'm going to awkwardly change the topic). It even explained the nonstop struggles I was facing with trying to stay in the Army.

That was my serendipitous moment to alter the course of my life, to change my bigger picture, or chose to continue struggling. While many of the patterns I discovered within my record clearly explained my entire life, the best part was, in that moment, I realized it didn't have to be that way! I had the power to change it.

I clearly understood that we create these karmic patterns through our everyday actions, then sustain those actions. Even if we don't realize we're doing it, it's still there. In that moment, I saw and understood how my actions upheld those patterns, and from that point on, I changed them.

We all have deeply rooted unconscious behaviors (or karmic patterns) that we continue to uphold through our daily choices. The problem is, 90 percent of the time, we're operating on autopilot and habitually going through the motions.

When we recognize a pattern or reoccurring event within our lives, it's important to step back and examine it. Having that awareness gives us so much more power over what we experience. I finally understood why meditation, mindfulness, intentions, and being "grounded" were important and taught all spiritual and sacred teachings.

It's because, within each moment, you have the power to recognize a pattern and make a different choice. If your attention is not in that moment, and instead you're living in your head, lost in thought or emotion, you miss that critical opportunity to step out of the cycle and make the change you're seeking.

Understanding the power and possibility of the present moment brought the puzzle picture fully into focus. The Akashic Records have helped me step out of struggle and stop repeating the same cycles over and over. I no longer must bear down and face the hurricanes. My life is freer and peaceful now, and I know I can create anything I want.

I started to give attention to my intuition and trust the

information given to me. That moment helped me recognize those smaller moments of divine serendipity.

What is divine serendipity? I think of divine serendipity as those special moments when a crucial puzzle piece is revealed to you. Whether it's showing you the part of the picture you're in or giving you the next piece to put in place to build that area, it's a sign or message from a higher source that's unmistakably intentional. It resonates deeply within your soul, sending visceral shivers through your body, and you know that moment was meant for you, and in that moment, you can decide to change the direction that the bigger picture is starting to form.

Those moments of serendipity led me to open my own business to help others turn their lives around, find their personal power, and take back the reins. It led me to create a life coaching business that uses the Akashic Records to find those patterns and guide my clients to step out of their cycles and recognize their own critical moments of opportunity. To find, see, understand, and embrace the power of the present moment.

Pay attention to those little moments that give you a glimpse of life's puzzle picture. Then, put those pieces back into their rightful places with attention and care, and soon you will be able to see the big picture you're building.

Remember, you have the power to choose the picture you want to create.

Ashley Hoobler is an Army veteran, single mother, and spiritual leader. Ashley spent 13 years in the Army, which helped her cultivate her leadership, mentorship, and communication skills through her experiences in working with people from all walks of life. In 2020 Ashley opened her spiritual business, Seeking Divine Serendipity, which was created to assist spiritual seekers in healing and transforming their lives, no longer living through struggle after struggle. Ashley focuses most of her work on newly awakened souls who have had their lives turned upside down upon their awakening, who crave a life of stability, peace, and fulfillment. Ashley blends the magic of the Akashic Records, NLP, Coaching, and psychology to help clients break free from old habits and create a new life for themselves.

Ashley has completed six levels of training in the Akashic Records through the Soul Realignment modality and the initial and mastery certifications through Soul Success Unleashed, which teaches aura and clairvoyant readings and energy healing and management tools. Ashley has also been certified as a Life Coach, Evolved Neurolinguistic Programing Practitioner, and Quantum Timeline Healing practitioner through Avalon Empowerment. She is working towards her master's degree in psychology before continuing to pursue a Ph.D.

To learn more about Ashley and her programs,
go to www.seekingdivineserendipity.com
or email ashley@seekingdivineserendipity.com

CHAPTER 11

Signs From Spirit

Reminders of Faith, Hope, and Love

By Laura McKinnon, E-RYT

When feathers appear, angels are near.
Many people doubt receiving messages from Spirit, thinking it's impossible or only happens for a select few. Not only is it possible, messages from Spirit are abundantly constant and showered equally upon everyone. They are sent to offer encouragement, hope, and comfort. To affirm our path or nudge us towards another. But above all, these messages remind us that we are never alone and always held in loving grace. The only requirement to receive is to believe that you can.

When the spirit world communicates, it speaks in ways we can recognize. Using signs and symbols, messages are sent through people, animals, and nature. They can even be felt as sensations in our bodies or voices heard in our heads. Impossible, you say? Remember what it was like to be a small child, the splendor of believing in magic and fairytales? Our minds were limitless then, insatiably curious of all that is possible in our world and of what lies beyond, the enchanting whisper of Spirit dancing around us. Then one day, we grow up. Influenced by everything around us, we begin to lose our whimsical way, and our ability to tune into Spirit fades. What once held mystery becomes mundane as the mind narrows and hardens. Special moments in our life now dismissed as nothing more than mere coincidence. Signs from Spirit become deflected like unwelcome raindrops bouncing off an umbrella.

Since I was a little girl, anytime I was afraid, in struggle, or worry, my parents would tell me to pray. "Talk to God," they would say, or "Ask your guardian angel for help; they will show you the way." During prayer, I always hoped that God or my guardian angel would come to visit me. I wanted to know for sure it was real. I wanted to *hear* an answer or *see* a sign, anything to let me know I wasn't alone. Even though God never visibly appeared to me, I still somehow knew I was heard. When I prayed, I felt an undercurrent of peace I can only describe as the flow of divine grace itself. I started noticing little signs.

One of the first signs I can remember came in the third grade. Our family moved and I started a new school. I felt overwhelmed, scared, and lonely and struggled to make friends. One afternoon upon leaving the classroom, my teacher, Mrs. Dubois, called me to her desk. As I cautiously approached, she met me with the kindest eyes as her hand reached inside her desk drawer. Out came a heart-shaped sticker she placed gently into my small hand. In the middle of the rainbow bordered heart was written, "God loves you." I looked incredulously at her thinking, *how did she know?! I hadn't told her I was feeling lonely.* I felt a warm sensation tingle throughout my body. Instantly I knew it was a reminder that I wasn't alone! Memories like these are plentiful, but it wasn't until my second child when signs from Spirit occurred in a more profound way.

Our first child, Cody, arrived in the summer of 2009. The first thing I heard as he was born was my husband shouting, "Honey! He's smiling, and he looks just like you!" Becoming a mother was my most joyful blessing yet. We had always desired more than one child, so we began discussing growing our family when he became a toddler. Unfortunately, we hadn't yet settled on a timeline when my husband almost died from a massive heart attack. He recovered physically, gradually regaining strength, but emotionally he was never the same.

Undeniably, it was an incredibly traumatic event for all of us. My husband constantly worried about dying. But never did I think it would change his mind about having more kids. Understanding his concerns did nothing to dampen the devastation I felt. For months I begged and pleaded with him to change his mind, trying every angle possible. I was distraught over the idea of our son being an only child, desperately wanting him to have siblings. But my attempts were futile. I would've had an easier time pulling an elephant out of quicksand than to change my husband's mind.

Suffering immense sadness, I mourned not having another child. I knew that if I didn't find acceptance, I would only grow in anger and resentment. So, one night, I turned to prayer.

Dear God, please help me with this as I struggle. I want another child so badly, but I know I cannot make my husband do something he is firmly against. Please know how thankful I am for our son. He is the biggest blessing you have bestowed upon me, and if he is meant to be my only child, I will accept this gift graciously and be at peace. I pledge to let go of the desire to have more and embrace fully the child I have. However, should it be that I am meant to bring another light into this world, I will know because you will tell this directly to my husband. I ask that you have him come to me and say, God has asked us to have another baby. Amen.

I began to feel peace in my heart that night.

I told no one of my prayer, months passing by. And then it happened. One bright and sunny morning, I returned home from teaching yoga classes, feeling energized and ready to tackle work from my home office. Slowing my truck, I pulled into the alley, gravel crushing under my tires. As I approached the house, I noticed my husband standing in the driveway with his arms folded across his chest, his facial expression completely unreadable. Instantly, I felt dread.

Why is he standing in the driveway when he's supposed to be at work?

Is something wrong?

Is someone hurt?

Did something happen to our son?

Panic set in as my mind raced. Feeling my heart sink into my stomach, pulse and breath quickening, I flew out of the car, barely remembering to put it in park.

"Scott!" I cried. "What's wrong?!"

A slow smile crept over his face as he said, "We're going to have another baby."

Relief and anger surged through me at the same time. Relief that no one was hurt, but anger as if I could punch someone in the face. The only thing that made sense to me in that moment was that he was playing a sick, cruel joke on me. He *knew* how badly I wanted to have another child; how dare he make a joke of it!

I screamed at him, anger seething in my words, "You jerk! April Fool's was two days ago! This isn't even close to funny. Why would you do this to me?!"

"But honey, I'm serious!" he replied.

Unconvinced, "What do you *mean* you're serious?" I asked.

"I'm serious! I already threw out your birth control. You won't find it. We're going to have another baby!"

Hesitantly, I began to believe him. I *wanted* to believe him.

"I don't understand. You said we weren't going to have any more kids."

He paused for a moment, then drew a deep breath and said, "Well, this is going to sound strange."

Immediately I felt my heart begin to swell while a warm, tingling sensation spread throughout my body. *Could it be?!*

As if preparing me for something completely inconceivable, he stepped forward and said, "I came home to grab materials for my job from the garage. I ended up going into the house, turning the TV on to the news where they were interviewing a priest. I had to go to the bathroom, and as I was walking back towards the kitchen, I swear I heard God say to me, *you are to bring another child into this world*. It was as if God was *in* our house!"

I stood frozen, unable to speak, just staring at him.

"I know, I know, you think I'm crazy," he says.

I fell into his arms, my mind trying to wrap around his words. "No, honey, it's not crazy at all. I have something to tell you."

As I shared with him about the night I prayed, we both knew something very special had just happened. Even though I was in the middle of my birth control, our second son, Bo, was conceived only three days later.

From the very beginning of his pregnancy, something *felt* different. I struggled with morning sickness much more than I did with my first, but it was more than that. I can only describe it as a very deep current of unease. It was an odd feeling, especially since I carried so much joy in the blessing of having another child. The pregnancy progressed normally, and while the baby and I were physically doing well, I continued to struggle emotionally, trying to ignore the distant whisper that something wasn't right. In my third trimester, I started receiving messages. With each one, time stood still, every hair on my body raising on end, as if a surge of electricity moved through me.

On an unusually warm November day, Cody and I were enjoying a day at the beach. Delighted to be wearing a sundress, I relished in the moment, playing and splashing with him in the cool, blue water. In every way, it was a perfect day. When it came time to leave, we packed up, brushed off the lingering sand, and started walking to our car. Suddenly, I felt wetness spread on my underwear. Knowing it wasn't my water breaking, I tried to keep myself calm as it could mean only one thing; I was bleeding. I quickened our pace, my mind narrowing its focus on getting to the hospital as quickly as possible. As we arrived at the parking lot, we had to pause for a car trying to exit. The driver, seeing us, stopped their car to let us cross. Upon waving a thank you, I realized I knew the driver. It was a friend I had not seen in a long while, a friend who when pregnant had lost her son when his heart stopped beating at 38 weeks. Silently I screamed, *No, no, no! Why am I seeing you now?! What does this mean?* Desperately trying to assure myself, I kept repeating, *everything will be okay, everything will be okay. My son will be okay!* With every fiber of my being, I pleaded for this to be a random coincidence. But, deep down, I knew that it wasn't.

I spent five days in the hospital. The bleeding stopped within a few hours of arriving, but doctors wanted to make sure I wasn't going into early labor. They suspected a partial placental separation, but ultrasound after ultrasound never determined the cause or source of bleeding. I was placed on bed rest out of an abundance of caution. Back at home, my mom came to help for a few days. Late one night chatting, I decided to tell her of my frightening encounter in the parking lot. I will never forget the eerie feeling, how the words haunted me as I said, "Mom, I'm so thankful her story is not my story."

Eight weeks later, in the dark, early hours of a stormy, rainy morning, Bo arrived. Labor at home was normal and uneventful until I woke from an intense contraction and began to hemorrhage. We rushed to the hospital and were immediately taken to surgery. Bo's heart rate was very low. Consumed with fear, I was certain I was going to die. So certain that my last thought before surrendering to anesthesia was a plea to God, *please take care of my boys.*

I awoke to sad faces standing over me. It took me a moment to understand what was happening as I heard, "I'm sorry. Bo didn't make it." Instantly I felt as if my body had been crushed under the weight of a semi-truck, unable to breathe or speak. A flood of tears exploded onto my face as I heard my midwife explain, "They did everything they could."

Bo wasn't breathing when he was born. Unsuccessfully, the NICU team worked for 27 tireless minutes to revive him. Oh, my sweet and precious baby boy. Perfect in every way, he looked only to be sleeping as I held his lifeless body in my arms. None of it made sense. I remember the anger and rage I felt towards God, spewing out like hot lava.

Why would you give me another child, only to take him away?! Why!? How could you have me go through this?!

I felt completely broken, shattered into a million pieces, without any hope of putting them back together. I had lost my son. An invisible, violent force ripped a huge and gaping hole into my heart and body, a hole that could never be filled. The weight of grief was immensely crushing.

The very next morning, I felt a strong urge to write in my son's journal. It was with me because I packed it in my birthing bag. Grabbing it, I fondly remembered the day I went to purchase his journal, how I asked him to help me pick it out. As I walked into the store, my eye immediately took notice of a journal sitting on a shelf. Everything else faded, my vision encompassing this one single journal. *Mom, I want this one!* I could hear my son delightfully say. It was incredibly cute; an owl with big eyes and a heart drawn onto its chest was on the cover. I circled the store to look at others but kept being guided back to the one with owl. Chuckling to myself, *Okay son, we'll get this one.*

As I started to write, moments of other signs during pregnancy came flooding back. The image of a dead owl flashed into my mind–the dead owl I saw the very afternoon after purchasing his journal. And the haunting words returning, *I'm so thankful her story was not my story.* Instantly I understood what my son knew all along; he knew he was not going to stay. God bless his little heart. He knew me all too well. Not wanting me to blame myself or carry the guilt of his death, he had sent me signs to let me know this. *Bam!* The door to the spirit world was kicked wide open.

After his passing, it seemed the skies of heaven itself cracked open, sign after sign pouring down with loving messages offering me comfort and hope and the strength and courage to move forward. Gradually peace began to fill my aching heart in ways I never knew possible, from the boldest, brightest rainbow on display the day of his funeral to his face shining through the presence of his spirit animals—the owl and hummingbird. I've even felt his small hand brushing my cheek.

He constantly reminds me that he's always with me, guiding me from above. His voice whispers, *Mama, I'm here.* The grace of his spirit quenches any thoughts of doubt and has opened my eyes to the greater workings of the spirit world. I no longer dismiss things as random or coincidental; rather I actively *look* for the coincidence in all things. I know when I'm receiving a sign because I *feel* it. It grabs me like someone on a bull horn saying, *pay attention!*

I even received signs for this book. The afternoon I met with the main author about writing for this book, I went out for a long walk with my dog. Coming down the hill as I approached our meeting time, thoughts of skepticism swirled in my head, *who was I to write for a book?* Out of nowhere, in that exact moment, I saw the tiniest little feather floating down, the breeze blowing it straight into my face. I reached out, snatching it into my hand hearing, *when a feather appears, angels are near.* I knew this was an affirmation, a sign of encouragement I was on the right path. As if to press upon me further to say yes to this project, as I met with the author, I learned the first meeting date for co-authors would be on the 18th that month. Bo was born on the 18th. Spirit provided me yet another sign.

The spirit world wants *all* of us to know how much we are loved, seen, and heard. Beings of light always surround and guide us, even in the darkest of times. In any moment, when something specific stands out to you, something that makes you pause and take notice, is a sign from Spirit. Don't question it! You might see numbers in repetition, hear a message in a song as you turn on the radio or see a logo on someone's shirt. If you *think* you see a sign, it's a sign! Have faith that simply acknowledging it enables you to see them more and more often. It also helps to ask! Spirit *loves* to be asked for guidance. Signs will always be sent, but when specifically asked, they deliver in great magnitude. Trust yourself, put down your umbrella and openly receive. It won't be long before you're soaking wet.

Laura McKinnon is a yoga teacher, writer, and mother. With her love of yoga and joy for life, she encourages students to meet themselves where they are, cultivating self-love and compassion to ignite the bright light within. Woven into her classes is the practical wisdom of bringing yoga into daily life. Her certification in Grief Yoga® helps her to assist others in moving through their grief, transform sorrow, and reconnect to love. She also leads workshops and teacher trainings at her yoga studio in Carmel, CA. As a lover of nature, you will find her most often outdoors in two of her favorite places, the ocean and forest. She resides in Seaside with her husband, three children (two earth angels and one heaven sent), two cats, and a dog.

To learn more about Laura's offerings and read her blogs on Life, Motherhood, and Yoga, visit: www.laurasrainbo.com

CHAPTER 12

Immerse Into Stillness
Connecting to Freedom and Peace

By Hayley Verney, ND Human Resource
Management, Certified Life Coach, Yoga Teacher

"When I discover who I am, I'll be free."

– RALPH ELLISON, *INVISIBLE MAN*

roll quietly onto my side to pick up my cell phone before the first of my five (yes, five!) alarms go off. I set these alarms with five-minute intervals to ensure that I wake up before the rest of the household-to relish the 4 am quiet time when I can connect to stillness and meditate.

There is little external and internal noise at 4 am, more silence between my thoughts, and connecting to stillness is easier as my parasympathetic nervous system, which focuses on rest and digestion, is more dominant. I usually resist delving into social media before meditating, as it can activate my sympathetic nervous system, which sends a flash flood of hormones and blood to alert the body to incoming stress, and this causes internal distractions.

On this particular morning, I inhale deeply for four counts, pause by holding my breath for five counts, and slowly exhale for six counts. I repeat this six times, then acting against all my instincts, I decide to open WhatsApp. My friends always tell me how strong my intuition is without any contact. I sense their pain or feelings of elation remotely. This is another one of those serendipitous moments as a message appears on my screen. "Can I call you? I can't breathe; I feel like I'm dying."

What should I do? Should I phone her back now?

I sit in silence for a moment, inhale for four, pause for five, exhale for six. I repeat this conscious breathing until I feel connected to my intuition. I phone her back, we explore her inner landscape, and she becomes aware of the fear of death she was attached to.

This encounter triggers memories of my first panic attack, which occurred a couple of months after my mother died. This was the start of my nightly tossing and turning and head spinning, with my chest and throat constricting as I struggled to breathe. I'd wake up in a sweat, not knowing whether I should collapse on the cold parquet floor or sit upright to allow more oxygen to my brain and lungs. I felt like a prisoner imprisoned in my own mind with walls crushing my breath as the same thoughts kept running through it.

What if I die? What will happen to my children?
Oh God, I don't want them to feel this pain of losing a mother.
I miss my mother's physical and emotional presence so much.
Why did she choose not to fight to stay alive, to stay with us longer?
How could she just leave us?

I was 28 years old and five months pregnant when my mother was ripped out of our family unit after suffering from a rare blood disorder for six weeks. The cause of death was due to unnatural causes. She died after her spleen was surgically removed, an organ we were told was not of much use in the body. The suddenness and the unnatural circumstances made it even more difficult to accept her death. Our mother was our rock, and we were her world. I could not accept that she would die without putting up a fight to stay alive, to be with us. I felt such anger as Mom was always overprotective and loved us profusely. I felt abandoned. It was two months before my brother's wedding, four months before my sister's wedding, and four months before the birth of my second son.

The sudden loss of my mother induced a fear of death and separation. I buried my pain by gathering information, desperately trying to contextualize her death, and learning how to communicate with her in the spiritual realm. My father was a priest, and my family is religious, so life after death was not a foreign concept. My quest for information came from reading many spiritual books and attending various spiritual and metaphysical courses, searching for ways to establish contact with the spirit world. I learnt how to quiet my mind through various breathing techniques, becoming aware of other forms of consciousness and dimensions that we live in.

I would lie quietly in the dark, looking at the ceiling for hours, connecting to stillness after breathing through layers of inner noise, with the hope of being able to do astral traveling and to connect to the spirit world. I had been always afraid of the dark, crawling into my younger sister's bed when I felt an unseen presence around me. I did not want any connection to spirits when I was a child; now, I hungered for it.

I've had some encounters with the spirit world, often sensing the presence of spirit beings through sound, smell, and movement. Most of these experiences have been during yoga and meditation practices. I have often felt my mother's presence, seen her at the foot of my bed, and smelled her perfume. I have connected to spirit beings, angels, and ascended masters. I channel Divine energy and light language through movement, meditation, breath work, mudras and have recently started expressing light language verbally. Light language, an ancient channelled cosmic language, conveys a message through the frequency of sound or symbols which emanates from the heart and speaks to the soul rather than to the analytical or rational mind. Energy fields are shifted to a higher frequency as the vibrations allow you to drop into feeling rather than words and thought.

> "Whenever you deeply accept the moment as it is—no matter what form it takes—you are still, you are at peace."
>
> ECKHART TOLLE, *STILLNESS SPEAKS*

After many years of attending personal and spiritual growth courses, having life coaches, meditating, practicing yoga, and going to mediums, I'm finally at peace with my mother's death. I understand the process of death and that souls transition through different dimensions. They detach from the three-dimensional world we live in, and their consciousness shifts to other dimensions with higher forms of consciousness. I have shifted my feelings of pain and anger to extending compassion for myself and thus found resolution. I'm grateful for the spiritual awakening which was triggered by her death.

Other pivotal moments in my life have led to a greater sense of peace, connection, and ultimately freedom. In this next part, I will share a personal story about an internal distraction (anxiety) that initially I felt might steal my freedom but ultimately enhanced it.

I invite you to awaken curiosity as to what your sense of inner peace and freedom may feel and look like to you once you have journeyed through all your layers of external and internal noise.

> "The equivalent of external noise is the inner noise of thinking, the equivalent of external silence is inner stillness."
>
> ECKHART TOLLE, *STILLNESS SPEAKS*

I was working as a Change Manager on a project when my contract was canceled rather abruptly with the announcement of South Africa going into complete lockdown due to the Covid-19 pandemic. The project involved introducing a new digital system to staff which would change the way that they worked. It would require a shift in mindset, and they would have to go through a process of unlearning whilst learning how to navigate the new system.

After this news, I lit tea light candles at midnight and placed them around the lounge floor. I placed all my crystals on the windowsill, dropped some orange aromatherapy oil (to assist with reducing anxiety) in my diffuser, and put in some frankincense (to induce feelings of peace and relaxation) resin onto a burner. I stood in the center of the room, connecting to the uplifting citrus fragrance and the ethereal energy from my crystals. I created my own sacred space to enable me to tap into my inner guidance system.

I lay down on the floor, flanked by my three meditating fur buddies, and stared into a candle flame, conscious of the scent that filled the air. The new silence was eerie, palpable, and subtle, a silence different to what I had experienced before, a dimension I had not connected to before. The normal noises of the busy road and revving cars were totally absent.

With the absence of the external noise, all I could hear was the inner noise of thoughts and the sensation of anxiety in my chest.

How am I going to cover my financial commitments?
How will the staff members transition through this time of great uncertainty?
How could the company just let me go without any further thought? Was I not good enough or of no value?
Was Covid-19 merely used as an excuse to end my contract?

I found myself reliving previous feelings of disappointment, fear, shame, and unworthiness. Observing my pattern of negative self-talk and being aware of the voices of my inner critic, I began coaching myself through a series of questions.

This is a practice you could use whenever you are feeling anxious too.

What emotion/s are you feeling now?
Anxiety, shame?

Where are you feeling the emotion of shame and anxiety in your body?
Anxiety, in my head and chest.
Shame, in the pit of my stomach.

What does the sensation of anxiety and shame feel like in your body?
Dizziness and confusion.
Shortness of breath in my chest.
Hunched shoulders and head looking down.
Clenched jaw.
Sense of weakness in the body.
Disappointment.
Hard, bloated stomach.

What color are these emotions?
Mixture of brown and black with orange and red streaks.

What does it smell like?
Ammonia.

What does it taste like?
Shit.

What texture is it?
Sticky tar.

What is it saying to you?
What the fuck is wrong with you!?

I was laughing out loud to myself, noticing the inner judge coming out again. I'm connecting to an old conditioned pattern of thought that no longer serves me.

I observed that most of my thoughts fell into the fear bucket. It was easy to connect to a collective consciousness of fear during Covid-19 as most people were experiencing a fear of death and/or of the future. A universal fear of death, lack, loss, inadequacy, and change can be observed in all of us.

When you step into a space of self-awareness of your thoughts, emotions, and sensations, you have the freedom to choose. You can either cling to previously conditioned thought patterns of not being good enough or step into the knowing that you are worthy.

Back to my personal story. After some time, the inner noise got quieter. I was aware I was revisiting old thought patterns of fear linked to lack, shame, and inadequacy.

I immersed myself into stillness, feeling its presence and pure source energy. The pauses between my thoughts were longer as I continued to focus on practicing my conscious breathing. This was a tool I used to navigate through the dark sticky times in order to emerge into lightness and clarity.

Stillness is not of this world; it has no form, no noise, no content. It is pure consciousness, pure creative energy. It is from this space that all thoughts form, and life, nature, and galaxies emerge. It is pure source energy used for manifestation and to create solutions; I know I cannot solve problems at the same level of the thinking that created the problem.

From this blissful state of stillness, I was connecting to inner peace. There was no external or internal noise, just awareness. I slipped into a golden stream of innate wisdom. I reached down to pick up my cell phone with no thought, just awareness. I navigated to my Facebook profile and created a life event, "Emergence." I had a deep inner knowing that I was going to do more than just transform. I was going to evolve. My body tingled with joy, and I had a sense of freedom. I could feel my energetic body expand with every breath. I searched for a visual image that would symbolize emergence as I was connecting to higher consciousness. I was free to create the life I wanted with a deep knowing that I was worthy of it. I release the shackles and stickiness of unworthiness, shame, guilt, and judgement and stand tall, embodying my sovereignty. I am worthy and free to shift collective consciousness through transmuting fear into love.

My palms tingle with heat, my arms rise above my head, and I begin to consciously move my body as energy streams through it and I begin chanting:

I am free
I am peaceful
I am an alchemist
I am, I am, I am

The combination of the Fourth Industrial Revolution, using digital systems and technology that will fundamentally alter the way we live, work and relate to each other together with the Covid-19 pandemic has challenged many conditioned thought patterns. As humans, we're often resistant to change, especially enforced change where we feel no control. Change is like death. It's a process of letting go and grieving for a familiar, comfortable way of being. It can be a messy process filled with a rollercoaster of emotions, starting with the fear of the unknown (anxiety), followed by depression, and arriving at a state of acceptance and adaptation. Over the past 20 years of coaching and leading people through change and making transitions, I have realized that change invokes chaos, and chaos invokes anxiety.

During the first two months of lockdown, I felt a great sense of inner freedom. Despite the external restrictions, I became absorbed by my spiritual practices. I was digitally guided to a diverse range of international yoga teachers, spiritual teachers, astrologers, and spiritual summits that nourished my soul and led me to a sense of wholeness and awakening.

I acknowledge the negative financial impact on the economy and the suffering resulting from the pandemic; however, there are also many positive stories of people becoming innovative and not just surviving but thriving.

The human race tapped into a collective greater stillness during Covid-19. We were forced to go within and become aware of the inner critic, the identity we created for ourselves from years of conditioned collective thought patterns. Staring at our perceived self-identity was uncomfortable. Letting go of who we thought we were and recreating who we want to be was a painful, scary process for many of us. With a desire to be of service to others during a time of going within, I taught yoga and coached online (something that pushed me out of my comfort zone) with a focus on anxiety and mental wellbeing to hold space and provide support while the world as we knew it, deconstructed.

Certain thought patterns are hard wired into families, communities, and countries. We all have the freedom to choose our thoughts and break free from thought patterns of not having enough, being enough, or being stuck in relationships that no longer serve us. Being busy, working hard for your money, going to work early, and leaving late were previous "norms" that people started questioning. Some people have nothing and yet have abundance, have no limbs, yet are free, have lost everything, and yet have found happiness.

Dear reader, I invite you to sit up tall, place your feet on the ground, inhale deeply through your nostrils and release your exhale slowly through an open mouth, directing your breath to the core of the earth. With your next inhale, feel your breath expand into your stomach, visualize white light entering all the cells in your stomach and then allow the white light to spread into all the cells of your body and slowly exhale black smoke, fear of lack, shame, guilt, unworthiness into the core of the earth.

Repeat this focused attention breathing for at least 2 minutes.

Now move your focused attention to your heart centre, inhale deeply through your nostrils, directing your breath into your diaphragm, feel your diaphragm expand, connecting to a sense of opening and allowing. Continue to breathe white light into your heart space, visualize white light entering into your heart space and then moving between all the spaces of the cells in your body, past the physical definition of your body and into the space around you. Become aware of how your breath creates more space to breathe, more space to create, more space to feel expansive and free.

As we breathe in oxygen gifted to us by plants, we gift plants with carbon dioxide to photosynthesize. We are the deep stillness of the ocean as the waves crash around us. We are made of stardust, and when our physical body takes its last breath, we shall be recycled back into the universe. We are nothing, and we are everything. We are pure source energy. We are free. I am no longer a prisoner of my past thoughts, actions, and language. I write my own code using a language congruent with my future self that integrates with my past self.

It is my soul's desire to live a conscious life increasing my vibration to be in my highest expression of love and light. I want to be of service to those who seek freedom and inner peace from anxiety. I offer a connecting point, a space for you to explore your inner landscape, tools, and breathing techniques to assist individuals. Take inspired action, set yourself free, contact Hayley through the below mentioned links, to schedule a free 20 minute introductory session.

Hayley Verney, a professional and spiritual life coach, creates space for individuals and groups to access their innate stillness. She facilitates the process, which allows them to connect with their intuition, strength, and creative energy when they feel stuck or uncertain. As a meditation coach and yoga teacher with 20 years' experience of leading people through change and uncertainty, she offers individuals a connection point to explore their inner landscape through conscious breathwork and movement. Organizing retreats and workshops is a passion of hers.

Collaboration and working with a shared sense of interconnected community inspires her. She has an enquiring mind, needing to constantly learn, evolve, and grow. This creates an alternative view that enriches any project or conversation. Hayley has also been blessed with the gift of friendship, attracting new people into her life and providing a safe haven of support to those in need. When she's not engaging with clients, she can be found in her vegetable garden, walking her dogs in the mountains, strolling along the beachfront, chasing rainbows and the next sunrise, or dancing under the moonlight sipping margaritas. She has a powerful, serene presence and a deep innate wisdom that facilitates healing through self-awareness and acceptance. Take inspired action, set yourself free and contact me for a free 30-minute introductory session.

Website: https://hayleyverney.com

Facebook: https://www.Facebook.com/HayleyVerney

Instagram: https://www.Instagram.com/HayleyVerney

LinkedIn: https://www.linkedin.com/in/hayley-verney-9613701b

Pinterest: https://www.pinterest.ca/hayleyverney

CHAPTER 13
Letters to the Future

By Joy Resor, Spiritual Mentor, Minister, Joy-Bringer

Bless you, dear human/divine spark, doing your best each day to navigate these wild and wonderful roads without an excellent map, perhaps.

In my case, I follow breadcrumbs, live in synchronicity, and allow my sensitive nature to steer me where it feels at ease.

Maybe you've connected dots a bit better than another, it seems to you, or grew despite immense adversity.

Somehow, some way, we evolve into better, higher versions of who we are. When those who knew us earlier notice that our consciousness appears wider and deeper, they marvel.

This is the path, as I understand it.

We're each born with potential.

Potential to live beyond wounded places that arrive at any age. We've been abandoned, neglected, bullied, burned, and broken. We've suffered hatred, death threats, slammed doors, swear words, belittling. We've escaped, tucked inside, and traveled far.

All of it, maybe.

Over lifetimes, we return as different humans to experience life differently, because as spirits, we're ready to do this anew.

With this groundwork, I'll share with humility and joy aspects of my spiritual journey in this chapter.

My prayer is that something I offer supplies you with fuel for your roads, that this tale of finding my way to love, peace, and joy serves you and your healing. Or you read an idea to pass along.

Each way we heal benefits humankind.

We bless souls through our vibration, through loving who we are. We become beacons of light for the darkness in another.

Releasing What We Can

My husband leads the way to buy property in the mountains of western North Carolina in 1995; he wants to purchase land with amazing, long-range views, which we'll build on when our sons are grown.

That year Andrew and Kevin are ten and eight. I feel lost to my center, immersed as chief cook and errand-runner while Wally (not his real name) has a big job with lots of travel.

Do I prefer living in the mountains or living on a coast? Who knows? I also wonder if we'll really live into this idea to move away from Ohio. After all, I'm a life-long Ohioan, aka Buckeye. I've been here since November of first grade when my teacher daily rolled a red pencil in her hands which made a cool clicking sound (as it crossed her rings, I later realized).

Feeling off-balance to my core, I settle into my sacred chair to write, allowing soulful desires to emerge:

A Journal Entry – December 1996

…I believe in You. I praise You. I live my life to please You and to grow into the Joy you intended—please help me be a joy to others and for others to see you in me. Amen.

I learn about *The Artist's Way: A Spiritual Path to Higher Creativity* by Julia Cameron, leaning into its pages to uncover and release long-held wounds inhibiting creativity.

A childhood memory returns. Each morning, I pull down a message from sleep that I'll write something that adds to the peace in the world. Yes, and along with the memory comes ego's eventual pestering. *Have you done it yet?*

Winter 2006

And, no, I haven't done it yet.

Our sons are away at school, Wally's at the office, and between interruptions from painters and remodelers, I sift through 17 years of memories (baby clothes, sports awards, artwork) as tears fall. Part of me misses crossing streets with small, warm hands entwined with mine. Part of me doesn't want to leave this familiar area, the closeness girlfriends and I have cultivated, and touchstones I regularly visit: Trader Joe's, the Metro Parks, and the Miles Farmers Market.

I'm not excited to move, yet I release what I can, navigating emotional triggers.

After Christmas break, the boys return to college as I muddle through a gray and white season of cold, looking forward to spring. May brings an annual journaling class led by Jenny at the Pink Pig (through Case Western Reserve's Continuing Education Department) that I adore. At the same time, with a heavy heart, I realize that this year signals the end for me of Pink Pig poetry and journaling classes.

Every time we write to Jenny's prompts, we're blessed through connections our pens reveal, awareness that broadens and deepens who we are, and the entries we share with one another. We delight that our perceptions, understandings, and gratitude enlarge beyond our imaginings.

Topics vary year to year: Tradition. Friendship. Raiment of Meaning.

The year Wally and I move away from Cleveland, Ohio, we write to journaling prompts on the subject, *Letters to the Future.*

What?! Can this be true?

Letters to the Future delivers incredibly perfect questions for me, especially.

Writing over six weeks, my energy shifts from fear of moving to a mountain top to a steady, core-deep faith.

Yes, I *know* to my depths that life in Brevard will reveal an amazing future and that new healing will enter, which feels stalled. God will bring me all I need, the right people, and so much more.

A Journal Entry – May 2007

...Life is bountiful, filled with the glory of spring, the ice of winter, the burned-out grass of an August day. That all feelings flow through us if we allow them to. That it's okay to be ticked off for a while, embarrassed, or joyful. It all passes. This bird song morning with a cool breeze through the windows, our pens moving across the page—privileged us! That we can take this time to feed our deeper understanding—what do we believe? Love is a verb. I will miss the friends I've made, but we will stay in touch. We'll write letters, emails. They will come for a visit. Glorious. My hostess persona will get to play the part. I'll cook in my new kitchen, read on the screened-in porch with the mountains watching on—ever grounded, ever changing—now dark green in shadow, now peeking from the clouds, now washed out from too much sun. I believe I'll have every feeling, finding my way to living in a new place. I know I wouldn't have chosen it. I would have stayed 'in my own little corner'… but this move will expand me in ways I couldn't have named…

No Voice, No Choice

I discover happy places to enjoy myself as a sensitive introvert growing up within an agitated, chaotic family: climbing a crabapple tree to commune with God, reading on my bed with a fan blowing cool air across my summer-hot body, and musing at my desk penning poems and letters before plopping onto the large rock to commune with God. Dad says, "Joy, turn on the news." I hurtle the pet gate, turn the living room TV to its nuclear noise level, and race back to my seat, where I slide despicable peas beneath the meat; no talking allowed.

Why don't we talk about our days at dinner? It hurts that we don't connect.

Dad asks where we'd like to go out for dinner. We name four options; he chooses otherwise.

Even when I speak, I'm not heard. Why does he ask us?

In marriage, life scatters painful accidents onto our sons when I voice impending danger that Wally won't abide.

When I speak, I'm not heard. He shuts me down.

Not only do I lack voice for decades, but I also lack power. I'm small, tucking into tight spaces. No one finds me during rainy day games of hide and seek.

Do they even look for me?

Commiserating with Cinderella, I often play 'In My Only Little Corner' on our basement piano, singing alone to the dehumidified air.

Despite feeling shut down at times, I live into moments where my consciousness expands, twirling in front of soul sisters to announce, "I'm going to take up space!" Or taking a journaling class, responding to a question, and seeing that *I'm the one* holding keys to the locked cages of a white-gloved childhood that runs my days as a mother.

Over and over in my journals, I pray to become better, more relaxed versions of who I am. I desire to be a more present mom, a more fun family member, and to live beyond self-imposed limits.

A Journal Entry – February 1998
...Age 40 – going on 41 in five months or so –it's time to reclaim Joy and to be joyful/playful/relaxed/fun/creative –wow. Such a tall order! Okay, okay. Slow down. Stay on the path of the Artist's Way and see where it takes you. You will not be perfect at this, and you will not be changed overnight. Remember that Rome wasn't built in a day, and you have a lot of undoing to undo. You need to dig deep and feel those places that stifled your creativity. And feel those places which keep you hiding your light. Can I be gentle enough to know that if I don't wake up early, I can still do this a little later in the morning?...

I find myself at age 53 in Brevard, North Carolina. Ben, my first post-divorce partner, sits nearby on the computer. When I name an aspect of my work that feels more egoic than others, an intense pain strikes my throat. As I scream to release it, Ben suggests I head to the laundry room so neighbors don't assume the worst. Behind a door near the washer and dryer, I scream and chant OM, intuitively clearing my throat chakra.

Ben's risen, awaiting my exit. I fall into him, collapsing by his feet. Rising for a hug, I say a few words about this crazy, surprising occurrence, and I babble about all the joy I will spread.

My voice of empowerment unfolds, grows, and evolves.

With support, the website for *Joy on Your Shoulders (J.O.Y.S.)* emerges. Writing with elation, I pen my first inspiring book called *Seven Ways to Jumpstart Your Joy*, which, to this day, is available as an e-book for subscribers to my monthly newsletter.

A friend in Ohio sends me a link to The Haden Institute, 20 minutes away. I'm in awe when I look it up because it aligns with a knowing I received a month earlier. Everything about the 21-month spiritual direction training program (journaling, dreamwork, meditation, prayer) resonates in my soul.

Enrolling, I love connecting with the community of students, reading the assigned books to report on, and leaning into divine contemplative practices. The program awakens feelings in me of reverence, sacredness, and time with God in silence.

I grow and change through the Haden Institute program. Halfway through, I feel I'm on the cusp of birthing a vision that knocked on my gut for so long: *birth me, birth me.*

The vision marries inspirational sayings with gorgeous fabric that I call radiant creations or stoles. Sayings include *Jumpstart your joy, Shine your sweet self,* and *Reel in a dream.*

A Journal Entry – July 2010

...The stole project occupies more & more space in my heart and head as I continue steps to bring them into the world. Bless my intention and action, those wearing them, and the whole journey. All's well!...

Checking the want-ads in our twice-weekly paper when intuition says today is the day, I drop the paper in astonishment when my eyes alight on:

JOY's Specialty Sewing Services

Really? JOY's Specialty Sewing Services to sew J.O.Y.S. radiant creations? I feel crazily embraced by all I don't see, loved beyond time and space.

A Journal Entry – August 2010

Oh, my!!

What a high to behold my longtime soul vision.

More radiant than I could have imagined. Wow. Anxious to take them home to show Ben. ...How wonderful! To be living into this new aspect of myself. Offering my soul gift to the world...finally—after what feels like a lifetime, beginning with the childhood repeating dream I would write something that would add peace in the world, moving to the vision of the stoles...

I sign up to vend at craft events...then larger venues...and eventually, spiritual conventions, spreading inspired beauty.

When we graduate from The Haden Institute, we wear Joy on Your Shoulders stoles that say *Summoned or not God is present.*

VOICE

Can your VOICE find a way
Like seeds that are sown

To speak in a VOICE
That's truly your own?

Without super loudness,
Whining or tears

May your VOICE land in place
To speak beyond fear.

Express what's inside
For it does matter so

May your VOICE speak right out
With wisdom you know.

With whispers, with quiet
A VOICE can find ways

To light a clear path
FOR ANYONE'S DAYS!

The Visit

"Joy, you're more aligned than ever; I practically see light beaming from your feet," exclaims Eva, my Pilates instructor.

Yes, there's a feeling of newness in my frame, as if I'm more whole than before, more integrated and connected. I feel heightened energy swirling.

As I finish noodles over dinner, the Universe sends a fortune cookie message over my head; no thoughts or decisions precede my announcement:

"Ben, I'm called to give myself a retreat at home this week; let's take time apart."

Oh, whoa. That's bizarre!

The next day upon waking, I receive a knowing to clear Ben's belongings from my house, so I zip through rooms before heading to Terra Nova Center.

During the meditation: *OMG, my wrists and ankles feel like they're being attacked by mini-lightning bolts*. This startles me to my feet.

Once I'm home, I walk around the front grass barefoot to ground myself and talk with God. Returning to "my own little corner," I feel best writing in my journal, praying, playing sacred music, reading cards from a box of Angel messages, shifting positions seeking comfort, slipping early under the covers.

In the middle of the night, I'm awakened with a backache while energy moves within my frame, sending me to bathe.

Soaking in the tub, The All addresses me without words: *Separation is an illusion. Oneness is all there is. You are in the Azalea; the Azalea is in you. Joy, you just don't get it. With you in matter and me with the power of the Universe, what WE can accomplish.*

And so, *WE* have.

We're sharing amazing years, years I didn't know were possible.

Years that are so wonderful, beautiful, and blessed.

At first, though, I mightily struggle.

Who receives visits from The All?

How does one live as a person after this immense, mystical happening?

One day at a time.

Early on, I'm awake at all hours of the night, scribbling in my journal downloads and ideas to live into.

A Journal Entry –August 2011
When we live in our heads, we miss the heart's wise beats.

From healing all separation within and without, a person is free to be in whole new ways. Without judgment, self-doubt, or feeling separate from anyone or anything, I'm becoming a little bit of a wild woman – Sunday I walked barefoot around my yard singing praise to Mother Earth….

> *What if all the people*
> *Named Joy healed into their names?*
> > *How life covers over the*
> *Sparks of Divinity we are.*

I cancel plans with my son and sisters to attend a niece's wedding in New York City, certain that my being is too fragile, as well as altered from the visit. It's awkward to explain I'm in a spiritual universe preventing me from joining them, though this is my truth.

As the days progress, I'm sure that I'll open a *Joy Center* where people leave their phones at the door, entering different rooms for unique experiences.

A few years later, I'm awakened with a divine assignment to use the lessons of my life to write a book called *Go In Joy! An Alphabetical Adventure*. After tussling with internal echoes, remnants of egoic naysayers, I'm able to settle into the writing. Essays, poems, and questions arrive through my heart and hands with effortlessness and fun.

And yes, I've done it, and so much more.

Additional books arrive. I serve clients as their spiritual mentor, marry couples as An Alliance of Divine Love Minister, bring the highest degree of love where I am, write chapters in collaborative books, and host Zoom gatherings to listen, share, and enliven women.

For years, the 'Joy Center' idea weighs me down, keeping me tethered to a narrow view for the unfolding of my days until I receive an epiphany.

I Am the Joy Center, a Center of Joy.

True freedom, fun, and flow arrive, allowing life to unfold in wondrous ways that align with who I am.

Who knew that we could be comfortable in our own skin? That we can breathe to receive solutions to dilemmas? That we can live without overwhelm? That we can love different partners over time, feeling when it's time to part? That we can attract who we need to heal aspects of who we are? That we become humans who offer space and grace to others who hurt, inviting them to share with us before they head off lighter, changed, and hopeful?

I'm in gratitude for my post-divorce partners who led me to heal into a woman who attracts this just-right partner.

Every morning, we begin with spiritual practices.

Michael journals on the porch while I engage in our room. When complete, I knock three times on the wall; Michael enters to sit on the edge of our bed facing me, open-heartedly listening. From my sacred chair, I read aloud from a Jesus-channeled text we love, *The Way of Mastery* by the Shanti Christo Foundation.

From there, we move onward and outward into our day, extending Heaven's gifts on Earth.

Postscript

Writing *Letters to the Future,* I dip into bins of dated journals from 1980 – 2021, thrilled to the moon and back that through multiple moves, I honored my intuition to save my journals.

These treasured books hold amazing words and feelings from decades of my life, revealing that I write *Letters to the Future* each morning, one day at a time.

How about that?

Joy Resor repeatedly wrote a daily prayer to become the Joy she's created to be. Her life has been a ride and a half of lessons, spiritual experiences, and synchronicities. After surrendering her will to Divinity, the All (God, Source, Universe) visited, teaching this poster child of separation for over 50 years that separation is an illusion and that co-creation is the way.

Joy lives in western North Carolina, where she's an inspiring author of books through her heart and hands, a contributing author in others, and an inspiring guest on podcasts and radio shows.

Ordained as an Alliance of Divine Love minister and certified in spiritual direction, she serves clients as their spiritual mentor, officiates weddings, and brings joy to everyone she meets.

Beyond pandemics, Joy presents to young people in a job corps program, leads classes and workshops, and offers a welcoming presence of love, peace, and joy at spiritual conventions as a vendor of Joy on Your Shoulders (J.O.Y.S.) Batik cotton wares and books.

Born in Brooklyn, NY, Joy lived most of her life in Ohio, where she and her husband raised two sons before moving south, followed by divorce. She loves her partner Michael, hula hooping in sunbeams, and co-creating to inspire others onward. She received her BS in Mass Communications from Miami of Ohio.

You'll enjoy a visit to Joy's site!

Sign up for her monthly newsletter, read articles, and look around to your heart's content.

https://www.joyonyourshoulders.com

And connect through social media:

https://www.facebook.com/JoyOnYourShoulders

https://www.linkedin.com/in/joyresor/

CHAPTER 14

Learning to Trust My Soul's Whisper

In the Midst of Chaos the Soul Speaks the Loudest

By Carly Tway, Certified Sound Therapist
and Vibrational Alignment Specialist

I t's the tail end of winter, the days feel short, and the weather is not yet bearable for my adapted, warm-blooded Southern California body. There's a chill in the air that reaches my bedroom in more ways than one. On a night like many of the nights before, I find myself teetering on the edge of two extremes. Do I let the fiery hot rage engulf my body and allow the last thread holding my heart together to rip, bursting my soul open at the seam? Or do I zoom out, further and further from reality, to lose all feeling, and float above my body until I'm no longer reachable?

This in-between surrender place was something I'd become quite familiar with over the years. It feels nearly comforting to be experiencing such turmoil once again. *That's just the way life is supposed to be for me. The chaos is just as prevalent as the blissed-out moments;* I convince myself as I slink my way into the abyss that is my bathtub. I lay there with my head tilted to the side because whoever put the bathtub in the house placed it backward. *It seems fitting,* I think as I chuckle half-heartedly.

The water surrounds my body, making me feel surprisingly heavy, much like the predicament I find myself in. The Epsom salts mixed with the scalding hot water begin to feel almost unbearably prickly upon my naked, vulnerable skin. *Is this a message or just a sensation?* I think to myself. Brushing off the thought, I stand up. I'm uncomfortable being naked at a time like this. A fear I had picked up in my teenage years, I presume. I flipped the lights off. A single candle flickers on the counter far enough away to still be seen but gives off almost no light at all. Sitting back down, I stare at the flame, trying to extinguish it with my mind to no avail, something I'd done since I was a kid. Like many children, I always wished I possessed some sort of psychic power. The only light being shed upon the bathwater is the dull yet shimmering glow of the moon that peeks through the tall, unmanaged avocado tree in my neighbor's yard. I'm surrounded by beautiful crystals and gemstones on the bathtub's edge, barely catching the washed-out moon's light. The stones feel so unreachable and untouchable as I lay dormant in the liminal space between the two extremes. It's hard for me to imagine how only yesterday I was convinced I was deeply connected to these exact stones like we were one. But on this night, I feel nothing of the sort.

As I soaked, I tried to remember the last time I felt so separate from the world around me, so alone. It must have been years prior as I was skilled at creating a life full of temporary connection and adventure, never staying in one place for too long and always seeking the next noisy, over-stimulating place I could exist in. I've loved loud places for as long as I can remember, concerts, fairs, and festivals being my preferred selection. Maybe it was because the loud, untamed places made me feel like part of something bigger than myself. Or perhaps it was because I couldn't truly be heard amongst the noise, especially when it came to hearing my own soul. In my eyes, the noise kept me safe, as I never trusted myself. *How could I trust myself if I was constantly experiencing such disorder?* If I couldn't hear the truth and I couldn't see the truth, then I could continue on wearing my rose-colored glasses, seeing life in the way I dreamt it to be. Not as it indeed was.

That way of life served me for eight long years, but it was only a matter of time before the excitement wore off and the lights began to fade. The reality was coming in fast and hard, barreling toward me like a stampede of wild horses. Deep down, I was trembling at the thought of being smacked in the face with the truth. A sting I knew would last for moments beyond comprehension, and yet I stood tall, not allowing myself to even dip my toe in the possibility of feeling weak or vulnerable.

On the other hand, I was calm. I was intrigued by the fast-approaching chaos. The knowing part of me understood I couldn't hide forever. The wise part of me saw the truth long before this moment in time. The sagacious part of me understood this was a situation that had to happen for the sake of my soul's evolution. The knowing part of me was the part I numbed out all these years.

The truth was always there, existing and speaking energetically to me, whether I looked at it or not. It always is. At some point, I would have to look it dead in the eye. I would be forced to let my guard down to feel it.

I found pleasure in bouncing from distraction to distraction, party after party, festival after festival. Of course, it was loads of fun, but even in the loudest, most exciting events, there was still an emptiness looming. That emptiness became such a constant for me in that world. It was so pervasive that I conditioned myself to ignore it. I taught myself to ignore my own soul. This longing for connection became the elephant in the room that was just an energy; I whittled it down to being just a concept in my mind. However, this energy kept me hooked, searching and searching for something outside of myself to fill in the hole that was so apparent. It never dawned on me that the emptiness could be coming from me, from my own soul. I was far too distracted and detached to think that way.

There was so much polarity and juxtaposition in this world I had so beautifully crafted for myself, but it was fleeting, and deep down, I knew it. After years of brushing off my own soul's desire to connect with me, I deemed myself not gifted and wildly disconnected. *Do I even have a soul or a higher self to connect to? Who am I to service energy work to others if I didn't even have a psychic gift?*

It was shortly after the last festival of the season that I found myself here, teetering on the edge of two extremes in my bathtub on this chilly February night.

"What the fuck is going on?" I screamed from my bathtub

toward the ceiling at the top of my lungs. The power of my voice carried way above my home and into the clouds. "If there's a higher version of myself or a guide or something out there, now would be a great time to show yourself!"

My life as I knew it had shattered in front of my eyes. Nothing was as I dreamt it to be anymore. The life I had so carefully crafted centered around those loud, wild places came to a screeching halt. The deep sister-like bond I had with my best friend of eight years, the relationship I was trying to mend, and all the other friendships I had so willingly nurtured during that time were deemed meaningless in an instant.

I had gotten word of the betrayal earlier that day, and I spent most of the afternoon in shock and going through the motions. It wasn't until night fell that I began to feel the weight of the situation. The deception was the kind you see in movies. The kind that stings even when you just imagine yourself in that position. This knowledge tore at my heart and cut me so deeply because these were the people in my delicately cultivated bubble that I trusted, the people I loved, and people I considered my family. The betrayal was simple, animalistic even. There were intimate relations between my former boyfriend and my best friend, and everyone knew and chose to keep it a secret from me for months. The deception, lies, and delusions were all bubbling up, bursting around me like suds in my bathtub. It became a communal breakup since it was not one or two, but almost all relationships of mine outside my immediate family. At that moment, I felt so alone. It felt like the entire world was plotting against me.

As familiar as the chaos was, I felt I had no other option but to choose since I wasn't about to be saved by any higher version of myself. *So do I let the fiery hot rage engulf my body, or do I zoom out until I'm no longer reachable?*

I began to do what I always did in challenging situations; I surrendered and began to zoom out. I lost feeling in my body first, relieving some of the emotional pain I felt. Soon enough, I was almost fully untethered until something stopped me at the very last second.

You experience so much turmoil because you do not listen to the whispers of your soul, said a voice inside my head. I say "a voice" because although I heard it the same way I hear my own thoughts, it felt like something otherworldly. This voice's power was clean, clear, and direct. It sliced through the heavy energy in my bathroom like a freshly sharpened sword. There was no choice other than to re-associate back into my body and listen closely.

"What? Hello? Is this my soul?" I said frantically, afraid that I would lose connection and the energy would disappear.

You have received countless indications and confirmations of another path. You have known the way. And now you will take the step. You are forever profoundly connected, said the effervescent voice.

In that moment of deep surrender, I was flooded with pictures, images, scenes, conversations, etc., all playing at the exact same time in my mind's eye, but I was not confused. I took it all in at once. I saw the signs my soul had sent me for nearly a decade, and I understood the message.

I have been psychic this entire time! My soul has been guiding me out of these relationships and this life I was hiding within for years!

I beamed! As excited as I was at that moment, I knew there was something more. Then I began to see my part in perpetuating the madness of this particular scenario and many scenarios before, and it sent a shudder down my spine. I cringed as I rewatched mistakes I made, words I spoke, past painful experiences, and all the times I ignored and betrayed my soul. I sat with those feelings for a while. It was easy to blame others for the pain I was in. What was hard was to take responsibility for my portion. It was hard to sit with the knowledge that I wouldn't be in this situation if I had listened to my soul. I wouldn't be experiencing such pain. I processed the sense of guilt of betraying my soul until I reached a beautiful light at the end of the tunnel.

This was the deep connection I was yearning for. Even though it was excruciatingly painful to arrive at this place, I was here, and I vowed never to let this trust and connection fade. The most confusing thing to me was that this situation with these friends barely even compared to the trauma I'd experienced as a teen (maybe one day I'll tell the story, but I'm not nearly ready for that), and even still, I was experiencing so much pain. Then, suddenly, I receive a ping from that energy again!

The pain you're feeling now is not only from the most recent experience but layered upon unresolved suffering from past experiences, extending from childhood and beyond. So you must continue to sift through the grief, learn to accept it, and then release the energy out of your body, my soul said effortlessly.

I took a deep breath and sipped in that message like ice-cold water on a hot summer day. The message struck something within me, and I felt it deep in my body. I was trained in crystal therapy, energy work, and sound therapy, all modalities structured around releasing energy. However, I didn't realize that nearly forgotten pain from the past could become stagnant energy stuck within the body, creating a more significant, more emotional, and somatic response to events in the present.

The most vital piece is to trust. That will pose as the most challenging for you. My soul was right. It was a challenge, but it was the type of challenge that once I sifted through, processed, and created closure for myself around the pain, the trust in my soul hit a point of exponential growth. Your trust can reach that point too.

Processing the suffering was extremely hard; accepting the reality of any painful scenarios was even harder, but the most challenging part of learning to trust again. We all go through tough times, and after experiencing pain at such a magnitude, it can be hard to find our way back to ourselves. If I've learned anything throughout my 27 years, it's that we are always intrinsically connected to our own souls. We are always divinely guided, even in the darkest moments. We directly communicate with the higher, knowing part of ourselves in ways we can barely fathom! All we have to do is listen, trust and believe. Whether we choose to act upon the messages or not, now that's up to us.

After that night, I began to listen to the whisper of my soul. I got the ping to lay low and heal for a while, so I did. When the idea of a particular crystal popped into my mind, I'd pick it up and start working with it, no questions asked. When I would hear ringing in my left ear, instead of ignoring it and blaming the many nights of loud music, I would quiet my thoughts and turn on my inner ear. When I felt a shift in my energy or body, such as a stomach ache that stemmed from being uncomfortable, I would immediately re-evaluate my next step.

I was busy laying low, rebuilding my life, and rewatching the TV show, *Lost* for the third time when I got a ping unlike any of the rest. It was the Fourth of July. There was an earthquake that morning. I wanted to stay home and watch *Lost,* but I got a phone call to come to a gathering over two hours away, and as much as I wanted to pass on the invitation, I couldn't. My soul was pushing me to go. I drove two hours south, my stomach feeling more and more fluttery and weightless as I got closer. Finally, after arriving, my stomach began to settle; I was combing through my emotions, confused by my soul's guidance to lead me to a party, and then, abruptly, I lock eyes with him. *Oh my god,* I thought to myself. The most gorgeous man, with the kindest eyes, appeared in front of me. He was tan and tall and looked as though he was glowing.

"Hello, Carly." His voice was smooth with a hint of gentle confidence. My entire body clicked into the most defined bodily yes I have ever felt. Every vertebra in my spine aligned, and I felt spiraling energy coursing through my being from my heart to my head. *This is what my soul was guiding me toward. All of that chaos was required to clear out enough space for this to come into my life.* My heart and mind were swirling, and in that moment, I knew.

That Fourth of July marked the beginning of something grand. I realized the chaos and pain had to happen to give me the courage to cut ties with the old paradigm I was living in, bound by distraction and temporary bliss. This new love I was stepping into required so much space in my energy field to come to fruition. I had to make room for it, but I wouldn't have done so unless I experienced that searing split from my past. Because I took the leap, my soul led me right into the arms of the most beautiful, unconditional, inspiring, timeless love I have yet to experience, and the divinity unfolds more and more with each passing day. *It all makes sense; I just had to trust.*

The secret to trusting our soul's message is so simple it can easily be overlooked. But, it's as simple of a matter as deciding so. My wish for you is that even amongst the chaos, you trust your soul is leading you along the way. May you trust yourself so profoundly that you follow your divine soul's guidance into the arms of the next beautiful journey the universe has for you. May you love hard, grow exponentially, and most importantly, may you trust the whispers of your soul.

 **Carly Tway** is a seeker and a mystic, just like many of you. She feels that her purpose here on Earth is to walk alongside people on their spiritual path to full embodiment of their highest, brightest, most aligned selves. Through intuition, sound, crystals, and energy, she dives into the portals of possibility so that she can guide people to claim the soul-led life of their dreams. Carly is the owner of Merkababe Designs, an ethereal online shop carrying crystals large and small, metaphysical tools, and creatively channeled handcrafted jewelry. She has a self-published oracle deck called Invitation to the Soul's Center that has a corresponding sound bath and guided meditation album that will guide you to your centermost place. She is the creator of Crystalline Confidence, an online mystery school consisting of classes on topics from crystals to self-confidence. Carly feels guided by her soul and the ancient wisdom teachings of the Divine Feminine. She has dedicated her life to spiritual exploration and the healing arts by studying and receiving certifications in Sound Therapy, Vibrational Alignment, Energy Healing, Crystal Therapy, Massage, Sound Bath Experiences, Breathwork, and Meditation from all over the world. Diving headfirst into the spiritual realms and sharing her findings with rawness, realness, and a bit of humor is her jam. Living in Southern California with her beloved and her soulmate cat Mr. Pinkerton, Carly leads group classes, works with students 1:1 virtually and in person, hosts Sound Bath experiences, conducts transformational sessions with Sound, Vibration, Energy and Crystal

Therapies, and much more. To get your free gift from Carly, join her online community hosting free weekly classes, check out Merkababe Designs, experience the Sounds of the Soul portal, or get in contact with Carly head to her website.

www.carlytway.com

CHAPTER 15

Listen for the Whispers

Learning to Trust Spirit in a Noisy World

By Shelly Roman

BAM! Witnesses said my body struck the concrete so hard it bounced twice before coming to rest.

It's June 1971; I'm nine years old, and I have just finished third grade at Grafton Bethel Elementary School. My brother, Phil, and I head to Windy Point, the community pool about a mile from our house. Swimming was always a big thing for us. We lived right on the Poquoson River and spent a lot of time on our boat or in the water. Heading to the pool was a near-daily activity. On this particular day, Mom was glad for us to go because she was anxious to paint the kitchen.

I loved the diving boards. There were two boards, a low one and a high one. I got in line for my turn to jump off the high diving board, and I excitedly climbed the sixteen feet to the top. After taking in the view from that height, I realized I never saw the person who dove before me come out of the water. I started looking over the edge to ensure they were not still in the water under the board. As I peeked over, I suddenly had a vision of myself falling. *I wonder what I'd do if I fell?* My mind flashed back to my third-grade classroom when Mrs. Haywood taught us how to fall safely. She put mats on the ground and had us practice falling forward and then backward. We were to turn our bodies to face front and put our arms out to break the fall. *Well, if I were really falling, I would turn my body and put my arms out just as I learned in class,* I thought. In my mind's eye, I saw my body doing this very thing.

Then I was on the concrete below the diving board.

There was a paramedic right there by the diving board. He

came over to talk to me, explaining I had fallen sixteen feet from the diving board, and began giving me medical care. I survived this incident with two severely broken arms, permanently damaged teeth, and a rather discombobulated summer.

This was the first time I can remember having my Spirit separate from my physical body. From that moment onward, I knew my body was just a temporary shell, and there was more to us than meets the eye.

Still, my stomach felt queasy every time I thought about discussing my experience. *Am I crazy? People will think I'm nuts if I share what I experienced!* How does a child get the message that some things are not supposed to be spoken aloud? I grew up in a wonderful church—St. Luke's United Methodist in Grafton, Virgina. This church did not deliver harsh messages but somehow, I still worried about being "different." At age nine, I didn't understand all the stories in the Bible about seemingly "crazy" spiritual experiences, but Dad did.

Later after I healed some, Dad and I were hanging out in the driveway doing something I can't remember now. I took a chance. I cannot regenerate the words of my child self now, but I told him. Dad's exact words are lost to time, but the way he made me feel is not. I felt believed and not crazy. I couldn't tell everyone, but I could tell my parents.

Later, in the 70s, I entered adolescence and began separating myself from the spiritual world. After all, church stuff was not cool, and I was trying to fit in. Partying with friends from high school was a much easier road to acceptance. Pouring alcohol on confusion, fear, and frustration helped numb all those feelings. I didn't spend much time seeking Spirit then nor during my college years. But while I was distancing myself from God, God was sending significant messages to remind me I was not alone.

I was gasping for breath from crying so hard. I was in bed, unable to sleep because of the fearful thoughts racing through my head. Suddenly, I felt the edge of the bed compress with the weight of someone sitting. But no one was in my room. Wide-eyed with fear, I turned to see who was there. I saw no one. Then I felt the comforting touch of some being laying hands on my back. Eventually, I let myself relax into the sensation and remembered the simple truth from my childhood experience—I am never alone; Spirit is always around me. This scenario played out multiple times during those high school and college years. God was still with me.

In 1988, I married my first husband, Jeff, and by 1993 we had two sons, Jake and Erik. Jeff always said he was an atheist, but he was willing to explore the spiritual with me. We tried a church that worked for a while, and I continued to dive into spiritual studies about eastern philosophies of healing. I learned about chakras, meditation, acupuncture, cleansings, channeling, and anything connected to the metaphysical.

As an engineer with technical degrees, a part of me rarely spoke of these interests. My life became divided, and I grew adept at compartmentalizing what I discussed with whom. The Shelly at work discussed highly technical problems, and the spiritual Shelly shared with a different group entirely.

"Mom, how does a person move a fork with their mind?" my son, Jake, asked one day at lunch. "Well, honey, there is the part of us we can see and touch with our fingers. Then there is the part of us not everyone can see. An energetic spiritual field surrounds us and connects us to everyone and everything in the world. If a person becomes good at using the non-physical part of themselves, then they can use their energetic field to move the fork without their hands," I explained. Jake looked at me wide-eyed, taking in my words. Then, my husband, Jeff, jumped in, "Yes, Shelly, if something like that could actually happen, then that is the way it would work." His words slapped me quiet, and I knew I couldn't talk about metaphysical topics anymore. Lacking the skillset to explain how this made me feel, I became more reserved about spiritual matters.

In 1999, behavior resulting directly from my alcohol use caused my marriage to implode. I still lacked the ability to discuss hard things in a real way, so I just left. Soon afterward, I entered recovery and began to deal with life at a new level. Recovery from addiction is a spiritual process, and it spoke to my heart. "How can I tell if something I hear is from my higher power?" I asked my dear friend Ellen. With a knowing look, Ellen said, "Just listen for the whispers, Shelly. God's voice can be quiet."

This awareness of subtle messages existing amid the cacophony of daily existence was life-changing. Until then, I only heard the loud voice in my head pointing out all things wrong and scary. Now, I started noticing the softer sounds. They were there if I just calmed my mind. Slowly, I began to understand that the ego wanted to keep me in fear, but there was also the higher self, encouraging me to become more authentic. My friend, Karen, explained, "The ego only knows about things in the past. Ego just keeps reminding you of everything that could go wrong—what happened before will happen again. The higher self knows the magic of what could be. You must ignore the ego and listen to the higher self to change."

The more I listened for Spirit, the easier the whispers became to hear. Sometimes I just asked for a message, closed my eyes, breathed deeply, and waited. Eventually, Spirit would let me know what I needed. Nature became my church. Hiking in the mountains or biking in a park made me feel as though I was in God's world, disconnected from man's illusion. Continuing to find paths away from the noise allowed me to receive guidance and do my best creative work.

"What a gift from God," I blurted out as I pulled the car into a prime parking spot outside the restaurant the boys and I were going to. It was the mid-2000's and my sons were teenagers. In the parking lot outside the car, Jake and Erik confronted me. "You say things like "gift from God" because you cannot accept we are atheists. You just don't accept us for who we are," they said with rage in their eyes. It took a minute for me to remember what I'd even said. "Guys, my comment was not directed at you. It was just my way of being grateful for the little things like a good parking spot," I replied. Of course, I didn't want my sons to be atheists. I wanted them to have a spiritual life, but I did respect their journey as their own. The moment passed, and we went in to eat. Inside myself, I registered this complaint and did my best to strike the words "gift from God" from my language when around them.

During my years between husbands, my confidence and

self-acceptance grew. My profile on the dating site, chemistry.
com, was entitled "Mystical Engineer." If I was going to date anyone, it had to be someone who could embrace both parts of me. In
2006, this profile attracted Bill. We fell deeply in love and married
in 2007. I knew I could no longer show just part of myself to my
husband, nor could I deal with conflict by cutting away a part of
myself. Bill had to be able to accept a fully integrated Shelly, not
divided or compartmentalized.

I could see Bill squirming in his chair while I reminisced with
some friends after dinner. We were discussing information received during a channeling session held some years back. "This is
fine for you, but I just can't believe it," Bill said. This time I didn't
silence my voice. I talked about it with him. A few days later, I noticed something taped on the bathroom mirror above Bill's sink. I
leaned in and saw a tiny piece of paper reading, "Don't take from
her what she believes in every day." "I put the paper up there to
remind me to let you believe whatever you want without argu-
ment," he explained. Many years passed when I suddenly noticed
it was gone. "I didn't need it anymore," Bill explained. My heart
sang from this unconditional acceptance from my husband.

In 2016, both my sons became engaged. We were overjoyed!
When the weddings were going to be at a Catholic church, I dis-
covered my sons had become Catholic. They had reached out to
Father Whatley, and he walked them through the whole process.
They had been baptized, and while their father was present, I was
not even aware it was happening.

My heart was torn with regret at missing this huge event in
their lives. *Why didn't they want me there?* "You have strong feelings
about things, Mom," Erik explained. I couldn't get any further details from Erik. It was clear I had said or done something causing
them to feel unsafe about sharing this life event. The knife cuts
both ways; I could be silenced, and I could be the silencer.

We are all wounded, and at the same time able to wound. *What
comes first—the wound or the ability to wound?* Pondering this has
never led me to an answer.

"That's the first step toward becoming a terrorist," I spouted off
while the boys, Bill, and I were sitting around the dining room

table talking about the journey of one of their boyhood friends, Dan, becoming an orthodox Jew. Dan had moved to Israel for a time and would no longer physically hug me or any other woman. Of course, none of those behaviors made Dan a terrorist, and I never meant to imply he was on the road to radicalization. Instead, I was blathering on about something about which I knew very little.

During Jake and Erik's atheist period, they made many jokes and snide comments about religion. I joined in with these jokes to fit into their conversations. As I think about this pattern of behavior, I realize I have done this often, not only with religion but with other topics as well. I would add to the jokes to be "part of" rather than being my authentic self. I was so used to compartmentalizing my conversation that I ultimately hurt my sons. *How many other people have I hurt?* This behavior made me part of the noise of the world.

"I am sad you have chosen to be atheist. I understand all people take an individual spiritual journey, and I do respect yours. I hope you can respect mine," I wish I had said in that parking lot rather than just silencing myself. "Dan is on a spiritual journey. I respect his choices, but I do miss being able to hug him," I wish I said during that conversation about orthodox Judaism rather than trying to fit in. "I believe we are all more than these physical bodies. We each have a higher self, a soul. I believe we are all connected by an energetic field sometimes called chi, the universal energy, Holy Spirit, and many other things," is what I wish I said rather than making any jokes about my husband being a "recovering Catholic." As I think about these missed opportunities, tears well in my eyes because I had not found my voice to authenticity.

After each of my sons' weddings, I thanked Father Whatley for helping them find a spiritual path. I will forever be grateful for his loving guidance to them.

It's August 2021, and Bill and I are hiking in the White Mountains of New Hampshire. My heart opens wide when I'm in the middle of God's creation for us, away from the noise of the world. We were exploring the impressive Flume Gorge. As we were coming down from the top of the waterfall, I saw signs for "The Pool – 350 feet. The signs continued to update as we walked closer. Finally, we arrived at the path down to see "The Pool." I gasped as I looked over the rail's edge at this simple pool of water. Under the surface, I could see the movement and flow of the fluid around all the rocks. "This is what energy is, Bill," I said. "Think of that pool of water as the energetic field connecting all of us. It moves and flows with such power. Everything we do and say affects that field and, hence, everything and everyone else," I explained. Gobsmacked, I stared down for a long while, taking in the scene.

This visual analogy grew in my mind as we walked further. Crossing another bridge, I looked over to see the waterfall, invisible from our initial vantage point, pouring water into "The Pool." "This is what it's like; God, source, higher self, or whatever word fits for you is always feeding the energetic field," I said to Bill. It's there even if we can't see or feel it. This added to the visual analogy in my mind.

Holding the image of the pool of water in my mind fills me with love from God and quiets the noise from this temporary world. It also helps me understand the danger of not growing authentic. I see the rocks in the water as the wounds and other obstacles we need to work around. Maybe those wounds are necessary for us to become authentic. The initial wound from the diving board taught me I am more than a physical being; I also have an eternal soul. The wound from my divorce pushed me into recovery and a new level of spiritual learning. The wound from missing my sons' baptisms led me to understand my part in wounding others. Each of these was necessary for me to find my spiritual voice.

As everyone else in this world continues to find their authentic voice, it will stop the collective insanity of pretending. As I stopped pretending, I stopped being silenced, and I lessened the chances of being a silencer.

During the last year and a half, God has guided me to put my voice out in the world. The whispers have led me to transition from work as an engineer to work as a spiritual healer. While in some ways, the evolution seems slow, in others, it seems rapid.

"Just slow down for a bit. I'm still stuck in this body," I say aloud while lying on the family room floor. I was receiving so much guidance from Spirit so quickly I couldn't take it all in. So in creating my business and my new life purpose, I just keep following the whispers. During the pandemic, it has been easier to find quiet; it just takes a click of the remote or the browser button to turn the news off. If I turn the negative off, I can focus on the creative flow from God. I'm following this sacred journey one step at a time and continuing to evolve into a fully voiced authentic Shelly. I invite you to come with me down this Spirit-centered road, following Spirit's guidance to help others and transforming the world.

Life has a way of bringing us to our knees. **Shelly Roman**'s life is no exception and took her from traumatic beginnings to professional career success. Shelly's childhood presented numerous challenges, including abandonment at birth, family violence, sexual abuse, mental illness, emotional abuse, and addiction. Yet, despite these personal challenges, she was able to sustain a successful 35+ year career as an engineer, engineering leader, functional manager, and program manager. Shelly is an exceptional leader with a particular skill of bringing order to chaos. She led large engineering projects that contributed to the safety and security of the public and our nation. Her first love being aviation, she became a subject matter expert in unmanned aircraft systems, and she led programs supporting the National Airspace System.

During her career growth, Shelly's life challenges continued and included motherhood, recovery from addiction, divorce, remarriage, step-parenting, grief, loss by suicide, tragic accidents, and rejection from her own family.

Shelly brought order to the chaos of her life by developing the concept of "sacred ground." As a result of her journey to wellness, her presentations, workshops, and retreats help others walk "sacred ground." Shelly is committed to helping others heal their deep pains, become resilient, and lovingly transform their lives. Shelly is a contributing author to *Find Your Voice, Save Your Life*

Volumes 2 and 3. Her forthcoming book, *Sacred Ground Walker – My Journey into the Light*, will be released in 2022.

Learn more about Shelly's work at https://www.sacredgroundwalk.com

CHAPTER 16

Music is Truly a Universal Language

And Songwriting is Truly My Earliest, Greatest Gift

By Maysha, Singer/Songwriter, Author, Vlogger, and Joy-bringer

With Just a Song

"I'm growing old before my time, and there's nothing I can do.
I let you mess with my mind because I'm so in love with you.
You used to be so sweet dear, with a love true and kind.
But now you've changed it seems and I'm growing old before
   my time."

As I finished the last note, I was unsure what to expect, but I'm positive it wasn't what happened next. Sitting across from me, clapping robustly and grinning from ear to ear, was country music legend Billy Walker. I was prepared for that part. Standing all around me, clapping with just as much adoration and approval, were also other people—spectators—who, moments before, were randomly sitting at the other tables in the Opryland Hotel Restaurant. That shook me to the core, which was the rare, surprising part.

Less than four minutes before, Billy had shifted his gaze away from my manager, Jay, to deal directly with me. "So Jay says you don't just play guitar and sing, but you write your own songs. I want to hear you do one of those."

I quickly scanned the table deciding how to proceed. Billy's wife and manager was about as engaged in the exchange as Jay was, and she was happily eating her salad. Momma was seated to my right, uncomfortably trying to do the same. Unaware that his comb-over was once again not doing its job, confidently oblivious, Jay was—well, he was being Jay, taking way too long to react, respond, or breathe. Skillfully hiding my frustration, like a perky cheerleader and a superhero rolled into one, yet again employing my unique blend of bubbly-adult, I replied, "Okay, great! When?"

Sitting as relaxed as someone at their kitchen table, the God-like figure I'd been raised to idolize used his striking brown eyes to hold my gaze. I remained calm and engaged, aware he was trying to pierce my well-entrenched defenses. "Well, if you're really a performer that can open shows for me, you'll do it right now."

Since I was raised to believe singing country music professionally was my duty and destiny all rolled into one, I couldn't hesitate. *What does everyone back home always want to hear? Of course.* I smiled, pushed back from the table a bit, and began to sing.

Ever the quintessential female country music performer, I stood and turned to face each direction, smiling graciously. "Thank you, thank you, thank you so much!" Finally, the applause stopped, and the adoring, approving strangers retook their seats. Elated, on some level, I was also shocked by the entire room's reaction. *Did they not hear what I was singing? Do they not see I am only fourteen?*

They *had* heard and seen. Still, their reactions were visceral. As I scanned the room, the looks on their aged—that is, aged in the eyes of a fourteen-year-old— faces and in their briefly rejuvenated tired eyes were not passive. They had connected to every word, just as every songwriter and performer would want. Those thoughts mostly went away, interrupted by God-man Billy Walker, "You've got the job! You tour with me, opening *all* of my shows this summer!"

This summer? What if he had said this evening?

More Evening and Another Idol

Later that evening, I was stunned again, as Roy Acuff announced to the other musicians in his dressing room that it was time for them to leave. They obediently filed out, one by one stopping as if to receive a blessing from the God Father. I remained seated, as the greatest man I'd ever been in the presence of had indicated for me to do. When the last to go closed the door, the room was like a tomb, when only moments before it had been vibrant with the energy of music, vocals, and laughter. *I've never been inside a mausoleum, but I believe it is like this.*

The entertainer extraordinaire—country music royalty—with whom I had unfathomably been playing and singing, now sat across from me, dignified but weary. I noticed his eyes, which had been dancing, now seemed filled with regret. Then, his soft yet confident voice began, "You are so talented—the whole package. You play, sing, write and have the personality and the looks. That may be the worst part." Then, after a barely noticeably pause, he added, "No, the worst part is how real you are."

I remained respectfully silent as he paused again. Obviously, he had something to say he didn't want to say, yet felt he *had* to.

Finally, "Your manager is a good man and well connected, but too new at this and not connected enough, especially for a young lady your age. If only you had come ten years ago. I was very powerful then. I could have protected you." He shifted his pale blue eyes to his empty hands, suspended mid-air. "But I have sold everything. I have no power now."

He slowly lowered and folded the wrinkled hands of an elderly man. *They had looked younger earlier when he was playing his fiddle.* "Sadly, for a woman—and certainly a young lady—this business is not about talent. I want it to be, it should be, and with someone powerful enough around you, it is. But right now, that's the only way it is, and that's the truth. I just don't know who that would be now. So, I'm going to ask you something that's very hard to answer at your age, but I believe you can. You have a decision to make: How badly do you want this? Is it worth what I'm telling you?"

The king of country music was saying to me—without saying it—exactly what Daddy had told me more times than I could remember. "Baby, to sing this music, you gotta live this music!" Only Daddy wanted me to live it. This great man did not.

Always confident *he just had to be wrong,* I'd reply, "Daddy, if that's what it takes, then I'll never make it in the business because *I will not* live out those songs I've grown up writing and singing."

Who in their right mind would?

Daddy, always confident he was right, would assure me, "Hell yes, Baby! That's what life's all about!" Then he'd sing about how God wasn't responsible for women becoming honkytonk angels— their cheating spouses were. Or, to drive the point home, he'd rare his head back, close his eyes, pretend to be playing guitar, and break into one of the songs I had written that glorified the life he so epitomized.

"If you want to meet me later,
Right here, in front of everyone, will be just fine.
I'll be waiting to meet you later.
Waiting for your eyes to meet mine."

I had entered the room older than my fourteen years—feeling old before my time—but excited and knowing who I was. I left feeling ancient and wiser, yet without a clue of what to do next. However, I did know that as I left that royal mausoleum dressing room, something within me had died.

Another Song, Another Death

"Yes, I'm sure he could hear it. His expression changed. I had it right up to Daddy's ear, and I watched his face the whole time. I just know he heard every word. He knew it was you, and you were singing his favorite song. He knew. He knew."

Fighting back tears, staring at seventeen inches of snow piled on my balcony in Washington state, I listened to my sister's voice. It was so clear, she could have been standing next to me, but she was far away in Southern Illinois.

Why had I not thought of this yesterday when he was more lucid? Why had he always loved that song so much anyway? How could that song have been picked for me to record in Nashville all those years ago? How could it have gone on to be recorded by an artist in England? How could it have been the only song from which I ever got a royalty check? How was that possible? I was always embarrassed by that song! Really? 'Grab a gal and go upstairs; that was the cowboy's glory!' Written by a ten-year-old! What were any of the decision-making adults all around me thinking? Why did that song have to be the perfect way to say goodbye to Daddy?

I didn't know if my tears were because I could not get to him, I'd never see him again, or because that song was how he would want to end his time with me. It didn't matter—I honored what my heart knew he'd want. I'd release that later, in another song. I just wanted to think of him smiling, laughing, singing, and dancing. He had loved music more than anything all of his eighty-seven years.

Although having a conversation on the phone with my sister, I could see him in his wheelchair. He was bent with arthritis after years of laying bricks and living too hard. There was some meaningful-to-him-picture or colorful proclamation on his T-shirt, and his blue jeans were now untypically baggy to accommodate his aging body. His ever-freshly-colored blond hair was perfectly combed. He was urging me on, mostly with praise, but demanding more because, like my whole life, I just had not done enough. "Sing 'Cowpokes to Gear Jammers' for me again, Baby!"

Music is Truly a Universal Language

"Music is my happy place, so thank you, thank you, thank you for reconnecting me to it! And to dancing! I danced around my living room a lot! Music gets me! It really changes my mood! It helps keep me in a happy place, so thank you! The combination of those two things is what has really been helping me this weekend!" That was the excited, jumbled, fast-spoken voice message playing on my phone.

I could hear how much higher the vibration of my friend and colleague—fellow lightworker, energy healer, etc.—was. I was so relieved. Grounding, clearing, meditation, light work, energy work, ancestral clearing—none of the modalities we had thrown at her very real-world situation had been effective. Finally, she was experiencing a shift in her energy! And of course, it was music! The movement helped, but she was dancing because of the music!

She understood the importance of the modalities I asked her to try. She was a regular practitioner of them already. Granted, this situation had thrown her out of sync, but she was open to my suggestions and knew exactly how to do them or participate. In the end, it was the music that turned things around. The vibration, frequency, and uplifting lyrics!

Not everyone is open to these modalities. Sometimes, even if they are, they have to be lifted to a place of preparation for them to work. Many people begin learning meditation by using guided versions with background music or listening to specific musical frequencies or binaural beats. Music, therefore, often serves as a gateway to meditation, leading to other healing options, like my friend and I were trying for her. Many of these modalities are practiced worldwide and have been around as far back as people can remember, like music.

The difference is, nearly everyone already likes some type of music. Look at all the people with headphones or earbuds. High vibrational music, high-frequency music, and upbeat lyrics are well known to make your day better, and you don't have to convince most to try it. It's not special, strange, or different. It's *just listening to music*. Music truly is a "universal language."

As a songwriter, I realize that we use our musical gift to purge or release pain, traumas, heartaches, disappointments, injustices, abuses, etc., that occur in our lives. Our songs move others with similar experiences, and thus the industry has become "big business." Some cannot find the words to express it themselves or did not realize or admit it until they heard us say it. These songs are often comforting because people relate to them so deeply. However, they also tend to be sad, and they can leave us in, or— even worse—return us to, that same feeling.

I have put songwriting aside in my life many times, only to pick it up, put it down, and pick it up again. I basically walked away from a career in music because of this. No, it is not just country music that can be sad. I became a Geriatric Certified RN/Long Term Care Consultant. Then, I faced a life of chronic pain and invisible illness—Fibromyalgia. I also became a poet, author, blogger, vlogger, teacher, speaker, and therapeutic journalist. I didn't understand back then that these were spiritual and energy healing modalities for releasing the pain, or stuck energy, that had permanently activated my body's fight, flight, or freeze defense system.

I didn't discover how to *fully* use the healing aspects of these gifts until I realized I was not having mental collaborations with myself my whole life but was clairaudient, claircognizant, and an empath. I'm also a medium, a light worker, and have various other related gifts. But then, we all have access to these gifts, to varying degrees, and we are certainly all healers.

I found we were stopping at the purging or releasing. Then we were revisiting what we had rid ourselves of over and over again, consequently re-poisoning ourselves with that which we were trying so desperately to no longer let affect us! We would tell the story and say it was the past but had wrapped it up so prettily, so artistically, so cleverly, so beautifully, etc.; many wanted to hear it again and again. It never got to be the past. To heal, once we purge, release, or move the energy, we must *move through* it—let the past become the past. Then *move toward*, embrace, and *integrate* the healing. Many of these songs, however, did not go that far.

I now write songs again, and blogs, vlogs, books, journal entries, etc. I write happy, upbeat, high-vibrational pieces with positive messages. If I write to release, I write to heal. I make sure not just to tell what happened but to identify what I want to be the rest of the story. If I'm dealing with a story that wasn't *the truth,* I identify *the truth* and make that part of it. I write these pieces with a purging section, but ending, even if it is just the last line, with healing! I encourage other songwriters—artists of all types—to include healing in some way as well.

The world is already listening to music. Let's take what we do as songwriters and performers one step further and make it healing! Let's do the same with other art forms as well. Maybe not every time—that may be a little overzealous for some. There is undoubtedly a place in the world for beautiful, moving, even sad songs. But if we all write with more awareness of the ability we have to include a healing aspect in each piece, imagine the impact we could make on our mental, physical, spiritual, and emotional health, as well as those who listen to or otherwise enjoy our gifts!

And Songwriting is Truly My Earliest, Greatest Gift

Had I seen the black and white photo in Momma's old handbag so often that it was not an actual memory? No! This happened many times. Momma, herself, tells the stories! And, so many details, plus all the feelings, are so vivid and real.

Ick and Chug-a-lug, two beloved mutt puppies, were right on my heels with every step. Momma sat on the jagged, rotted edges of our front porch. It was still early, but the sunlight had become a bit too much for a blue-eyed, fair-skinned little girl with toddler-fine, blond hair, and I was in serious mode. Momma, all too aware of what that meant, was hanging on my every word. Trying not to trip again, I was looking down intently at the makeshift walkway we maneuvered daily to avoid the mud and coal dust. With Teddy Bear tucked tightly beneath my arm, I paced back and forth. This process somehow facilitated the lyrics that rushed from *somewhere,* into my head, and then out of my mouth, as quickly as they came.

Have I ever met another mom that would take dictation from a three-year-old songwriter?

I honestly don't remember the words I was spewing, but I still feel my furrowed brow as I rattled them off to Momma, faster than she could keep up with. Thoroughly frustrated, I could not wait until I could write my precious songs down *all by myself!*

Why would the Divine give me the gift of songwriting at the age of three?

Regardless of the words, the intent was to release the fear that caused me to squinch my eyes tightly each night and try not to breathe too deeply or scratch an itch. I was *supposed* to be asleep. Instead, I replayed episodes of Gilligan's Island in my head for the company—and sanity. I was trying to sleep. I was always trying to do whatever it took for Daddy not to get mad.

Diligently taking down every word, Momma's head was dropped low—like pretty much always. A fervent three-year-old Maysha paced and purged, writing songs and singing her little heart out on the beginning of her journey to save herself.

Maysha is a singer, songwriter, vlogger, author, joy-bringer—a title given to her by her Arch Angel guides she lovingly calls The Angel Squad—avid traveler and the founder of the platform As Long As You're Breathing, Keep Living.

Since Fibromyalgia ended her career as a Geriatric Certified RN/Long Term Care Consultant in the late 90s, she became a life-long member of the Chronic Pain and Invisible Illness Community, living her desire to learn, better herself, serve others, and encourage others to do what they think they cannot.

Maysha uses her unique social platform to host educational and inspiring online interviews with those the world needs to hear, bringing together seekers of information on spiritual awakening, spiritual gifts, and healing modalities and those wanting to share such information. Having worked in healthcare, then having experienced it as a Chronic Pain and Invisible Illness Patient and Patient-Expert, she has come not to view science and spirituality as *either/or*. For her, it is truly about the reintegration of the two: *both/and*.

A spiritual healer herself, Maysha is claircognizant, clairaudient, a medium, and lightworker. She does Chiron Wound Healing, leads meditations, and other modalities with emphasis on releasing the past while focusing on the present to facilitate healing.

Maysha believes that by spreading unconditional love, we can raise our vibration into alignment with our authentic selves—the person we came here to be. Her desire as a joy-bringer is for everyone to live their "best and highest good" and watch the world change accordingly. This is Maysha, as long as she is breathing. You can connect with her at AsLongAsYoureBreathing.com and Facebook.com/AsLongAsYoureBreathingKeepLiving

Maysha warmly welcomes others with similar gifts and desires to contact her to be featured on her platform.

Email: Mayshac1965@gmail.com

CHAPTER 17

Embodying Strength, Courage, and Love
Moving Forward by Freeing Yourself From the Past

By Lyndi Picard

As the shadows danced across the bedroom wall, I was entranced by the way they moved. Then, as they slowed down, taking shape in human form, they began to look familiar and comfortable to me. I realized each one of the shadows was me! Each one held a painful memory of what others did to me or what I did to others and to myself.

I was born a medium and healer. I quickly realized I knew things were going to happen before they did, saw things that no one else could see, and was able to connect with the spirit world. These are the gifts, that through time and conversations, I know were passed down to me from my great great grandmother. The biggest gift I received was a fire in the inner depths of my belly, yelling at me, trying to guide me away from the shadows or lead me to a brighter light. It was called intuition. I am happy and excited to tell you that we all have this gift.

Over the past 40 years, I have embraced, honored, and listened to the inner wisdom that embodies us all. That inner wisdom remains strong until our shadows cover it with a cloak of silence. When we become still, we can start to hear the whispers of our souls, the guidance and love that helps us turn the shadows into light.

Intuition is meant to be felt, listened to, and followed. It's not always easy to do, especially if we have lost hope, feel the world is against us, or wonder when our personal nightmare will end. Following your intuition is trusting that what you are feeling or hearing is for a reason. You may not see the results immediately or at all, but trust me, the fire burns for you.

Shadows began to form early on in my life. My grandmother's chaotic, alcoholic, and schizophrenic behaviors, which can only be explained by the torture of not following her own intuition, opened the space for my shadows to enter. I heard the fear and worry in my mother's voice when my grandmother would ask for me to visit her. "I'm not sure," she would say into the phone. As I watched her tortured face, I would also feel that fire in my belly telling me not to go. But as a child, without knowing what I know today, I dismissed that fire and begged to go. My need to go was so strong, it washed over the fire and doused its flames.

I needed to make sure my grandmother was okay. When I was with her, we would simply be. I closed the oven door on the chocolate zucchini cake only to realize we had left the zucchini on the counter. "Grandma, let's listen to seventies music." We filled the kitchen with our dance moves and the freedom of it just being us. There were movie nights, sweet treats, and crafts galore. She made it all so fun. *I can't ask for more than what I feel when we are together like this.*

But as the day went on, the smell of rye became stronger, the ashes from her burning cigarette would hit the floor, and her head began to bob. That was when, even at a tender age and full of fear, I knew I needed to make sure that both she and I were safe. I would carefully get her into her pajamas, one arm and one leg at a time. I moved oh-so-carefully so she didn't fight me and helped her get into bed and pull up the sheets over her weary body. Then I would wait for the alcohol to finally take over, for her eyelids to firmly shut, and her breathing to become rhythmic. I waited for her to be completely passed out. Then I would climb on the kitchen counter, stand on my tippy toes, grab the 66 of rye and drown it with water.

My first shadow arrived during this chaotic time, in sixth grade. The fire raged in my belly. *Something serious is happening; it feels like a hundred pounds of weight.* "Lyndi, you need to go down to the principal's office." What waited for me was the confirmation that the feeling I had was right. My grandmother had a gun and was looking for me, blaming me for her divorce from my grandfather.

Hello to more shadows. Alcohol was and still is used to cope with stress in my family, and it was a normalized way to deal with just about any emotion. Life is tough enough for any teenager, but I was layered with reasons I shouldn't care or honor what was good for me. I was confused, and my emotions were heightened and inconsistent. Turning to alcohol and drugs was an easy way to numb my pain and confusion. *I don't care what might happen; I just want to be somewhere else than with myself.* My body became disposable, not honored, as I took part in risky behaviors to detach from my feelings. I know I hurt my family and friends, "We are afraid and worry about you!" *That's not enough to make me change.*

But my lack of self and soul care had unwittingly opened the door to even more shadows. One night out with some friends, the fire in my belly was so strong, telling me that something was not right. *What's happening? What should I do?* I asked those questions in my head, looking for clarification. Nothing more came to me, so I ignored the feeling, pushing it aside every time I felt that fire starting to burn again.

The evening was beautiful; we drove down a dark gravel road, the air filled with the smell of the summer wheat fields that flanked either side. My heart started to race; the fire in my belly was exploding as the car came to a stop, then everything turned into a fury of chaos. I watched a knife plunged multiple times into my friend's body by another friend while another let out frantic screams for him to stop. He and the knife turned to me as I stood shielding myself with the car door. My heart raced with fear, my breath rapid. From the corner of my eye, his arm raised, gripping hard on the handle of the large knife that was now coming down with force toward my back. Paralyzed by fear, my body surrendered, ready for the piercing. As my young life flashed before my eyes, I heard a blood-curdling scream.

Instead of my back, three stab holes appeared in the roof of the car. The two assailants fled. Adrenaline kicked in; I was able to get my friend into the car and help. Covered in blood, feeling like I was staggering in a horror movie, I sat in the hospital, waiting for my parents. *Their daughter is a fuck up.*

My intuition was so on point that night; I felt it but did not obviously listen to it. Knowing what I know now, I should have literally pumped the brakes, turned the car back around, and headed back home as soon as I felt it.

But shoulds don't always mean we will. A few years later, still inviting more shadows, I met a guy. We were in love, or so I thought, and moved in together rather quickly. After a short time, my intuition clearly told me the relationship was not a healthy one. I doused that fire in my belly again, looking for love I didn't have for myself. I soon became pregnant, then felt more compelled to stay. My intuition didn't stop, continually telling me that I couldn't trust him. When my son was three months, I left.

On a cold Sunday night, the days when my son would see his biological person, I was out with a friend celebrating a friend's birthday. This friend knew my history and wanted to tag along to pick up my son on the way home. The fire in my belly was so strong I could not ignore it. I knew he couldn't come with me; it was undeniable.

Opening the door, the fire and fear it told me about was strong. *Am I seeing this for real?* The man who supposedly loved my son and me, sat causally in an armchair, my son in one hand and a loaded shotgun in the other. Somehow, I was able to leave the house without either one of us being physically harmed. That cold winter air hitting my face as I carried my son to the car never felt so good.

Thank goodness I listened to my intuition that night. It made it possible for one less shadow to appear that night.

A small sliver of light began to shine. I started counseling; I was reluctant at first. There was a stereotype for people going to counseling, and I did not want to be painted with the same brush. This made me avoid going. After a few cancellations and the next appointment scheduled a few days away, I picked up the phone to cancel again. This time my intuition was loud and clear that the need to go out was more important than what people think about me. I gave it a chance, then another. Listening to my intuition to go made the opening a little bit wider for more light to shine through on the life I found so hard to endure.

"Lyndi, I've met this new healer, and I think she might be able to help you," Mom said. I went to see her. Entering the room, I noticed a wooden box filled with vials of potions. She intuitively picked which ones to use with me. My mind went in a million different directions, but I was intrigued. *This is right up my alley.* She put the potions on my tongue; some tasted awful and made my nose curl, some made me scream at the top of my lungs. I could feel my heaviness being replaced with peace and calm.

She just pushed a reset button for my soul.

Everyone's healing journey looks different, although most of us have similar events in our lives, with similar emotions and fears attached to them. I started quietly sitting with myself, clearing my mind to listen to that fire and the spirits that have been there the whole time. *I see you, spirits, shaking your head and laughing at me for not listening sooner.* I laugh a bit too, then seriously wonder, *how the hell I am still here?*

In the end, it doesn't matter why we're still here. What matters is that we are. I ask you, what are you going to do with this next day given to you? Healing takes work, which is the reason most of us don't do it. It's much easier to stay in that lower energy of fear, anger, and regret. But it's so fucking rewarding. I would cry for days, get angry, and beg for forgiveness. Who I was begging to was unknown; I was just hoping that someone was listening.

Forgiveness was super important to me. I wanted to make sure the people I hurt forgave me. The truth is, the only person it's truly important to spend that energy on is the one you see when you look in the mirror. Forgive yourself for being too young to comprehend that the abuse was happening. Know it was not your fault. Forgive yourself for not knowing how to process the emotions that came when the shadows began. Forgive yourself for knowing better but still making the same fucking wrong decision over and over again. Finally, I got to a point where I could look in the mirror and like what I saw.

Healing would be so much easier if there was an easy button. But if there were, we would never be able to learn or discover anything about ourselves. Walking is one coping mechanism that helped me process my emotions and connect to my inner self. One day I heard this big booming voice from Spirit say, "You need to meditate." *I can't do that.* All I saw in my mind's eye was me sitting in the lotus position, with my fingers touching each other, humming ohm. It looked so ridiculous to me. I could see the Spirit literally shaking his head and saying, "We have much work to do." I never know what wisdom is going to be bestowed on me. We are all guided and watched over; becoming still and listening is where the healing can occur. While walking, I could let the tears flow and listen to that inner voice, listening to the messages coming through.

After years on my healing journey, it has changed in many different directions, each twist and turn leading me somewhere different that I needed to be. It brought amazing people into my life and kicked some to the curb. Listening to my intuition and trusting it made it possible to make positive changes in my life. But the biggest, most amazing thing to happen to this Cancer baby who is ruled by the moon is to know our lives are in a constant state of change. We cannot control anyone but ourselves. We cannot change a goddamn thing about the past. And we can never tell anyone else what or how to feel.

Trauma, projections, and guilt have played a huge part in forming the shadows. To connect and trust our intuition is one of the best things we can do for ourselves. It may feel a little uncomfortable at first like we need to get a larger size of pants, more headroom to breathe, or larger trash cans to put our shit in. All we have to do is listen to that inner fire burning in our bellies, process the emotions of our past, and know that time for ourselves is imperative so we can connect, listen, and heal. This is the way to finding peace, joy, and happiness.

Our feelings matter; our stories matter. Unfortunately, we have been made to feel that we were less than, undeserving, and weak because of the shadows. That is far from the truth. Just like a phoenix rises from the ashes, we can take the weakness that overtook us and become stronger emotionally, physically, sexually, and spiritually.

At this point in my life, I'm not afraid to use my voice. I'm not ashamed of my story. Without the chapters in my book, I would not be who I am today. I'm more confident than ever by listening to my inner voice and honoring my emotions and story. I honor every part of my journey. I may have taken some detours, ups and downs, and a few 'I fucking give ups' along the way, but it's all been worth every moment. Each moment I learned, released and grew. I have the strength when shadows creep in, knowing now that they have no power over me.

Finding my voice has enabled me to have the strength and courage to have hard conversations. This allowed me to understand the circumstances that brought my grandmother to where she was years ago. Without my healing journey, I would not have been able to have the relationship we had over the past 20 years. It was full of love, spending time together, and total understanding. Finding my voice made it possible for me to shine a light on every shadow formed with the relationship with my grandma. I have no anger, regret, or sadness attached to the relationship. We were able to make loving memories that I will cherish. It was my honor to hold her hand as she passed away peacefully after I turned off Home Alone and switched it to Christmas carols. I could not have her last moments be listening to, "You guys give up? Or are you thirsty for more."

My hope for you as you find your voice and shine your light is that you become stronger, more courageous, and live in your most authentic self, regardless of how many shadows you have dancing on your walls. We all deserve to shine our beautiful soul lights on them.

Lyndi Qu'Appelle Valley
Medium & Energy Healer
Born a healer and medium over the years, my gifts have evolved into my soul's passion. Walking beside people to help them become the best versions of themselves brings me joy and fills my heart, whether it's through a reading, healing session, or teaching a class. Learning how to connect

with one's emotions and feelings is the avenue needed to begin to heal. I have learned over the last 20 years helping beautiful souls that we are all writing a book of our lives. The title of our books will be different, but if we take the time to connect with people, we will find that some of our chapters are the same. Connecting to ourselves and others will aid in reducing the shame, guilt, and fear that holds us back from finding the strength to heal.

I am a daughter, granddaughter, sister, mother, auntie, partner, and friend; a Cancer baby ruled by the moon. I don't beat around the bush, I will give you a kick in the ass if needed, but most of all, I will guide you to find your authentic self. I am feisty, real, been broken, bruised, scarred, and healed. Being a spiritual healer has helped me find my voice; I am honored to help people find their voice; we are all deserving to be heard.

Website: quappellevalleymedium.ca

FB: Lyndi Qu'Appelle Valley Medium & Energy Healer

Instagram: @quappellevalleymedium

Email: quappellevalleymedium@gmail.com

CHAPTER 18

Healing Through Loss
How Our Dreams Guide Us

By Dr. Jessica Chardoulias, PharmD, BCPS

It was early on a chilly December Sunday morning, and I stood in my towel absent-mindedly thinking about what kind of dim sum I might have at lunch with visiting friends when my cellphone blinked to life.

I plucked the phone off my nightstand, "Morning, Papa. What's up?"

I heard him draw in a deep breath, and then his words came out in random spits. "Honey…" "Could…could you come over? Lynne. Lynne. Lynne passed away overnight, and I don't know what to do."

I couldn't breathe, but I squeaked out, "I'm on my way."

I went on autopilot but managed to find mismatched coverings for my body. My hair was unbrushed and soaking wet as I stumbled out into the hallway.

In the elevator, my neighbor looked me up and down and said, "You do know it's below freezing out, right?"

I think I nodded. It dawned on me then that I'd left my jacket, mittens, and hat next to the door as I'd left. But I didn't have the energy to go back for them.

I probably won't freeze, I thought.

My phone buzzed again. I had left an unintelligible message for my boyfriend, and he was calling to beg me not to drive myself and instead take an Uber. But the effort that would require seemed gargantuan and intolerable. So I pulled myself up into my vehicle and drove across Denver through a blur of tears. As soon as I arrived, I threw my car into park and ran into the house, straight into the waiting arms of my father. It would be hours before I realized I left the car on with the keys inside.

After disconcerting conversations with a police deputy and the coroner, my father and I stood together at the top of the stairs as we watched a stretcher containing our collective hearts roll out the front door.

And life simply stopped.

It stopped making sense. It stopped feeling right. It just stopped.

Together we began to understand what it means to lose someone we'd never considered losing. We began to understand how ill-prepared we actually were.

One of the first gut-punching lessons: loss shifts everything. And as that day and the coming weeks moved forward, I realized that all of the things I thought I knew had ingloriously, spectacularly, wholly imploded. The parent I knew would be my no-nonsense, loving counselor until deep into my days as a gray-haired elder was gone. My absolute certainty about my ability to handle anything that came my way without flinching was but a naive memory. And my family felt frozen in time even as the winter thaw was beginning around us.

Three weeks later, I woke up cursing the world. I was livid that the heavens had ignored our plans as a family. I was fuming that I couldn't call Lynne to tell her the stuffed puppy she gave me at Christmas wound up perched protectively on my head overnight. It broke my heart that my dad would be picking up her ashes instead of doing the crossword puzzle with her that morning.

I went about the better part of the morning seething.

My boss, Marilyn, called to check on me. As the conversation closed, she said, "Jess, how are you actually doing? To an untrained eye, you look like you and even sound like you, but I know some part of you is entirely muted."

I didn't know how to respond, or perhaps I wasn't brave enough yet to be that transparent, so I simply said, "Today just feels tough. But I'm okay, I promise."

I also knew it was a lie. I wasn't okay. On my best days, I was sleep-walking through life. On my worst days, like this day, I was a wrecking ball, angrily smashing whatever I encountered. But I needed to face the day, so I stomped into the corridor outside of my condo.

After slamming and locking my door, I looked down the hallway to see my friend Francisco carefully dusting a painting.

I found a way to mask my fury and waved and smiled like normal and prattled, *"Como estás?"*

He stopped dusting, turned my way, and walked toward me with a quiet purpose. I counted each step he took and told myself, *Jess, no crying today.*

He stopped just short of me, looked straight into my eyes, and said, "I'm so happy you are here, my friend. I hoped I'd see you today because I dreamt you needed a hug."

In that instant, every bit of anger coursing through my veins dissipated, and I collapsed into his warm embrace.

I realized I had spent my whole life wondering where our loved ones go when they pass. And while I still didn't definitively know the answer to that question, I knew one thing. I knew that Lynne found her way into his dreams. In that dream, she planted a seed of love. And for the first time since her passing, I knew I'd find a way through the grief. But I also knew it would be with her help.

Months later, I found myself tear-stained and tender in the days before Mother's Day. It would be my first without one of the women who raised me and the sixth without the son I miscarried, my precious Peanut.

But on the eve of Mother's Day, while I slept, I received the perfect answer to a prayer.

Somehow they both visited me.

I dreamt of a warm afternoon on a sunlit patio. It wasn't a place I knew from memory, but it was a place my heart recognized as home. Together we feasted our eyes on miles of emerald rolling hills and what seemed to be a super bloom of poppies. Lynne and I sat side by side while she cradled my little boy.

She didn't say a lot of words, but she did say, "You know I love you. And miss everyone so much."

After that, we sat in silence for what felt like an eternity. I smiled and watched her rock my Peanut on her lap. For years, I carried a heaviness in my heart about how I'd lost him without ever really knowing him, and those thoughts were again swirling as we sat together.

As if she knew what I was thinking, she looked up and said, "He knows you, Jess. We are safe here. We are together."

I blinked rapidly but still felt tears trickle down my cheeks.

As the afternoon progressed, I found a way to speak. I told her all of the things I knew I never said enough while she was alive.

After each statement, she just said, "Jess, I know."

In the blink of an eye, my son went from a swaddled babe to an unsteady toddler in a Tyrannosaurus Rex t-shirt.

He crawled up into my lap and nestled in so gently. After that, by my estimation, time stood entirely still.

And I was able to tell him all of the things I've said each night in my prayers for six years. He held my eye while I spoke and just smiled.

Lynne reached over and ran her fingers through his wavy brown locks.

In another blink, the toddler on my lap vanished, and I found myself standing on the patio's edge, looking down at the grass below.

Instead of a toddler, I saw the six-year-old prince my son should be chasing bubbles through the grass.

He squealed with delight over and over. And I couldn't help but wish that I didn't have to leave them. Every ounce of me wanted to stay forever.

I felt Lynne's hand gently rest on my shoulder, and she said, "Jess, he loves you and will always be here. But, I promise, we are okay."

I crumpled down onto the deck.

And she finished, "You will have an eternity with him. Time isn't linear here."

After she passed away, I sobbed at the reality that neither my brother nor I had given her a chance to be a grandmother.

But the next morning, I awoke to feel only one thing, peace. The peace of knowing she continues to find a way to help me process her loss and heal from it. The peace of knowing that she is the wonderful and warm grandmother I always envisioned after all. It just happens that her opportunity for that role is out in the beautiful unknown of life after life. The peace of knowing my sweet boy is aware of every second I've spent loving him since losing him. And the peace of knowing he will be there waiting for our own infinity to begin one day.

It would be almost a year before she found her way back into my dreams.

But a cool night in the following March, I crawled into my bed early. I pulled up my meditation app and nestled in for twenty minutes of centering for a good night's sleep.

And I spent the entire night dreaming of fantastic things. In the last dream of the night, I found myself standing in a snow-kissed meadow just outside Telluride, Colorado. My dad and I were shoulder to shoulder, staring up at an unsteady cornice on the mountain above.

Strangers surrounded us in snow gear.

He shook his head and said, "I hope no one is in the backcountry today. That just doesn't look good."

We were still standing with our gazes fixed on the mountain when a line of moose began walking along the cornice.

I remember thinking, *how strange. I wonder what those guys are doing up there.*

As that thought cleared my mind, the moose at the end of the line triggered an avalanche.

Chaos erupted around us. The strangers crowded around us were screaming and running and wildly pointing at the snow as it barreled down the mountain toward us in the valley below.

I was strangely calm; I knew the snow wouldn't reach us and that we were safe.

But in the chaos, I lost sight of my dad.

I was spinning in circles trying to find him and, in the blink of an eye, Lynne appeared and placed her hands on my shoulders.

She pulled me into the kind of embrace she was famous for, deep and strong and bursting with love.

And she looked me in the eye and said, "I'm safe and happy, and I miss you. I miss your dad."

I just leaned into the hug more because I couldn't find words.

The chaos around me dissolved into nothingness, and I felt the same warmth I'd felt on our patio encounter.

But she pushed my shoulders back, so we were eye to eye and repeated, "I'm safe and happy, and I miss your dad."

Then I woke up. It was well before dawn, so I tossed and turned before falling back into a dreamless sleep.

The following day, I called my dad.

I told him the story of the dream I'd had the night before. I told him I was missing her extra today as a result, but I also felt comforted because she had reassured me she was safe and happy and missed us back.

He was quiet for a pause and responded, "I understand how you feel, honey. I spent the entire night awake, screaming at her urn for leaving us. For leaving me. I miss her extra today too."

I had initially thought her visit this time was again an effort to help me process my grief. But after he spoke, I knew that this time, she visited me to reach his still actively breaking heart.

I believe that she felt his pain. I believe she found a way into my dream in an effort to comfort him. I believe her energy and her love surround us. I believe she is safe and happy and misses us.

I believe.

They say dreams are simply a random succession of images, emotions, and sensations that involuntarily occur as we sleep. Scientists are conflicted about their purpose and meaning but don't suppose they are much more than an attempt to calm and heal our neurological pathways.

Normally, as a woman of science, I'd trust the opinions of scientific experts above all. But this time, I trust my own.

In the almost two years since we lost Lynne, I know dreams have been a profound source of my own delicate healing. I know that when my heart and mind were closed to her, she found her way into my friend Francisco's dreams in an effort to calm the angry storm that was growing inside me. As I took slow, careful steps through the lengthy process of grief, she found a way to visit again. This time she was with my son, and it was as if she knew I needed to face the lingering grief over his loss. During that visit, I took bigger steps in healing my own very broken heart than I ever imagined possible. And as I continued down that slow and steady path of healing, she found her way in again to help as the love of her life struggled to make peace with the colossal hole created by her absence.

The veil between states of living seems thinner while we sleep. Where we are open, dreams are a conduit to all we have lost, and more importantly, a way to heal the wounds that plague us while awake.

Dr. Chardoulias holds a Doctor of Pharmacy from the University of Nebraska Medical Center and is a Board-Certified Pharmacotherapy Specialist. She spent the first decade of her career working as an Ambulatory Care Clinical Pharmacist for the VA Sierra Nevada Health Care System in Northern California and the Department of Defense in Landstuhl, Germany. In recent years, she took a career pivot and now works as an educator and relationship builder. She's passionate about comprehensive chronic disease management and is particularly devoted to the cardiometabolic space. She believes that the most profound healing can be found where we marry traditional medicine and spiritual healing. Her life experiences have taught her to trust both the answers she finds via faith and also empirically via the scientific method. She's been blessed to live and learn on three of the planet's continents and aspires to, at the very least, sleep soundly on the other four. In her free time, she enjoys landscape photography, hiking whatever mountain she can find, writing, and traveling. In 2018 she followed her heart home and now happily resides in the shadow of the Rocky Mountains in Golden, CO. You can catch up with her on:

Facebook: <u>Jessica Chardoulias Writing</u>

Instagram: <u>@jessicachardoulias</u>

CHAPTER 19

Decluttering Magick and Empowerment
Letting Go and Getting Free

By Ashley Moon, MA.

My Story

I felt my heart heavily sinking downward as my impressionable ears, desperately seeking solutions, perked up. He paced the stage with grace, continuing his magical way with words, "... and so it's one thing to have wisdom and awareness. It's another to take *action* that aligns with it. *That* requires real courage and faith."

Oh my God, he's talking to me—about my relationship with alcohol. Because I know better, but I keep doing it anyway. I'd been harboring this deep, dark, confusing-as-fuck secret. I wanted this demon monster off my back, to demagnetize myself from its insatiable grip. But how? The night before, I'd been fantasizing about slitting my wrists after drinking red wine all day. For the first time, the wine wasn't taking the edge off. In fact, it was making it worse. My workaholism had been gradually intensifying too, alongside this general sense of *it's never enough because I'm not enough.* Something sure wasn't right inside and needed some serious attention, like now.

What I didn't realize at the time was that I was in the thick of an identity crisis, feeling like a fraud with imposter syndrome. I was about to co-star in a pretty major online series sponsored by a big-time brand, and yet I felt so alone, ugly, confused, and terrified. Here I was—the "declutter expert"—feeling deeply wounded, overwhelmed, and ironically *cluttered* with emotions. Mainly, I was riddled with guilt and felt defeated by this freakish substance that wanted its way with me. If I was so smart and spiritual, why couldn't I figure out how to moderate?! What a shame!

My best friend came over and suggested I go to a meeting. An Alcoholics Anonymous (AA) meeting! *Who, me?!* Yea, girl. Well, I was desperate and in a lot of pain, ready to try anything. I'd crawl there if I had to and do whatever it took to unburden myself from the weight. That day was Sunday, September 2nd, 2018, just hours after hearing the magical minister's morning message. What serendipity. What a blessing. Now here I am today, three years later, still sober, having just returned from co-hosting an adult sober summer camp in nature, where I felt beautiful, free, connected, clear, and confident, celebrating who I truly am with a community that gets me.

I want you to understand that it's not simply abstinence from alcohol that made this transformation possible. It's the power of decluttering magick and empowerment *as a way of life,* every single day, whatever the thing or thought may be. We are consistently releasing and receiving and thereby continuously rebirthing. We let go of what no longer serves us, making space to receive what truly does. And we do this on every level: physically, mentally, emotionally, spiritually, and energetically. They are all interconnected, allowing for what I call *Inner Outer Space Magick.* It's full of promise and potential; it's what encourages our human evolution and soulful expansion.

From a pile of bills or to-do lists to an entire home, toxic relationship, or career you've outgrown, you get to face your truth, desires, and fears, and trust that you can let go and manifest the next version of you. And let it be the *you* that aligns with your ever-expanding inner wisdom. Will it be easy? No. Will it be worth it? Yes.

Let's explore some concepts and tools so you can practice the art of decluttering magick and empowerment, too! We all have clutter on some level, coming in and out of our lives. Yet, the journey, destination, and gift of liberation have so much magick in store for you. I can't wait to see where your decluttering journey takes you!

Physical Decluttering Magick

The fastest, most efficient way to declutter and organize anything (*yes, anything*) happens in three steps: sort, purge, organize. The first two are how we declutter and downsize, ideally only keeping what we love or use, or what Marie Kondo would say, "sparks joy." I encourage you also to explore whether it feels magical or brings magick into your life somehow. The third step, organizing, simply means making a home or system for the keeps, based on access needed.

This is how we get to know our inventory and make conscious, empowered decisions about what we keep in our lives. We can choose what items to display intentionally (i.e., shelves, walls) and what to store and put away (i.e., closets, pantries, bins). Ideally, these items make our lives easier, more beautiful, or enjoyable. Knowing your inventory and working with the resources you already have before buying something new is medicine for you and the planet. It's how we practice eco-sustainability and slow down the consumerism machine. Plus, finding things easily and returning them to their designated home can mean less stress, more focused flow, and potential.

One way of being less cluttered and more minimal is by keeping *current,* or in other words, keeping what reflects who you are today. With clothes, this could refer to the current size, style, and season. With foods and items in the kitchen, you want these to match your current health goals. Imagine if everything in your home encouraged you to be the best, most authentic version of yourself. Imagine the moment you realize something doesn't align with that, and you practice the art of releasing. This, my friend, is decluttering magick! It requires rigorous honesty, a strong sense of self, dedicated focus, abundant mentality, trust, courage, mindfulness, and consistency. Keep it simple. It's progress, not perfection; you've got this. Patience and compassion are key.

To help you immediately make this a way of life, I can recommend keeping a year-round release bin. The moment you realize something is no longer *you* or serving you, you drop it in the bin! Then, when it's full, you give it all away. Boom! Yes. Yes. Yes. Thank you and goodbye.

With less stuff to clean or manage, there's more time for other matters, perhaps the less physical ones, like relationships and life experiences. Time is precious.

Mental Decluttering Magick

Too much mental activity in the brain can become exhausting and even dangerous. If thoughts aren't calm, focused, supportive, or inspiring, they have the potential to add stress, overwhelm, panic, anxiety, or depression to our lives. You've heard it said before: you are what you think. Your thoughts lead to actions, and so on.

Meditation is a beautiful tool that allows us to declutter our minds by making space between our thoughts. It's also an opportunity to get out of our forced self-will and allow more divine influence or inspiration to come in.

Yoga is an ancient, empowering tool for decluttering the mind as well. It honors the divine union of the mind, body, and spirit. When we get out of our head and into our body and breath, we allow more flow, harmony, and grace. We're telling our nervous system that it's okay to rest our brain, that we're still safe and will be okay.

As mentioned earlier, *getting* organized happens by sorting, purging, and then organizing the keeps. On the other hand, staying organized requires mindfulness (being present and focused) and slowing down, which is often easier said than done. Many who struggle with clutter, chronic disorganization, compulsive shopping, or hoarding may also struggle with mental challenges like Attention Deficit Hyperactivity Disorder (ADHD). Like with anything, knowledge is power, and patience is key.

Everyone's decluttering journey is unique. While some (those with ADHD, for example) improve with medication, others prefer alternative routes, such as meditation, yoga, or working with a coach or specialist.

Mental decluttering magick means downsizing brain clutter, so you can better manage and organize your thoughts and priorities. This allows more focus, flow, and success between the ears, reflecting itself all around you.

Mental clutter can also look like limiting beliefs not serving you, but I address this type more in the next section on emotional decluttering.

Emotional Decluttering Magick

Years ago, I went to a women's full moon circle and released this idea that I was too damaged to be loved. Talk about emotional decluttering magick and empowerment! It's hard to believe this now, but I really thought I was broken. I felt ugly, like a monster on an emotional rollercoaster, taking my boyfriend hostage, which I learned later was a highly codependent relationship. I just didn't know any better yet.

Today I get to enjoy a happy, healthy, harmonious relationship with someone putting in the same emotional inventory work I am through our 12 step program. It's not perfect, but we know how to communicate and find a way through our trauma responses into love and honesty. What a gift!

Decluttering emotionally is also why I have a relationship with my mom again, after many years of turmoil or no communication at all. I don't take everything so personally. I have a better sense of my boundaries, with a stronger sense of who I am and how to forgive, with compassion. I don't get triggered so easily because I've been releasing emotions that no longer serve through therapy, twelve-step, journaling, creative expression, and various spiritual art forms.

One of the greatest tools for emotional decluttering magick and empowerment is the ability to *pause*. When we're triggered or feel completely out of control, we must pause before we say or do something impulsive or irrational that we may later regret. We can even take it a step further and ask ourselves if perhaps we're hungry, angry, lonely, or tired (HALT) and then take appropriate action.

Practicing the *pause* can mean breaking a vicious shame cycle of overreacting and then regretting it, which is what I was in when I went crawling to that women's full moon circle. And that AA meeting. My decisions and actions about who and how I dated began to change after that. The relationship with myself became much more important to me as well, and I'm forever grateful.

Just like clutter, emotions don't go away, but our relationship with them changes. You are not your emotions, but they do want your attention. There is often a shadow side, and you can love her just as much as the sun side. This is how we find balance, truth, and harmony. This is how we work our emotional decluttering magick.

Spirit / Soul Decluttering Magick

If you're learning the spiritual life lessons meant for you, you're spiraling outward, ever-expanding, and evolving. You are practicing decluttering magick on this wild, cosmic soul level. You are doing your karmic work. Whatever you don't learn or navigate through in this life, you may have an opportunity in the next one.

Sometimes we know we need to let go and release, perhaps when we're feeling in a funk. But we don't know how. This is why it's key to remember that God, or whatever you choose to call a power greater than yourself, will do for us what we cannot do for ourselves. We can pray and ask for miracles. So long as we listen and take aligned action. That, remember, is where courage and faith come in.

Energetic Decluttering Magick (and Beyond!)

The law of attraction and manifestation is wild and real. It became more popular when the movie *The Secret* came out in 2006.

However, what's often not discussed is that it's not merely about focusing on what you want. It's also learning to let go, intentionally, from an empowered place because that is how we convey to the universe that we *trust* her. We trust we'll be provided for, that there is plenty and more to come. This is an abundance mentality. This is decluttering magick and empowerment. They go hand in hand so beautifully.

When we get to know our inventory, whether physically, mentally, emotionally, or spiritually, we empower ourselves to live our most magical, authentic lives. First, we recognize what is serving us with gratitude. Second, we realize what's not serving us and develop the courage and faith to let it go. Finally, we can see what needs an upgrade or wants to manifest into ourselves, space, or life.

Rituals for releasing as well as healthy, proper grieving are important, too. Allowing death without pressuring yourself to re-birth again right away gives you the space needed to heal and move forward.

I grieved that alcohol. Red wine was my friend for a long time and comforted me at home alone many nights. My sponsor had me write a letter to it, thanking it and telling it goodbye. I cried hard many times. I've written many letters these last three years, most of which I'll never send because they were *for me* to grieve and process. Whether it be anger and confusion or sadness and despair, the letters were for me to release.

Twelve-step recovery literature explains how we alcohol-ics have a spiritual sickness. We are learning how to trust and strengthen our relationship with our higher power, whatever that means to us, and how to surrender and give things over, especially when we're in fear. My getting sober and working a spiritual program also allows me to be of maximum service to others, to live with purpose, without being distracted by the poi-son and the shame that comes with it. I got keys to the kingdom, freedom, my authentic voice, and truth in exchange for a bottle. I get to wake up each morning feeling clear and creative, excited for another day. I go to bed with more peace of mind and self-re-spect. It's truly a miracle, and it is priceless. I wouldn't trade it for anything.

Just like my approach with decluttering, twelve-step programs are holistic, which I find necessary. We address the clutter on a physical, mental, emotional, and spiritual level. When I was crav-ing alcohol, I was trying to feed all of those aspects of my being. The ironic thing is that while I thought I was relaxing and numb-ing (decluttering my mental chaos), I was doing the opposite, making cloudy the connection between myself and my ultimate truth, higher self, and power. But, like the lotus, I keep rising from the murky waters, returning home to myself.

And that's what we do every time we declutter. We get closer to finding our voice and improving—or even saving—our precious lives. So whether it be coffee or sugar, toxic thoughts or communi-cation, or piles of stuff everywhere, if you're willing to see your part and lovingly explore what you're ready to release, there is a beautiful path of possibilities, hope, and resiliency eagerly awaiting you.

So now it's your turn. What are you releasing? Write these down. Burn them too if you like. Then consider what you're making space to receive, internally and externally, when you let these go. Align your actions with this inner wisdom, and you're golden. Release. Receive. Rebirth. Beautiful!

The full moon is a potent time to reflect on what you're releasing. The new moon is a magical time to name what you're calling in. However you choose to go about it, be sure to make it yours. Work your beautiful decluttering magick. Let go and keep getting free. And may your freedom light up the way for the freedom of others.

Ashley Moon is a Decluttering Witch, Healer, and Coach. She helps artists and entrepreneurs organize their time and space to master their potential and truly live their purpose. As a reader of the Tarot and Akashic Records, she intuitively blends the practical with the spiritual, providing a profoundly empowering and sustainable experience.

Miss Moon dedicates her time toward helping people let go and make space for the best version of themselves, in every aspect, as a way of life. She is an artist, activist, author, speaker, and group facilitator – often helping bridge the mind, body, space, and spirit. She has organized over a thousand clients in person and has reached millions more online. She has been featured on OWN, Buzzfeed, Hoarders, LA Times, WikiHow, and Youtube's favorite social media influencers. In addition, she has offered intuitive sessions at HBO events, Kiva cannabis parties, fabulous festivals, and intimate private gatherings.

She has an MA in Human Development, BA in American Studies, and extensive certifications within coaching, business, productivity, psychology, leadership, community organizing, and healing modalities, including yoga, reiki, and the priestess path. And always she remains a student of life!

CHAPTER 20

Forging the Phoenix from the Fires of Perfection

By Jennifer Highmoor

t's my fault. No one forced me, made me, or pressured me! Don't blame them! I chose to do the drugs! Blame me!" I screamed in his face, with fire from the depths of my core.

As I reached the end of my fierce expiration, I felt his hot, calloused hand clench around my neck and became weightless in an instant. The back of my skull impacted the cold, hard countertop, and I laid there, dumbfounded, staring at the stippled ceiling, reeling from the shock that I'd just been choke-slammed in my kitchen. At this time, I popped out of my body again and witnessed the rest of the scene from above.

"You little fuckin' bitch!" he exclaimed, head red as a fire engine and looking like it contained enough pressure to explode.

Hi! My name is Jenn. Welcome to the climax of my intervention. I don't really recall much after that. I'd popped out of my physical form and been taken by yet another wave of psychosis. I think Dad released me when he realized what he'd done. It was the only time he'd ever been physical with me, beyond a deserved spanking as a child. In his defense, just thirty minutes prior, he'd been broadsided by the news that his golden child had been addicted to methamphetamine for the last year. He was terrified, in denial, confused, frustrated, and disappointed; he was all the negative feelings that manifested in anger and rage when they appeared for him, and he'd never felt so powerless to help or fix someone he loved.

I am the eldest child, a natural leader, Daddy's little boy-girl with a secret rebel side. For him, the sun rose and set upon my head. While my siblings and I all felt we lacked praise and encouragement from our patriarch, somehow that got mixed in with the pedestal he placed me on since the day I was born. In his eyes, I could do no wrong. School came easily to me; I always had a natural talent for athleticism and was socially developed from a young age. I was the child with an angel's face, the girl with a propensity for helping others with anything they may need. But beneath the surface of my good girl facade, my darkness developed, and the wild child began to emerge, in secrecy, throughout my teenage years. I love to be bad. I require a regular hit of adrenaline and excitement, but I confess I had let it go too far and seriously needed to find a balance point.

I've come to know that my rebel child was born of desperately trying to make myself look bad so that perhaps he would notice my sister and brother. I spent much of my childhood hoping he would develop a closeness with them as he had with me. I was very like him, personality-wise. He could relate to me. He could understand me. I was able to meet his anger with my own. Instead of being wounded by his rage, I would step up and take it all, so no one else had to.

Somedays, he would come home after a stressful day at work, and the house would walk on eggshells, knowing he was on edge. Each time, I would step up to the plate and intentionally poke the bear until he blew his top. My mom and siblings would retreat to their bedrooms while he and I staged war in the living room, and once he'd adequately vented and cooled off, we could carry on about our peaceful lives. Always the line-walker. The warrior who fought on the front lines of the battlefield then tended to the wounded when it was over, just like Brigid: the primary goddess I resonate and work with.

Our relationship was complicated. He and I have been married in prior incarnations. His soul is also a fair bit younger than mine. Sometimes I felt as though I was the only one he understood or related to in our house. I inherited his fire. When we spent time together in the barnyard or on the rodeo trail, he sometimes confided in me, and the family often elected me to broach difficult subjects with him. His mother and I were the only two who could potentially sway him to change his mind or see things from another perspective. We shared secrets. It was a fucked up dynamic, but I'm grateful for our unique relationship.

After losing him this past year to depression, I've gained a great deal of perspective and grown through it, as I've chosen to do with each personal tragedy befallen upon my chaotic path. After all, he taught me how to be a strong, independent leader. Someone who takes no shit or abuse from anyone, who fiercely cares for her people, and who is prepared to defend them to the ends of the earth. My androgynous soul chose him to mold me into the efficient, resourceful problem solver I am today. Thanks to his example, I've managed to connect with and earn the respect of a demographic most consider hard and impenetrable, especially by women. It was the fire that helped me create a name for myself in the Alberta oilfields, where I keep tabs on everyone and lovingly, assertively lifeguard my work crews, providing medical standby for remote and high-risk work operations as their "medic."

I offer my workers natural remedies, homemade creams and salves, healing, and muscle work and always ensure their physical needs are met and maintained, because I know they don't have adequate time to seek practitioners outside our long workdays. My safety meeting topics include relatable information on body mechanics and body systems to learn to be aware and read their own dials. Many of them call me the witch doctor; others call me Mom. After a decade of honing my skills in groups consisting mainly of very grounded, hyper-critical, tangibly oriented men, I found the courage to rent a space (lovingly named Celeste) and begin to conduct formal sessions on a part-time basis. After all, if I could make believers out of them, I must have some serious gifts to bring to the world!

When the fire raged out of control.

Until I was about 16 years old, this occurred fairly regularly and unpredictably, always directed at someone very close to me during a disagreement. One day, in mid-conflict with my sister, I spoke a hateful statement I regretted instantly. I witnessed her soul shatter in front of me as she crumbled to the floor in a sobbing pile of tears. It winded me. I was speechless and felt as though I'd lanced myself with the dagger. She was my closest confidant, my partner in crime, my sidekick since the day she was born. It wasn't okay to wound her that deep. I couldn't take back the words I had said. No apology was going to reverse the damage I'd inflicted in my malice. I vowed from that day forward to never use someone's insecurities against them, especially not someone I loved.

For the next decade, I shoved the fire down, inside. I lost myself fully in the service of others and people-pleasing without knowing it. That's what led me to my addiction in the first place: the inability to say no and a magnetism that attracted more responsibilities than I could handle in the 16 hours a day most people spend awake. So I forfeited sleep to make enough time. During the course of my drug use, I also lost my grandmother—with whom I was living while working EMS in our small town—to leukemia. In fact, the intervention took place in the home my boyfriend and I purchased from her estate. I must interject here that I did not agree to get help for myself in the beginning. It was my three-year-old son, Ryder, for whom I did that. They told me that if I wanted to get him back, I had to straighten up. And they were right. So, I went to rehab for him.

After completing the program, I moved home to live with my parents. My common-law spouse had vowed he'd quit using while I was inside. I was granted a weekend pass and arrived home to find an array of scattered beer bottles. I realized my guy and our friends had been there, doing meth and drinking all night before he picked me up. The drugs were gone, but the empty alcohol containers combined with his paranoid behavior strongly indicated what was occurring in my absence. I was too fresh in my recovery to be around that. I'd lost my job, my kid, my friends, my house, my boyfriend, and the respect of my community and some family. I lost everything. And once I graduated from the program, I spiraled into a deep, all-consuming depression. Darkness. Isolation. Sleeping all the time, lacking motivation, I started thinking the world would be better off without me. Still, being the spiritual creature I am, I didn't have the balls to prematurely terminate my contract and return for a do-over in my next life. I was stuck wading through quicksand until Mom found a book. Bless her heart;

she always found a way to teach us, even when we couldn't listen. *A Return to Love* by Marianne Williamson is the book that saved my life, helped me flip the switch, and changed my perspective. It reminded me I have a purpose to fulfill and encouraged me to forgive myself for my choices. It helped me consider that perhaps my addiction occurred so I could become a lighthouse for other addicts. And so I did.

While I no longer condone the use of chemicals in my body, I will admit that my experience with them opened up my brain to new possibilities, perspectives, and abilities. Don't get me wrong; I was naturally gifted from childhood without realizing it. I've always known things without knowing how. I remember once picking up the phone to dial someone, finding a lack of dial tone present, and after saying hello, I was surprised to find the person I was calling had dialed me first, and I picked up before it rang. The same thing still happens now, except it's me hitting the send button at the same time they call my cell. I often predict events and occurrences, but I've learned to set healthy boundaries and intentions around the incoming information because I have no want to preemptively know about an illness, injury, or death of which I can't alter the course.

The bottom line is that rehab taught me how to start setting boundaries in all aspects of my life. I learned to say no when something didn't feel intrinsically good. I learned to discern between the people who deserve my care and attention and those who were so self-involved and toxic that they couldn't return the favor. But I was still missing joy. I used the essential oil blend daily to support my endocrine system in its fight to recover its dopamine, oxytocin and serotonin. Eventually, that vibration, paired with the crystals I packed around, led me where I needed to go.

The next step in my journey was to recover my inner child. Bless her heart; she had been suppressed since I was nine, at which time my little brother fought a two and a half year battle with leukemia. I largely took on the household managerial role because Dad didn't know how to operate the washing machine or dishwasher, and Mom oversaw my brother's care during the week. When they swapped spots on weekends, we wanted

Find Your Voice, Save Your Life 3 | 169

to spend quality time with Mom, not lose her to an endless list of chores. So I tucked away the playful, fun little sprite for over 15 years and took on the role of matriarch. Finally, a dear healer friend took me on a meditative river journey to retrieve her and emotionally welcome her back to the fold. Since then, she lightly tugs on my hair if she thinks I'm taking life too seriously and reminds me it's okay to let go and be silly. She's the best with kids, and it was her genuine curiosity and sense of wonder that brought me to the next puzzle piece.

I attended a rainy weekend workshop/retreat with my mom, sister, and sister-in-law. The setting was a neighbor's beautiful country acreage with forest trails, a hilltop view, gorgeous gardens, flowers, decor, and healthy, delicious food. Remember, at this point, I've been stuffing anger for a solid decade, and anxiety is something that's been gradually mounting since my recovery. I struggled with vulnerability, period. I came in with my armor, as I often do in group settings, especially if I don't know and trust everyone present. That day and all the ones leading up to it, I was conditioned to believe crying was weakness, the opposite of strong. And I'm one tough bitch, so that didn't fit into my persona.

We were assigned an hour of silence. *Well, shit, this means I have to be by myself.* It was raining outside, and I do love that smell. I wandered out and was mildly annoyed by the droplets distorting the view through my glasses. I scurried under a little tin roof on four legs to shield them from the spatter and found myself seated on the quad beneath. I breathed in the smell of the rain and listened to the tiny pings it created as it splashed on the metal sheeting above my head. I began to look around the property. I was facing the front of the house and began to marvel at the rain barrel. I love an old wooden rain barrel. An old wooden anything, really. The skies had been intermittently showering the prairies with heavy doses of rain for the past few days. As the gutters and clouds poured more into the already full container, it simply overflowed gracefully, gently. I pondered water's affiliation with emotions and the metaphor the goddess laid before me.

Could it be that simple? Could it be that tears are the way to release all the emotions that feel too big to be housed in this tiny body? Could I just let them overflow onto my cheeks when my feelings overwhelmed me? Could I be the rain barrel?

So began the journey of reconnecting with my emotions. Embracing my darkness. Learning to sit in it, to feel it. Being comfortable with my joy, sadness, disappointment, frustration, etc. Reaching the threshold, which builds from the center of my diaphragm and gently releases any extra pressure in droplets to the earth, for she will transform it into something beautiful. That burning feeling, my fire. The answer has always been to let water balance my fire. Once I began to create space for that—first privately and now in circles where I feel safe, loved, and understood, as well as occasionally in public speeches which can bring a new level of power to the house, and also in client sessions (the last few years I've been known to cry with or for a client on the table)—I started to feel what others felt mentally, physically, emotionally. Not just the people I was closest with. Now I was feeling the feels of my clients and workers, enabling me to understand where they're at and how I can best serve them. I've since allowed myself the grace to love without bounds. I've discovered true self-love in the practice of self-care, and my marriage to my husband has grown to find deeper levels of intimacy than I thought possible with a spouse. I've realized I'm a perfectly imperfect human, just like everyone else, and if I have no judgment for their choices, why should I judge myself for my lessons?

I know that I've walked through fire and fury for a good reason. I've burned it all down and rebuilt from scratch on more than one occasion. I genuinely believe I'm here to facilitate change, help alter systems that fail to serve the good of all, and share my tools and experiences with the people drawn to my magical ways. I feel a sense of purpose when I guide someone else navigating a similar experience. I honor my callings and treat each client very differently, pulling from a vast toolkit ranging from two handfuls of healing modalities to bodywork, stretches to exercises, intuitive psychology to supplementation, crystal therapy to belief reprogramming. I've spent my entire existence studying the facets and tricks of the human experience, both because it fascinates me and because I wish to master it while I lead others to do the same. I will continue to learn and grow until my last breath, and now I do it because I love myself more than I love them. I know I need to honor my needs and myself before I can take care of them. I know that I can show up for my favorite people as the best version of me every day, as long as I cry, take my baths, do my exercises, drink water, eat food, breathe, meditate, enjoy nature, color, write, garden and let my spirit guides walk me through my human experience. As much as I love a raging fire when it's warranted, I'm grateful for the phoenix who's emerged from the ashes of my life. She's strong, compassionate, empathetic, and understanding but perhaps greatest of all, she's found peace in forgiveness and the balance of her elements. And she's going to willfully fulfill her contract on this earth with as much power, intention, and purpose she can muster until the gods call her sovereign soul home.

Jennifer Highmoor is the owner/operator of Witch Way to Heaven. She is a caring empath with a knack for helping others create empowerment and positive change in their lives. She has extensively studied all aspects of humans, with the single goal of using that information to help them navigate their earthly experiences with as little turbulence as possible. She considers herself a human body mechanic, uniquely tailoring her treatments to the individual's most pressing needs and working on whatever level of the self is causing the problem. A natural counselor all her life, she's a safe space for anyone to unload their emotional baggage, and she offers perspective on their experiences that aims to facilitate forgiveness. She's a wellness warrior, inspiring others to take care of their human bodies via nutrition, mindful movement, and regular exercise. Her androgynous soul enables her to connect with all types of energies, earthly and otherwise, to facilitate the highest possible healing for her clients. She enjoys spending time in nature, especially near water and the Rocky Mountains, clearing spaces of energies and entities, hosting groups, events, and retreats. She teaches classes in natural pain management, magick, spirituality, healing modalities, and wellness. She loves working with children and animals, especially horses. She's grown through more than her share of negative and traumatic experiences, choosing to focus on the lessons learned and how she can create something good by openly sharing her stories. Jennifer's wish is for everyone to understand themselves and the world around them better, to share tools and navigational tactics because we're all in this together.

https://www.facebook.com/witchwaytoheaven/

witchwaytoheaven@gmail.com

CHAPTER 21

You May Love Differently
Healing Through Trauma

By Tiffany Marie Boerner, Light Channel,
Evidential Medium, Energy Mentor/Teacher

He straddled my upper torso while strategically pinning my arms to the kitchen tile floor with his knees. I've seen this battle position between two people before. A rush of survival charges my cells. My head was awkwardly lodged between the refrigerator and oven. We had torn the place apart. At this point, I was completely trapped. I felt his hands wrap around my throat. His thumbs crossed over one another in the front, and the tips of his fingers touched in the back. The same hands that gently caressed my skin to help me fall asleep. The same hands that I've proudly held as we walked down the street. His grip on my throat tightened. My heart was pounding, my breath was heavy, yet I had to slow my breathing. *Focus.* He seemed to have let go of himself, blindly strangling me. My only defense at this point was to communicate with my eyes. His eyes weren't his. They had gone hollow. This isn't who he was or how he was raised. But all he needed was a spark to ignite any lingering pain. Our unhealed trauma collided. *Uh, I am so reactive. But I am so angry. He needs to understand what I am feeling.* I think this to myself. He projects, "she's just like every other woman in my life. Dissatisfied with me. She thinks I'm incapable, and she doesn't trust me." Together, we recreate scenes and feelings from childhood.

I was slowly fading. No longer able to fight, I was exhausted. My muscles weren't firing; I was disoriented and forced to surrender. I was losing this fight. I couldn't breathe or hear, and my vision was closing. I remember trying to see and find something to grab on to, a last-ditch effort of saving my life. I had tunnel vision, and the dot of light I could see was completely blurred. I could feel my body softening. My legs settled, and my hips lay flat. There was a moment of weightlessness. Just before going unconscious, the darkness that was my sight became a magnificent light. A gentle, compassionate guiding voice resounded loudly within me, running through every cell of my being, of my essence. *My Dear, you may love differently.* You may do things differently. I lay on the kitchen floor lifeless. He fled.

In retrospect, I now see clearly how the supportive realms of spirit made a conscious connection with me, taking and holding me. Time and time again, one traumatic episode after another—a viable energetic defense—I fled my body until it was safe to return. I separated from the physical pain being inflicted or the emotional pain generated by abuse. Energetically I expanded out, reaching for light and softness, departing from reality. I was ungrounded, but more importantly, connected to realms of pink hues, softness, and true love. I fled my body each time the blow hit, creating a well-honed pathway to the spirit realm, a pathway I am much more familiar with than I realize.

Is this a pathway that you've unknowingly established in times of trauma?

My roommate came home early from work and saved both my boyfriend and me that day. Unbeknownst to him, his unannounced arrival home was a slap of awareness, the pause we needed. It was the relief our hearts needed. And this was the day my soul reminded me of *my* truth. It rang my freedom loudly, guiding my remembrance to love and co-create differently than from what I've only known.

I was 22 years old at the time, and I desperately needed to experience those words spoken to me. *I get to do it differently.* I choose to do it differently. Our relationship ended that evening. Our togetherness served us both brilliantly. We were able to highlight truth in each other. Did it have to happen through violence? For us, it did. It was a pivotal moment in our relationship experience that shined upon areas that needed healing and nurturing. Through our pain, we lifted one another to new heights of self-realization.

How do you wish to co-create in your relationships? How are healing opportunities shined upon in your relationships? Do you see them but just aren't quite yet ready to nurture those areas?

I was in a relationship before this one with red flags and exchanges that didn't sit well with me, but I still wasn't quite ready to do the healing work. Our togetherness had expired. We were complete. We both needed to step back and see ourselves in truth. We individually needed to resolve within our hearts how we were going to choose to live with love.

When I came to, my boyfriend was gone. I have never seen him again. Both of us were ashamed and filled with uncertainties. My roommate slowly helped me sit up and handed me some water. I shared what happened just hours before and how things quickly escalated. In that moment of explaining the details, none of it made sense from a rational mind. "I don't even know why we were so mad. Or who was physical first or why it even became physical."

How did this happen!? Why did I allow it to happen, and even more, why am I letting myself co-create like this! This was my moment of I AM present, here, able, and willing to do this work. To connect to truth and honor my being. My truth of living differently. My honoring of being, willing to hold loving patience with myself as I navigate what feels right to my heart and release from what had been spoken to me throughout my life. In pursuit of freedom from untruths, I release.

I remember jolting episodes of rage, abuse, and violent energy spewing from bodies from a very early age. These were bodies that held the hearts of two that held, loved, and nurtured me. A lot of painful moments have been forgotten until I am unknowingly mirroring suppressed moments of my childhood. There's always a heightened intensity at home. Emotions surge, catapulting the ego into disassociation. Nails bit down until they bleed. Their minds were deeply consumed with wild scenarios. I can feel how none of this is true to them. My body feels the emotional weight of the atmosphere. I know when to hide. I know when to defend and when to protect.

It was 2:00 AM. I'm now half asleep as I hear my dad fumbling through the front door, staggering to the back of the house where their bedroom is. The vibration of my heartbeat begins to fill my chest. Ba-boom. Ba-boom. My breaths are now quick and short. I'm fully awake. I listen. My heart gets louder, Ba-boom. In a panic, *uh I can't hear.* I press myself. *I need to hear. What if she needs me? I need to hear her.* Swiftly my toes hit the old hardwood floor, and I rush to the top of the stairs. I sit and listen. *I need to be closer.* I move to the bottom of the staircase and listen. The silence is killing me. It's not this easy. He doesn't just come home and go to sleep, not on nights like these. I move through the formal living room and then the dining room, impressed not to make a sound. These hardwood floors are older than my grandmother. They have stories to tell, and they speak through every creaky step. I hold my breath, standing still on my toes, but my heart is loud.

I hear something big hit the wall. The house shakes a little. Loud whispers. Then loud yells. A fist hitting the flesh of someone is a sound, a very specific sound. Now a rhythmic pattern behind his punching. He's beating her. It took seconds to make it through the kitchen and into the family room. He's on top of her. He's spitting and slurring words, unrelated and exaggerated. I hear calls for reason amid cries for help and rationale. Deaf ears. He just never fucking stopped hitting her until he was exhausted, or she stopped defending, violently releasing the dried blood of the pain harbored. I refuse to wear the stains of others' blood. It's these moments amidst fistfights, broken hearts, blood, and fear, that I learned I'm a courageous lightworker. I'm a lightworker who has an incredible amount of love and a heart that's capable of great things. I'm a warrior, as are you, and you, too, get to do it differently.

My mother is a mighty woman, emotionally, physically, and spiritually. I'm not sure if she ever truly celebrated her brilliance or even permitted herself to do so. I wonder how her soul speaks to her and in what brilliant, magical ways it does. I wonder how she's listened and honored the divine messages that delicately swirl about her. Ignoring divine messages can be a rather daunting experience. The pain may seem to deepen the more you push away your connection. The path before you may seem to be littered with emotional debris, suffocating your senses. Yet, in all of her internal turmoil, I know she listens.

I know she moves effortlessly, fooling those around her. When there is real, deep love, a mother has the motivation to endure all sorts of hardship. There were many times she energetically tented me, protecting me from the day-to-day happenings. This I know, as I find myself naturally doing just the same for my daughters. With pure, light-filled intention, I expand my energy field out like a blanket to dress them with the light of the highest realms, protect them and raise them from the darkness of an atmosphere. My mom did this often. I could sense her energetically sending out protection for our home, my father, and myself.

Have you felt this before or done this yourself?

What is fascinating is that my mom and I never spoke of such practices, the how-to, or even the concept. We simply do this naturally. This is innate wisdom. We all invoke, at some level, energetic practices that clear, protect, and heal.

I understand how my parents didn't expect to show up like this, how generations of violence and emotional trauma captured and entangled them. Experiencing physical and emotional abuse alters how your brain and body operate, as well as how you think, learn, and behave. It affects the ability to make well-considered choices. When something in their atmosphere slightly resembles a dangerous situation, it causes one to be triggered, similarly to someone with PTSD. A trigger is an automatic response, an instance that sends one back to the very moment of trauma, a foundation of reaction. It's a response meter if you will.

Tendencies, characteristics, resilience, addictions, and probabilities are woven from the very fabric of our upbringing and atmosphere. A product of your experiences, your mind consists of limiting ego-constructs by which you identify yourself. Over time, these patterns and beliefs become so deeply ingrained that they congeal or crystallize into a solid form in your energy field, all of which can be softened, lifted, released, and healed through intentional acts of nurturing love. You create your future through free will, and by changing your patterns and beliefs, you change your destiny. Awareness is the greatest agent for change. Here is where it becomes vital to learn how to unravel from such experiences. Through self-witnessing and self-love, you can profoundly transform congealed forms in your energy field instantly. You can soften your grip of learned pain patterns to understand better what truly does and doesn't belong to you. This realization is an opportunity, and it's not to be denied.

Let's take a moment to practice energetic awareness by connecting to your energy field. Your energy field is directly connected to your nervous system. Understanding this may bring forth a new awareness for you. For example, visiting a stagnant, depressed atmosphere or working alongside an angry, stressed-out co-worker may deposit unwanted energetic residue in your energy field. This residue certainly will not serve you, or anyone for that matter. You may also experience sudden moodiness, anxiety, headache, or brain fog, depending on how sensitive you are. This is a small example of how your everyday environment and interactions with others affect you in big and small ways. Being present with yourself grants a higher sight to realize sudden emotional and/or physical shifts. Nurturing your relationship with your intuition and energy field will be key in your discernment. You will be able to cleanse your energy and release what isn't yours with confidence.

Through my intuitive mentoring and healing courses, I encourage students to be like a spider who can sense the vibration of even the slightest shift of frequency within their intricately woven web or, in this case, your energy field. May the following exercise and meditation support you in this intention.

Exercise: Sensing your energy field

I invite you to close your eyes and let go of expectations; breathe for a moment and imagine a brilliant sphere of light around you. Begin to open your awareness to the area just outside of your body. Pause and breathe for a moment. Settle in and open to receive. With the guidance of your intuition, sense joy and love in your energy field. Trust the very first thing that comes forward. Love may show itself as a color, memory, symbol, or all-knowing. Notice where love is in your field. Great! With the same intention, sense emotional pain or trauma in your energy field. You may immediately sense a person(s), place, and/or event. Notice where trauma is in your field. You may even be able to sense the colors and vibrancy of your chakras. The more you sit with this connection, the more you may witness unresolved emotions, impressions, and love. Possibly unrealized, altering how you interact, respond, and operate with yourself and others. You may even be able to get a sense of the patterns that have kept you from calling in a more harmonious and balanced life. As you explore your energy field, you will realize what a powerful, radiant light-being you are. The amazing world of your luminous sphere will continue to open as you continue to discover the multiple dimensions of your being. This is your healing journey; may you welcome the wonder and awe of your brilliance.

Meditation: Healing thought-forms

You may want to record yourself reading the following so you can completely relax and go within. Or you may log on to my website www.bodyandsoulconnection.com for the pre-recorded version of this healing exercise. Find a comfortable, supportive space that will act as a safe container for you today.

Now, close your eyes, taking the deepest breath you've taken today. Treating your following breathes equally, inhale for five and exhale for five. If you wish to take your breath deeper, you may inhale for seven and exhale for seven. Filling your body to the top and slowly releasing to empty, repeat this rhythmic breathing now. With each breath, your shoulders drop further from your ears, you become heavier in your seat, your tongue releases from the roof of your mouth. You are honoring several minutes to welcome a state of complete relaxation. Place your hand to your heart and speak: *I call upon my highest consciousness of the highest good to work through me. I welcome clarity for resolution in my healing. I am a divine being living a human experience whose heart is open to the highest frequency of love. I hold myself with deep compassion as I allow such wisdom and truths to be revealed. I open to receive higher self-realization as I unravel from falsehoods. I begin to set myself free from restrictive patterns and structures that no longer serve my highest timeline. I courageously give myself permission to live in accordance with my highest path for my highest good. I invite the spirit of wholeness, love, and truth to illuminate my innate wisdom upon any and all forms, patterns, and structures that obscure my truth. Thank you. So be it, and so it is.* Bask in the radiant light that surrounds you, supporting you as you integrate this heightened energy. Continue rhythmic breathing, but this time see yourself inhaling healing light. Invite this healing light to fill every area of your body. Now your chakras, one by one, see each chakra receive this healing light, trusting in your perfect approach. Release every bit of stagnant energy on your exhale, knowing that every bit of your essence is fully supported and guided.

Take your time coming back to your space. Enjoy a glass of water and welcome rest.

Daily Permission:

To be still. To truly see myself. To keep promises to myself. To celebrate myself. To honor my feelings. To honor guiding messages. To self-reflect. To heal. To break patterns that do not serve me. To feel. To listen. To nurture myself. To rise. To unravel. To believe. To live. To speak. To rest. To love myself.

In what ways do you give yourself permission?

_____

_____

_____

_____

_____

_____

Beloved Sister, you are not alone. There are days when the water is clear, settled, and calm. Those are the days when it is most easy to listen. Yet, when the water is boisterous and overpowering is when it's of utmost importance to be in your stillness. To see and listen beyond rushing currents, which are a mere distraction. Your waters will calm upon being beyond the chaos. It is quite a sobering experience. The water rushes by, yet you are unscathed. Be still to create calm. Nurture inner trust to harness your birthright gifts.

My high love to you.

 **Tiffany Marie** is an intuitive mentor and teacher, evidential medium, channeler, and energy healer whose purpose is to guide people in reawakening their soul's wisdom and innate connection. She's been certified as a Reiki teacher, ancient shamanic timeline healer, sound healing and breathwork facilitator, and Integrated Energy Therapy practitioner, which have all unlocked her purpose-led and heart-filled work.

Tiffany hosts virtual community gatherings for intimate healing to guide self-awareness, healthy thought-forms, intuitive abilities and welcome greater self-love and wholeness. She's a life-long student who loves to write, think outside the box and connect to Mother Earth through plant life and the animal kingdom. Tiffany is a sage light channel dedicated to transcribing forgotten ancient healing scripture. She holds a strong passion for guiding others through their personal journey of healing through self-discovery. With extensive study, classwork, and community shares, Tiffany has come to deepen her understanding of the foundation of energy healing and emotional and physical healing possibilities. With a heart of being of service, she connects with Divine Source consciousness of the highest realms to guide her work. Her personal story continues to motivate others to reclaim their Divine power. She is excited to be publishing her next collaborative book, Sister Armor, Healing in Community (to be released in the spring of 2022). She grounds herself by spending lots of time in nature, lifting weights, creating intuitively, and being with her family.

Connect with me at www.bodyandsoulconnection.com

CHAPTER 22

The Voices in My Head Said I Wasn't Crazy

How They Proved I Was Sane

Melissa Jolly Graves, L.P.N., ORDM, Seer, Priestess, Shaman, Reiki Master, Documentarian, Philosopher

It's 11:22 p.m. I'm just getting home after working a 16-hour T.C.U. shift. My next shift starts at 6:00 a.m. and I'm ready to kiss my kids and go to bed. I walk through the entrance door leading to the living room. Sitting on the couch is my neighbor, babysitter, and close friend Drew. He pauses the movie and explains how the night went. Afterward, he asks, "Can I finish watching the movie? There's only 28 minutes left. I don't have Netflix."

"Sure," I say as I sit on the couch. *I can stay awake;* I think as I fight my heavy eyes from closing.

Hours go by, and I wake, laying down, my head on Drew's leg. He is sitting up, sleeping with his arm and hand over my shoulder, chest, and arm. I try to move. Before I can, a lighted spirit enters the room, pushes me down, and says, "Stay."

I lay in shock as the adrenaline charges through my body, waking every cell. *Did that really happen? No, I must have been dreaming. I wasn't fully awake. Open your eyes; it was your imagination.* I open my eyes and nothing is there. Hoping what I saw was a dream, I put my hands on Drew's arm and slowly start pushing it away. The figure hovers at me again and says, "Don't get up."

I go back to my starting position, now feeling protected by Drew's arm.

"Don't get up. He needs you." I hear the spirit speak.

Nope, this isn't real, I quickly tell myself, hoping to believe it. But the woman in front of me won't go away. In fact, she is more predominant than before.

Her brown hair flows past her shoulders; her kind hazel eyes look at me with concern; her body is of light, and it flows around her like a dress made of electricity.

"I'm not here to hurt you. You are a gift to my son. I have spent years bringing you together." The spirit says.

My body won't move. I lay silent, trying to convince myself this moment isn't real. I've been through enough counseling and medication to know this is not normal. I close my eyes. That doesn't help. This woman has imprinted herself in my head. *I must be hallucinating, like when I was young. What's wrong with me?* I question reality as my mind fades into the darkness. Memories of the past fill my head. I remember seeing angels, ghosts, spirits, demons, and creatures not of this world. I recall having Déjà Vu, premonitions of the future, experiencing other people's dreams, and seeing energy around people.

Flashbacks of my stepfather saying, "Welcome back from La La Land," triggers memories of times my spirit left my body. During those times, I would blackout in a trance, stare into space, run into walls, fall down steps, and forget my surroundings. Sometimes I didn't move at all; I was catatonic. Sleepwalking happened day and night. As a result, my parents had to lock the doors to keep me from walking out.

I remember going to worlds with the angels and ancestors. They fed me, told me stories, kept me company. I would even sleep with one arm in the air, convinced I was holding their hands.

I was an undiagnosable disruption—a guinea pig for medication. Often, I would end up in the special education classes or the counselor's office for my behaviors. By fifth grade, I trained myself to act "normal" and hide what I saw. Mom made the decision to take me off medication, and I was placed in regular classes. I did a great job until I was 14 when I started dating Kemet.

He, too, believed and had experiences with ghosts. The Ouija board was the fad at that time and Kemet wanted to connect to his deceased father. We were ignorant and didn't understand its power. After using it, I was in a trance. I didn't talk to anyone except Kemet. I said things his dad would have said if he were alive. I spoke of things he never told me. I channeled my friend T. J.'s dad too. The gates were open. I knew things again. I began challenging and correcting teachers, finding my own ways to solve problems. Mom and the teachers would often argue. She said I was never wrong about the things I said.

The counselor said it was attention-seeking behavior because of depression. I got put on medication, again. I didn't feel depressed; I felt unheard. Blackouts now happened from the medication, not my angels. I ran away, stopped the medication, and acted "normal" enough to be accepted in society.

When I was 20 years old, Kemet bought me a new car. While driving home from Iowa, I looked over to the passenger seat and saw the ghost of a young boy, who later moved into the house. He would open and close doors, turn on our appliances, play with my son's toys, cry, and yell for his mom. He scared guests away. Kemet ran a vehicle report, and found the car was totaled at 5,000 miles and had been hit on the passenger side. Someone fixed it up and sold it to us.

Eventually, I started nursing school, we moved into a new house, and the boy stayed there.

In 2006, I got my first nursing job. Ironically, dying patients and those diagnosed with cancer or mental illnesses would report seeing and experiencing the same things I did. They, too, saw ghosts, angels, demons, and energy, which I chalked it up to hormonal imbalances. Kemet and I divorced in 2008. Being a nurse and single mom meant I had no time for things science couldn't explain. I did such a good job at ignoring my intuition that I shut it off completely.

But this hallucination feels real. It can't be. I get out of my head and come back to the moment with Drew on the couch. I open my eyes. The spirit is looking at me with love in her eyes, knowing I'm scared, she says nothing and just points to another spirit entering the room.

At that moment, every emotion a human being can feel encloses my mind, body, and spirit. The year is 2012, now. 2006 was the last time I saw the man standing before me. It was my brother

Danny; he drowned six years ago. He looked at me, tears running down my face. He was my heart. He understood me. He knew of the angels and demons that fought over families. Although his Bipolar gave him the ability to see things I couldn't, we still had similar visions and occurrences.

Why haven't I seen you until now?

"Sis, you closed me out and turned off communication. She is here to help. This is Drew's mother, Laurel. She has a message for you. Listen."

The woman looks at me. "You are a great healer, Melissa. You have known this all your life; your angels and God told you so. You weren't meant to be a nurse. You were meant to do faith healing, like Jesus. Many people need your help, including my son. Help him heal, find the love in his heart, and remember who he is. In return, I will guide you back to your angels and ancestors. I will teach you how you were meant to heal."

My brother stepped in. "Sis, Drew is like me. He will challenge you in ways you never thought. Accept him, and you will accept yourself. Listen to your guides and angels. They are real. You're not crazy; you were just too innocent to understand. It will make sense soon enough. Trust, have faith. I will be here to fight the demons with you." Without giving me a chance to speak, Danny left the room, and the fear inside me subsided.

"Please listen. We need you, and you need us. Remember who you are," were Laurel's last words before she left. I laid still in the silence, eyes wide open, trying to make sense of what I witnessed. *Remember who I am? But I've worked so hard to hide it.* Eventually, I get up to use the restroom and go to bed.

I woke up feeling energized. My body tingled, my vision was blurry, my hands were hot, and I had high-pitch ringing in my ears. I didn't feel sick, just different. Drew was still sleeping on the couch when I left for work. He would get the kids ready for the day.

I replayed the vision in my head during my drive. I made every excuse to rationalize what happened. I tried to pretend it wasn't real, but there was no ignoring it. When I got into work, my "crazy vision" activated again. I could see things, and I knew things people didn't share with me. I tried to turn it off. But Laurel came back.

"Trust what you see and feel. You are right." She spoke.

What if I am wrong, and they say I'm crazy?

"They won't," she said confidently.

My soul knew she was right. I had to trust her. Throughout the day, my intuition was correct. I asked for the exact labs, tests, and treatments needed for my patients. I found three hidden diagnoses, including gangrene, cancer, and diabetes. Every time I trusted my vision, angels, or guides, I was right!

When I got home, I told Drew about my night and workday. He said Laurel visited him too. He explained his mom could see the same things I did. She saw auras, angels, demons, and good and bad energy. We bonded over her visions.

"I believe in you. Embrace your crazy," Drew advised.

Those words changed everything. Someone finally believed in me.

Within the next few months, the doctors came to depend on my visions and moved me to harder cases. I was never wrong. Not only could I see energy, but my patients also reported feeling better when I touched them.

One day my supervisor asked me to cure her headache.

"I don't know how."

"Just put your hands on me and do your thing," she replied.

"But I have no control. I don't know what I'm doing."

"Just do it."

"I'll try."

I placed my hand on her head. My hands got hot. I blacked out and came back.

"I know what you're doing. It's a Chinese medicine called Reiki. I've had it done before; that's what it feels like." She spoke.

Immediately I looked up Reiki on my phone, and I registered for the next class.

After my Reiki one attunement, my abilities to see and wisdom of this universe increased. During Reiki level two, I could answer more questions than my teacher. Intrigued, my teacher Mertha asked, "Can you work on my ankle?" She was standing with a soft cast on her left foot.

"Of course," I replied.

As I worked on her, my hands got hot, my body felt weightless, and all I could see were black and blue colors. The blue guided me to where the healing needed to be done. *Heal, please, God, heal,* I repeated to myself over and over as I followed the blue light through a black hole. In the black hole was a tangled mess of colors and shapes folding in on itself. The image was like looking in a kaleidoscope or a moving mandala. There were many sounds going on, too. It sounded like an orchestra playing fifteen different genres.

My guides filled the room like a coliseum full of spirits, waiting to see my next move.

"Untangle the shapes," "separate the sounds," "change the point of contact," "bend the light," "change the color," "exchange the light," "cast a shadow." I hear them chant.

While they chant their advice, I realize that every single point of my body changed the internal structure of Mertha. As I bent my pointer finger, a square moved. When I lowered my head, it changed the tone of the frequencies. My hips controlled the wave patterns. Each fingertip was a point of light. When I moved my extremities, I stretched the light. I started moving and dancing with her energy. Everything I did affected her. I took the guide's advice. With concentration of the mind and movement of the body, my spirit separated the mandala in front of me. Her muscles twitched and contracted as I did this.

I was left with nothing but shapes, which all had their order. When I put them back into sacred geometry formations, her bones clicked into place. When I moved and flowed with the frequency, I could feel her mixed emotions running through me, like music. If a rhythm was off, all I had to do was dance in the rhythm pleasing her soul. By the time I was done, she sounded like a professional orchestra, and her soul was calm.

"Now, finish with a smile and open your eyes," the voices instructed.

I smiled and looked up at my teacher.

"You are magical. I have never felt energy move like that before. I felt the bones shifting." She got up from the massage table and stood, her eyes big. She stared at me, walked away, and came back with a piece of paper. "I have nothing more to teach you," were her words to me as she handed me a Reiki Masters/Teachers certificate with my name on it.

Who will teach me? I panicked.

"We will," the voices in my head responded.

How?

"Any way we can."

That night when I fell asleep, I met the voices in my head. They began training me during my slumber. Each morning when I woke, my clarity and truth became more evident. The churches, scientists, and spiritual guides failed to wait for the entire story and present the facts in ways all points of view could understand.

The meaning of religion is to have faith, belief, interest, or worship of some kind. It's a very personal thing. The Creator you worship or connect to should be found by you alone.

The word "Cult" is defined by a group of people getting together with the same religious beliefs. The same churches that told me I had "cult-like thinking" were themselves, cult. Churches are a group of religious people gathering. Yep, I said it: churches are cults!

When I realized this, I researched 504 religions and 52 subjects to include science, math, history, culture, photography, astrology, sacred geometry, video games, and more. I found that all subjects speak of the same thing at their core. Everything is frequency, colors, and shapes. Red, blue, green. Square, triangle, circle.

In 106 religions, when asked what God is, this was said: "I am male and female," "the darkness and light," "the ins and the out," "the first to live the last to die," "I Am that I Am," "I am Alpha to Omega." Put all that together, and you'll see The Creator is energy! G.O.D. can be broken down into Generator, Organizer, Destroyer.

If we tap into any energy, we are connected to G.O.D. Good, bad, ugly, we are all accepted if we're connected. There was war, life, death, chaos, light, and darkness in every major religion before there was peace. The G.O.D.s demanded sacrifices of the living, started wars, starved, and plagued humans. We were born from sin because our G.O.D. before us sinned. If G.O.D. didn't experience pain, loss, rage, anger, sadness, or fear before us, we would have never received those emotions in our D.N.A.

So why were the people condemned? G.O.D. was upset with

people for rejecting its love. It wanted to make others feel how it felt. But humanity was made from the Creator's heart and with with love, so when you truly find yourself, you find love. You realize anyone not exhibiting love is exhibiting behaviors of rejection and resentment. Resentment is the mind's way of preserving the soul from feeling pain again. Resentment is also the first form of fear and fear of not being loved is the worst evil one can face.

Humans like Jesus, Sanat Kumara, and Muhammad were the new testaments to how much love can change G.O.D. Without loving G.O.D., you have no permission to have love. But that's another story for another time.

My point here is love. Let vulnerability be the new sexy because we all hurt, even G.O.D. And if we were truly made in the image of the G.O.D.s, then all of us are G.O.D.s, including your worst enemy, your family, friends, and strangers. Every human being is a G.O.D.

Yes, you are a G.O.D.: Generator of your idea, Organizer of your storyline, and Destroyer of the energies no longer needed in your life.

Life is a puzzle. The middle can't connect to the corner, they depend on the pieces between them to connect. Use your voice; make connections. If something doesn't fit your life, move on, and appreciate both of your narratives are useful for the puzzle. My voice is a piece of the puzzle. Yours is too.

Here I am today, free from all fears that once held me back. I'm connected, brave, honest, raw, and real 100% of the time. I don't hold back what I see, hear, or feel. Instead, I use my voice to help people find a new perspective they haven't considered.

I thank the Creator and the voices in my head every day for doing the one thing counselors, doctors, medication, and teachers couldn't do. They gave me my sanity. Without them, I'd be lost. Looking back, I see they were the only ones I should have trusted. To this day, they have never been wrong.

Call me crazy. That's okay, my guides will tell me otherwise, and I trust them above any human walking this earth.

P.S.: The voices in my head have a message for you too: "Remember who you are. We forgive you."

Melissa is the one-of-a-kind associative thinker who can visibly see and feel energy. In 1979 she was born a healer, but she didn't start her journey until 2006 when she became an L.P.N. She practiced several fields to include Behavioral Health, T.C.U., Alzheimer's, Mental Health, Senior Care, and Chemical Dependency. While working for Hazelden, she was called to do a different type of healing. Through meditation, prayer, and the guidance of her Angels and teachers, Melissa was taught how to do faith healing. She furthered her training in energy healing with schooling. In 2012, she started the study of Reiki. In 2015 she became a Reiki Master and teacher. From there, she went on to train in the arts of Qigong, Kundalini, Shamanism, D.N.A. healings, genetic modification, source coding, spiritual counseling, and quantum and frequency healing and has had the privilege to work with native healers. Currently, she holds 24 healing modalities.

In 2015, Melissa opened the doors to her business, Euphoric Source, which has received many awards. In 2016 Melissa was one of the 30 people in the United States asked to speak at the National Symposium for Holistic Arts Practitioners held at Harvard University. From 2016-2018 she hosted her own radio show called Euphoria Radio, where she began to learn how to communicate with people about her abilities. Soon after that, Melissa was on Local Insider T.V. for being one of the most effective healers in Minnesota. From 2017-2019 she was busy working in many temples, hosting ceremonies and spiritual events. Currently, Melissa is healing, teaching, advising, hosting spiritual events, writing her books, doing a documentary, running her business and science lab, being a mom and wife, and living life to the fullest.

More information at
https://www.euphoricsource.com/resources

CHAPTER 23

Disarm Your Fear

Complete Freedom
In One Circular Breath

By Atlantis Wolf

"To love oneself is the beginning of a lifelong romance."

– OSCAR WILDE

Like a sea turtle that glides to the surface of the water to inhale and peek above the line between the worlds of ocean and air, I peek into the physical world of clients, kids, bills, and social calls before submerging back into the slow, quiet depths of my interior ocean—a mystical world of peace and reflection populated with spiritual guides, power animals, and galactic dragons. But once, in a single breath, I became a haven for other people and their invisible oceans.

As I was taking the back stairs two at a time to get to work, carrying three bags and my purse, I was four steps from the top when I smelled perfume.

Mmmm. I love the smell of women.

I heard a voice, a woman's dark caramel, Australian voice in my right ear: *Manifest your destiny.*

Cate Blanchett!

I stumbled on the last step, fell forward from the weight of the bags, and caught myself. I stood at the top of the landing, startled and jangled. I breathed one circular breath and looked around the stairwell.

Big D, did you hear that?

I looked to my constant companion, a black guardian spirit dragon named Big D, who replied: *Yes.*

What was that?

He replied: *Cate.*

I know it was Cate, but it was just a voice. Voices need bodies. Disembodied voices don't just appear from nowhere. That's crazy. Never mind. That probably didn't happen. I'm going to be late for work.

I opened the hallway door and hurried to my office, unlocked the entrance to the chiropractor's suite, and made my way to my room, a windowed corner room that I painted hibiscus pink. I switched on my orange Himalayan salt lamp at the center of the long, wooden, rustic-style table. It also held my massage oil, incense sticks, black shiva lingam stone, Hathor statue, turquoise vase with peacock feathers, hematite dragon, and HiFi speakers.

Hello, room! I brought you some friends today—apophyllite and arfvedsonite. These two high-vibe high-flying ladies asked to be part of the action today. So we'll see what that means.

After unpacking the two crystals and placing them on the window shelf, I leaned my laptop bag against the wall beside my cowskin drum and walked out of my room, passing the washer and dryer on my way to the fridge to stash my lunch.

With the room ready for a long day of nine clients, I greeted my first client, then left the room to let her get undressed and comfortable before I returned. Then, standing between the massage table and the long wooden table, I opened the space in silence with closed eyes and open arms.

Great Spirit of Healing Light, I greet you with love and gratitude. Open a healing space here.

I breathed in through my nose and out through my mouth in a slow, steady, silent whistle of air, three times, three circular breaths, drawing an imaginary circle with my hands each time up and back between my heart and the earth energy, my heart and the sky energy and my heart and my soul energy.

I gather the energy of Mother Earth, Pachamama, into my heart.
I gather the galactic and celestial energies of Father Sky into my heart.
I activate my invincible soul seated in my aquarian shaman's heart.

A spiritual temple opened, encircling the room. In my mind, I saw the inside of my Egyptian pyramid from a favorite past life filled with dark-skinned bodies and voices. Bare-chested men walking in loose white linen covering them from their waist to their knees carried scrolls and incense while women with black hair walking in white loose linen dresses carried baskets of cloth. I waved and smiled at them, and they waved and smiled back.

The room was bright and dusty, with one enormous door across from me with two sentry statues of Horus on each side and two smaller doors to my right and left. No windows. The inside walls were covered with hieroglyphics of healing prayers, tincture recipes, and stories. The floor was well-trodden earth.

In front of me was a bathtub-shaped, un-lidded sarcophagus filled with holy water for my client. The client's spirit rested in the tub to receive healing from my Egyptian helpers and her guides while I worked on her physical body on my massage table. Today, I saw my client's deceased sister peering over her to the right of the tub and her Kodiak spirit bear sitting on top of her using one bear claw nail to scoop out little black flecks from her lower abdomen where she had surgery for bladder cancer.

I asked the spirit bear, or rather his rump since he was facing away from me, what he was doing.

He didn't look up, just responded: *Chemo. Black is chemo.*

I massaged my client and met her outside the room after she was dressed.

"Have you thought about your sister lately?" I asked.

"Funny you should say that," she said. "I thought about her this morning when I was making coffee, about the way she used to say 'sissy up' to mean: add cream and sugar."

I smiled.

"Maybe you could make some coffee later today and imagine she is sitting across from you," I said. "Make her a cup, too, and have a conversation with her."

"That's a nice idea," she said as we hugged goodbye. "Thank you."

I worked on my next three clients, working on their muscle aches and pains, holding trigger points, and letting them speak their thoughts into the room while their spirit guides healed them in spirit in the Egyptian healing temple.

At my extended midday break, I changed the sheets and pulled the table closer to the corner leather club chair, preparing for the ultimate indulgence. The Intuitive Writers and Speakers class was a six-week gift to myself for a secret, ongoing passion of mine— writing.

I brought my lunch into the room, arranging it on the humidor next to my corner chair—black garlic hummus, cauliflower chips, a Honeycrisp apple, and a cup of Earl Grey tea. I sat in the brown leather chair with my laptop open on the table. With both hands, I lifted my hot cup of tea to my nose. The smell of bergamot oil on Assam tea leaves slowed time from hare to turtle as I closed my eyes and inhaled the smokey vapor.

Mmmmm. I love Fortnum & Mason tea.

Big D smiled as smokey vapor curled out of his exhaling nostrils. *Me, too.*

I decided to introduce myself as my spirit name for no reason more than Spirit told me it was time to take one small step out of my cave and be myself. One.

"Hello, Atlantis," said the facilitator of the writing class, wrapping the greeting around me the way people do when they meet a stranger, using their intuition to answer the social question: friend or foe?

I waved a silent acknowledgment and looked at her for the first time in the Zoom box, meeting her at a distance the way I always meet people—closing the door to my house and walking down a few strides to greet them at my garden gate behind the wrought-iron fence.

She had a long wave of dark hair and an air of business, a tone of direct honesty. I liked her. She had a boa constrictor over her right shoulder. Powerful spirit guide.

"Is Atlantis Wolf your name?" she asked.

"Yes," I replied, not expecting the question.

"That is my name in my spiritual community, my shamanic name," I said, "given to me by my teacher, Linda Star Wolf. I carry the lineage of the Seneca Nation Wolf Clan. It's my YouTube channel name, website name, and the name I intend to use if I ever publish any writing."

"Sounds like you're good at marketing," she said.

I leaned away from the screen, happy to retreat into the quiet folds of my chair and let the other twenty participants lean forward and speak into their laptop microphones.

One step, Spirit. I'm done.

Big D smiled, looking down at my upturned face with his thousand-tooth gargantuan grin, the golden scales on his belly rising with pride. *Brave.*

I reached up on the spirit side and scratched the scales under his chin.

Thanks, D. At least it's a writing class. Not much talking, I imagine.

The Zoom screen filled with faces as I munched on snack lunch.

This is so much better than an actual class. I can see clients before and after, and I can nosh and slurp without having to chit-chat. Perfect. This is like watching twenty TV channels at once. I never watch TV.

Checking my phone, I see Sable texted me:

Adele wants her next Shamanic Breathwork on The Day Out of Time. Thoughts?

Also, Mike wants to know his name when he was your past-life teacher. Says you forgot to write it down.

I replied:

Please tell Adele 1 pm is fine. Remind her to order the Galactic Calendar Journal. It's out.

To Mike: "Genshe." It was in China, which might have been Mongolia then.

Thanks, Sable!

"Okay," said the facilitator, "Let's get started. Give me your name, business name, and how you help people, plus one thing you learned in the last year or something you are grateful for."

She moved down the list until it was my turn. My stomach migrated up to my throat in a fluttering motion, feeling as if a millipede's throng of tiny legs were carrying it up to the top of my throat.

I like being the eyeballs. Why do the other eyeballs have to look at me?

"Hi, I'm Atlantis Wolf," I said. "I'm the owner of Sano Totum, which is Latin for heal the whole. I'm a medical massage therapist, and I help people by finding the source of their chronic pain. I'm grateful for my kids."

Big D looked down at me sideways with one of his tiger iron eyes.

What? I just met these people. It's a writing class. I don't need to tell them I talk to people's bodies and let my hands go where their body wants me to go. That's weird. I just want to get better at writing.

What will you write about? he said, rubbing his chin back and forth on top of my head.

I have no idea, I replied, reaching for my tea before absentmindedly reaching in spirit to scratch the tip of his golden chin scales again.

"We talked about desire, how desire for your business and your life are really the same," the facilitator said. "Now we're going to talk about purpose-driven fear. What are the fears keeping you from achieving your deepest desires?"

Fear. Fears. Frights and scares. Spookles.

I don't have time to be afraid. I'm a single mom, self-employed.

All the scary things are over:

Lost my mom to cancer.

Lost 84 pounds.

Filed bankruptcy.

Divorced.

Stood up to my dad's rage.

Almost lost my house.

Lost Gram to old age.

Lost all my income after the exodus from Cube-Land.

Built my private practice.

Dying and not having a clean basement? Yes, those are legitimate fears that have not happened. Oy! Please, no.

My big spirit dragon shrugged his shoulders as I scanned my potential fears.

"What is your greatest fear?" the facilitator said.

Oh, greatest! Um, there is one. I was hoping to avoid it for a few more years or so until, well, I don't know. I don't need to write about it.

I wrote two words in my journal: I'm weird.

My armpits started to sweat. I remembered my anatomy and

physiology teacher, Dr. Boyd, in massage school talking about apocrine sweat, ape sweat, the kind that is smelly and thick, lipid-rich. I tried to wriggle out of my body and into my brain —or beyond—to escape the uncomfortable, spiraling sensations.

Is there any dark chocolate in here?

"Okay," said the facilitator. "We're gonna share a fear with the group. Pick one and know you are supported. This is a safe space. Any volunteers?"

Pick one? I only have one. I'll make one up. Something normal. I'm afraid of normal things. What's a normal fear? Insufficient retirement funds? Wrinkles? Not traveling to Nepal?

The muscles across the top of my back tensed. My diaphragm didn't exhale enough air, and the sides of my throat were getting jumpy.

Big D leaned closer, *It's time now.*

Share out loud? Isn't this a writing class? Mostly?

My stomach curled into a fist as I sat still with crossed legs in my corner chair in my closed room with walls painted the color of a womb. In my temple to healing, my hidden cave of safety, looking at the calm strangers, I evaluated the question: *How safe is safe?*

I don't have to say anything. I can stay quiet. Hidden. Small.

But I'm not small. I'm a vast ocean in here. Sacred. Galactic.

I raised my hand that held my blue pen to the Zoom screen lens.

"Atlantis?" said the facilitator.

Two words arrived in a pop, like a bubble that bursts on the surface of the water from a crack opening in the ocean's floor.

"I'm weird," I said.

"What do you mean?" she asked in a direct, steady gaze from her dark eyes.

Breathe in. Open the circle.

I gather the energy of Mother Earth, Pachamama, into my heart.

I inhaled my last breath of anonymity and focused my eyes just above the small white circle of my laptop camera lens, my cheeks as red as the setting sun.

Breathe out. Close the circle.

"I see things, spiritual things. Spiritual beings. And talk to them," I said.

"When I work on people, I see the spiritual beings around

them, the animals that are working with them to guide their life journey, the settings of their past lives, and the spirits of their family members and ancestors who have passed through the veil. Dead people," I continued.

Breathe in what you need.

I gather the galactic and celestial energies of Father Sky into my heart.

I also see people's spirits which are sometimes not in human form," I said. "I have a client who is a mermaid, one who is a pixie, and one who is a dolphin. I also see people's original form if their first incarnation was not on Earth, their extraterrestrial form."

Breathe out what you don't need.

I looked above the camera lens into my beautiful room, my pink shell of protection, my sea turtle shell.

"Also, dragons," I said. "I work with a council of fourteen galactic dragons. One is a big black and gold dragon with tiger iron eyes that teaches me to travel in different dimensions. So, that."

An invisible hand started to close my throat. My eyes were hot and watery.

My head hurt. My heart pumped in thumpy, lumbering drubs. I felt self-inflicted.

Breathe in love.

I activate my invincible soul seated in my Aquarian Shaman's heart.

"And I feel called to say this out loud," I said, "to normalize my experience and let other people know that what they see or hear or feel beyond their five senses is a gift, an awakening. We are all waking up to these experiences. We all have these abilities. We are all remembering who we are!"

Breathe out love.

Warm tears overflowed my barricades. I felt like I was exiled on an island with no bridges.

"Awesome," said the facilitator, Laura Di Franco. "Who's next?"

I reached for Kleenex, naked and wet.

Big D rested the tip of his chin on top of my head, pulling me close to his chest. *Bravest.*

Well, at least they don't know me.

I reached for more Kleenex, then glanced at the screen again. Six private messages in the chatbox. More tears.

Here comes the stones and torches. I'm going to pretend I don't see them. It's my first Zoom call. I'm still anonymous. I can turn away from them.

I read each message:

> *I talk with angels,* said the first person.
> *I see colors around people,* said another.
> *I talk with trees,* said a third.
> *I see my grandmother when I go to sleep,* said another classmate.
> *I feel crystals,* said one woman in a purple top.
> *I work in the quantum field to heal past life wounds,* said a new friend.

My heart was lumpy-thumping again, and new tears fell for all the people in the world who are hiding.

How many of us are waiting to confess secret lives? How many people live with a fear of being seen?

My island became a haven. Boats sailed to my shore, and I welcomed them into a place where they could be unburdened from who they thought they needed to be to find love and acceptance.

That's why Spirit sent Cate. My calling, my destiny, my purpose-driven fear, is to be seen, to be a living field of safe sharing and a haven of acceptance and love. I'm extra weird by divine design. And I get to be the one who speaks first, the way-shower, the medicine woman.

The dragon.

That first writing class was an initiation that asked me: Can you stand in a circle of strangers and show your weird, wild self to them—just once—knowing in your heart that you are weirder and wilder than most people? Sacred yes. And one more thing I don't fear anymore. I am free.

You, my friend, can use the circular breathing technique in my story to connect to your spirit guides, too. Or go to my YouTube channel, and I'll walk through it with you. https://youtu.be/Pffk-o3o2Gc

Thank you for reading. I'm Atlantis Wolf. And I believe in you.

Atlantis Wolf is a Shamanic Life Coach and workshop leader who supports people seeking answers to their medical, spiritual, and emotional questions in collaboration with her spirit guides, power animals, and galactic dragons. Her specialty is pain — chronic physical pain or mysterious medical conditions.

Atlantis grew up on a single-lane dirt road in the country, sure her mother was an angel in human form, whistling to birds and asking the question: What am I supposed to do on Earth? She walks into the forest at sunrise in all weather to answer that question every day.

As a young girl, she would daydream and write poetry in school. She was told to follow in her family's footsteps to become an engineer instead of pursuing writing, which was not a lucrative future. She compromised by pursuing a dual major in civil engineering and English with a minor in environmental engineering.

Her joy is helping people discover their power — walking with them into their interior labyrinths, their dark castles, and their forgotten stories.

She has worked as a civil engineer, technical writer, business analyst, project manager, licensed massage therapist, marketing consultant, and entrepreneur.

She was spiritually asleep until events around her mother's death awakened her gifts to see and communicate with spiritual beings and remember her past lives as an Egyptian healer, Toltec curandera, and Ayurvedic traveling shaman. She is the Dragon Medicine Woman.

Atlantis is a single mom with four kids and five cats. She lives on Turtle Island.

AtlantisWolf.com

DragonMedicineWoman@gmail.com

YouTube: Atlantis Wolf

Instagram: @DragonMedicineWoman

CHAPTER 24

Stepping Into My Light with Faith, Trust, and Intuition

By Judithann Walz

There I am, seven years old, standing in front of the congregation, and the pastor is asking us kids, which is worth more: faith or a handful of pennies? In my heart, I want to say, "Faith."

My relationship with God was meaningful, and I knew that faith always trumped wealth, but I had a niggling feeling in my belly that the pastor expected me to answer, "Pennies," because don't all kids love money? My intuition shook my body as it did when I knew I was on to something.

Rather than say, "Faith," however, out popped, "Pennies."

Disappointment filled my belly as the congregation chuckled. The pastor corrected me and then asked the children to sit down to continue with the sermon. I had known the answer but lacked confidence.

That night my great-grandmother consoled me, telling me it was okay. She and I talked for hours past my bedtime. The conversations deepened our relationship. Sometimes other relatives joined in. The funny thing was no one could see them except me.

One day I mentioned the conversations to my mother, who looked at me incredulously. There was no way I could know the details of people I had never met, minus my great-grandmother, whom I had known before she passed on. There were other things too. For example, I told my parents who were calling before the phone rang. I could also see people walking through the neighborhood. They were there, and yet they were not, but they knew

I could see them. They did not always look at me, but I "sensed" they knew I knew.

At school, I played a game where a classmate flipped a coin into the air, and before it landed on the back of their hand, I called heads or tails. We played this daily. I only got them wrong when I doubted myself. Those were the days when I trusted my intuition.

Elementary through middle school, I had vivid déjà vu. These experiences came from dreams. I loved sleep and, if given the opportunity, could take three and four-hour naps. While I slept, I had dreams within dreams and only upon waking realized I was in my bedroom and not living a life on another plane of reality. These adventures turned into stories I wrote for pleasure. The déjà vu events in my waking life, however, came to fruition after I experienced them. That is when I realized I had dreamed the events before they happened.

I once confided in some cousins about my déjà vu moments, but they did not believe me, and I never brought it up again. I did not dare tell anyone outside of my family that I could see and talk to dead people. When I got to high school, I could no longer use my physical eyes to see spirits, and my déjà vu lessened. All I had left was my faith and intuition.

By the time I got to college, I had left the spiritual world behind me. I attended a small Catholic school with solid principles and ethics. Although raised as a Lutheran, I wanted to be in an environment with a religious focus. I joined the theater club and choir and took communion every Sunday. I also attended guided meditations with a nun whose self-awareness rivaled my belief of what I had heard about nuns from my mother, a Catholic turned Protestant.

During the fall of 1997, I experienced an awakening of sorts. As Sister Mary Joy led a guided meditation, a swirl of color danced behind closed eyes. Flowing between the colors were three-dimensional geometric shapes. As I explained everything I saw, Sister Mary Joy fervently took notes (before it was common to type on a computer). To this day, I remember the exact images. With her guidance, I learned how to strengthen my meditation and listen within. I left those sessions exhilarated, the spot in the middle of my forehead sore from concentrating. It was my third eye, but at the time, I didn't know what that was. This guidance system strengthened my intuition and faith, which was good because I would need it soon enough.

In the spring of 1998, Father David called me into his office for a conversation. He had heard that I was a Lutheran who saw spirits. Nausea gripped my stomach, sending waves of panic up my spine. I surmised that he must have heard it from Sister Mary Joy. After one of the sessions, I confided in her about seeing and hearing the dead. It surprised and worried me that Father David knew of my gifts. Would he accept or reject me?

He asked me why I chose this school and listened intently as I told him about my dream of becoming a teacher and that this college had the program I wanted. He then asked about my seeing spirits. Swallowing my nerves, I told him about my visions during the guided meditations and how spirits came to me about wanting to pass messages on to loved ones.

He waited until I finished before switching gears and quizzing me on my knowledge of Martin Luther and the Ninety-five Theses. I wiped damp palms on my pants. I hated tests and was not confident in quoting scripture or any other book. Memorization was not my strength. The minutes ticked by until he changed topics and told me the two religions were different. A non-Catholic could not accept communion. I had committed a cardinal sin. He explained why Catholicism was the one true faith and suggested I think long and hard about what I had done. Father David encouraged me to think about my relationship with God and what *He* would think of my transgression.

I fought back angry tears as I nodded my head. He added that the only people who had visions and could hear Spirit were Jesus Christ and those in religious orders. He assured me my experiences were tainted, and I was encouraged to purge my heart. Shame filled my soul. Faith in my gifts and intuition had come into question yet again.

My freshman year was already on a downward trajectory, and now this. I was dealing with a pot-smoking, partying roommate with whom I had nothing in common and whose cronies bullied everyone in the dorm, especially me. I could not handle losing the support of the church. They were my community, my people. I withdrew from everything, including Sunday mass, and my grades plummeted as I slid into depression.

I finished out the year, but just barely. There were many lonely nights when I thought about ending it all. Was not a religious college supposed to be better? Where was the support when I needed it most?

By the fall of 1998, I transferred and began attending a state school closer to home. I made new friends, held several work-study jobs, and even had a boyfriend. I also joined a new choir that was part of a non-denominational Christian group on campus. The depression and loneliness disappeared. Hope returned.

One night while lying in bed, I read a passage in my student Bible, a gift from my parents that would travel the world with me less than ten years later. As I dozed in and out of sleep, a voice spoke to me. The voice sounded like my voice, except it spoke with authority and compassion. A ripple of excitement flowed through me. All was not lost!

The voice said, "Go to bed, Judithann."

I strained my ears in hopes of hearing more, but nothing happened. Pulling the covers over my head, I switched off the light and went to sleep, but not before a smile crept across my face.

Three years passed, and I graduated with my bachelor's degree in English. Finally, I was ready to take on the world as a high school teacher. The only problem was that I struggled to pass the subject exam for the state license. Unable to secure a satisfactory score, I took a zigzag path to become a teacher that eventually led me overseas. Faith and intuition took a backseat as I was too busy worrying about money and job satisfaction.

The years between graduation and relocating to Asia were a mess. I held several unfulfilling jobs, some in education and some not. The only guiding light was the graduate degree I earned in business. If teaching did not work out, I could enter the business world with all my transferable skills!

In 2007 I moved to South Korea to work as an English-as-a-Second-Language teacher. It was the start of a new path. Within months of settling in, my spiritual senses re-emerged. I caught glimpses of people on the edges of my vision, but no one was there when I looked.

I also heard my nickname, "Judith," said out loud while running errands.

As I drifted off to sleep, I heard complete conversations reminiscent of a cocktail party that had taken up residence in my bedroom. It happened so often I kept a notepad next to my bed; if I had enough energy to jot down pieces of dialogue, I could. I never did.

One rainy Saturday, as I lay on my rock-hard twin bed in my studio apartment, the hair on the back of my neck stood on end. It is as if someone took a fine-toothed comb and gently brushed the nape causing goosebumps to prickle across my body. I shivered and turned over. The light in the kitchen blinked furiously. On. Off. On. Off. On. Off. Standing up, I walked over to my small kitchenette and flipped off the light. Laying back down, I turned to face the wall when something brushed my neck again. I whipped around, and the light was flashing on and off as if possessed. Another shiver went through my body as I attempted to shake off my nerves.

Several days later, I replaced the bulb to no avail. It was the only one in the apartment that blinked, but never when I had company. This continued for a year until I moved back to the States. I chalked it up to faulty wiring. A few years later, I moved to Bangkok, Thailand, for another teaching contract. I secured a one-bedroom condo off Sukhumvit Road in a hip part of the city, popular with foreigners and young, successful Thai professionals.

The condo came furnished and included an open concept kitchen/living room, a bathroom I could dance in, a large bedroom with a king bed, a double wardrobe, and a soft yellow light above the bed. At night I enjoyed reading before sleep until that light also began blinking furiously. Every night I said a prayer that it stayed on long enough for me to read, but it never happened. It also never flashed when I was not in bed. How infuriating!

I requested the bulb be changed, but like my experience in South Korea, it made no difference. Then one night, as I stood in the doorway between the bedroom and living room, I watched as one of the recessed bulbs dropped out of the ceiling and shattered onto the floor. Sweeping up the glass against the pale wood was tricky. This replaced bulb broke one week later.

It was long overdue that I figured out what the heck was going on. By this time, I accepted that I was a psychic medium but did not understand how to control the energy. When I was a child, I was innocent of the ways of the world. It was not until I got older that my surroundings dictated what was acceptable. I had to heal past traumas so that I could understand what was happening to me.

When I needed guidance, I turned to books. I often visited Kinokuniya, a large bookstore not unlike what we have here in the States. My favorite section was New Age. Here I found topics on religion, philosophy, and angels. I read Lorna Byrne's, *Angels in My Hair* and, later, *A Message of Hope from the Angels*, and yes, these two nonfiction titles were in that same section. These books profoundly affected me and altered my understanding of the type of help available to humans. I put her ideas into practice and saw immediate results. I asked the angels for all kinds of support, and they *always* delivered.

One night, I opened my book, and the light above me blinked furiously.

I said, "I hear you and finally understand."

Unconditional love filled my soul. It was an overwhelming sensation. Then, the blinking stopped, and none of the lights flashed again for the remainder of my time overseas.

Living in Bangkok was the start of my spiritual journey, although some may argue that it began long before. It took seven years to figure out that the flashing lights were my guides desperately trying to get my attention. With each step, I trusted, and as I trusted, my intuition grew.

By the time I found myself in Southeast Asia, I had a fundamental understanding of a world that most people had difficulty accepting as real, so when the lights began flashing in my condo, I sought help. I found the OM Room in Chitlom and underwent several hypnotherapy sessions to expand my awareness and understanding. I also learned how to speak to God conversationally.

In July 2015, I returned to the United States after a harrowing experience in Saudi Arabia. It took me several years to overcome the panic attacks and fear, but because of my previous experiences, I knew how to call on divine help. It is through the power of God, faith, and intuition that I survived.

Today, I teach people how to develop their intuitive gifts through faith. A specific religion is not essential, though belief in a higher power is. I show them how to *feel* into their heart space and trust the messages they receive. It is also vital to have fun — self-discovery is part of the journey. There are no wrong answers with God. He/She/They want us to live abundantly on our divine paths, knowing that we can always call on them for guidance and, when we are ready, to step into our light with faith, trust, and intuition.

Born a writer and medium, it has taken much of **Judithann Walz**'s life to step into her spiritual gifts. Armed with an MBA in Marketing from the University of Phoenix, a BA in English Literature from Worcester State College (now a university), and lots of naivete, she jumped into a career as a globetrotting English-as-a-Second-Language teacher.

After two decades as an English teacher, Judithann stepped away to become a business owner and full-time writer. She teaches creative writing workshops on Learn It Live, Zoom, and in-person (pre-COVID and hopefully post-COVID too). Her favorite subjects are:

- Story arcs
- Character development
- Writing structure
- Show versus tell
- Dialogue and grammar for fiction and nonfiction

An avid traveler, Judithann is most at home when in a culture where English is not the first language. She blogs and podcasts about her travel experiences and dealings with Spirit and spirits on Joy Among Wonder.

This is her second book. The first one, *Find Your Voice, Save Your Life 2*, is a bestseller on Amazon. She is also a core blogger for The Wellness Universe (TWU), an organization comprised of light-workers, healers, life coaches, and writers. Judithann moderates a room called "Channeled Readings in Unconditional Love" on Clubhouse every first and third Saturday of the month and joins a talented group of moderators in the room, "Voice Your Intention: Collective Consciousness." Both rooms are on the Feeling Good club and part of the TWU. Because of the success of her first room, Judithann has had the pleasure of having read hundreds of people and has met with over two-hundred offline in private sessions. She has been an active member of Clubhouse since February 2021.

Judithann loves meeting new people, so please reach out to her via the information below with any questions or comments.

www.joyamongwonder.com

https://www.thewellnessuniverse.com/world-changers/judithwalz/

https://blog.thewellnessuniverse.com/

Instagram: Judithannwalz

Clubhouse: @Judithannw

CHAPTER 25

Acceptance

Sometimes Our Spirit Has Other Plans

By Michele Tatos

have never felt more helpless in my life. *I am a healer; I should be able to heal her cancer,* raced through my head for the millionth time as I ran calming energy through my big sister and talked her through another panic attack that hit her in the middle of the night.

Kathy or Kat, who I have always called Sissypoo, was battling cancer again, but this time cancer was winning. The metastatic breast cancer had spread to her brain, abdomen, and lungs. The lungs were the worst because she constantly struggled to breathe.

"I better not die after all this hell I'm going through. This suffering better be for a good reason." My sister said this a lot during the year and a half she was fighting cancer.

She never once gave up. She did every treatment offered to her, no matter how sick or exhausted it might make her. She was a warrior until her last breath. She didn't want to die. She didn't want to leave us. Unfortunately, her spirit had other plans.

By nature, I'm an optimistic, happy, friendly, and energetic person, annoyingly so at times, which I have been told on occasion. However, losing someone close to me temporarily changed that.

My sister called me the day before my 51st birthday. "Hey Sis, I hate to ruin your birthday, but the cancer is back." I immediately responded, "We will fight it together and beat it again! We've got this!" That's me, the forever optimist.

That night, we went out with our husbands and pretended we were happily celebrating my birthday. Our hollow eyes and tight body posture told a different story. Dinner was a blur, but I remember vividly walking into Behan's Bar hand in hand with my sister. We had plastered on our party faces and were determined to drink and dance our fears away. I remember singing at the top of our lungs, swinging each other around, and then looking into her big, lovely, golden cat eyes and seeing the utter terror that resided there. I knew it was also reflected in mine. We were both faking it. We pretended this was the last time we'd be able to party together for a while, and we never once let ourselves admit it could be the last time ever.

A few months later, I had just pulled into the supermarket parking lot, and my caller-ID said Sissypoo. My heart dropped into the pit of my stomach, my mouth dried up, and time froze. I knew she was calling to give me the latest result of the CT scan.

"It's now in my lungs and abdomen, and there are more spots on my brain." I started shaking and immediately shot out of my body. I somehow knew this was coming, but hearing it out loud was devastating.

As each doctor's appointment brought more bad news, I thought to myself, *I can't survive losing my sister.* The thought was beyond comprehension. I loved her so much. I talked to her almost every day of my life. She was my only sibling. We had never lived more than 25 minutes from each other. She had always been there for me. We went to college together and took the same classes. I was with her the night she met her husband. I was in the delivery room when my nephew was born. She flew with me to Texas when I was meeting the birth mother of my adopted daughter. The list goes on and on. *How could she leave me?*

It wasn't about me. A healer's role is to support a spirit's journey. Support, not try to change or control.

As the year and a half of hell progressed, I remember one day walking into my house after another night sleeping at my sister's. I didn't know how to face my husband or children. I wanted to hide how drained and sad I was, but I knew it was visible in my posture and speech. I was so frustrated that I couldn't heal my sister. Nothing I did seemed to help. That's when it hit me: the awful truth that healing from the illness may not be part of her spirit's journey.

I hated this *aha* moment, realizing that, as a healer, you must honor a spirit's journey, which may conflict with their personality and emotional desires and what *you* personally want to happen. I want everyone to live a long, healthy, and happy life. I also know that if we all did that, our spirits wouldn't be learning and growing. We inhabit our bodies to facilitate lessons for our spirit's development over many lifetimes. I believe this wholeheartedly, but I don't always have to like it. Especially when it means I'm going to lose my sister.

I firmly believe that if we eat right, exercise, meditate to harmonize and rebalance our energy body and physical body, and are mindful of our actions and patterns, we have a much better shot at living a longer, healthier, and happier life. But sometimes, it seems like even when you are doing everything right, disease can still strike! It enters our life to teach important lessons. This can be a hard one to grasp, right?

The last healing session with my sister will always be a vivid, painful, and incredibly beautiful memory. Kathy's graceful and divine spirit showed up immediately, front and center. *What? That's not supposed to happen! I am supposed to be working with my sister's guides, not her spirit. Why is her spirit telling me to leave everything as is and to just surround her with unconditional love?*

A typical healing for me (if there is such a thing) involves working with my guides as well as the guides of the person participating. After I'm settled in and have received permission, I intuitively perceive the person's subtle energy system. I start by making sure they're deeply connected to the earth and that their shielding, which protects their energy body, is solid and undamaged. I also make sure that there are no attached cords or uninvited energetic guests. I then work my way up through the chakras. I receive information that I may or may not share depending on the guidance, and I direct and amplify various divine energies (compassion, calm, forgiveness, grace, etc.) to clear, rebalance, and realign the chakras. Body systems also light up, such as the nervous or endocrine system, lungs, or kidneys. There is usually a lot going on and a lot to do.

This last healing with my sister was different. I was not given any direction other than flooding her with unconditional love. I felt terrified as the meaning of this hit me. I didn't want to accept what it meant. I wanted there still to be hope. I wanted to be able to do more.

In hindsight, I did what I was meant to do. I spent countless hours with her, listening to her process her life, the good and the bad. I held her hand and helped her catch her breath when she was struggling. I surrounded her with unconditional love and helped ease her pain when I could. But I wasn't meant to heal her cancer. I finally understand that, and have released my guilt, which was almost as heavy as my grief.

I received *the call* from my brother-in-law early one morning. I knew what he was going to say. The scream that came out of my mouth can only be described as a primal, heart-shattering, full-body, raging howl.

Two minutes later, I'm in the car, trying to focus and not get in an accident. I'm dreading the act of knocking on my parent's door to tell them they lost their baby girl. I feared facing my nephew, brother-in-law, and my sister's lifeless body. Suddenly, I felt my sister's strong presence in the passenger seat of my car. Her spirit had chosen this moment to visit me. It felt like she was physically sitting right next to me. My sister always did know how to make an entrance.

Kat's spirit began calmly speaking to me and asking that I do several things for her. It was like we were just two sisters, sitting in the car, having a normal conversation.

In response, I screamed at her for leaving me and the rest of us. This is not how I imagined myself handling this kind of situation.

After my sister passed, I snapped into *healer* mode to support the family: my amazing twenty-four-year-old nephew, who considered his mom his best friend; my parents, who were shocked and devastated; and my two kiddos, who were ordinarily happy and carefree but were now grieving and depressed. My kids adored their aunt, and to add to their grief they were in lockdown and away from all of their friends due to Covid.

You might be thinking, "But no! You need to take care of yourself!" I felt utterly broken, but I did take care of myself. I realized

I wasn't going to be able to support anyone if I was a complete mess.

I powered through. I made sure I kept up with my intuition and energy management classes. I increased my exercise regime, which has always been critical to my emotional well-being. I even joined in on my remote Zoom soccer practices. I didn't feel like it, and I told my coach and the team I was too much of a wreck to talk to anyone, so I muted myself, turned off my camera, and did the workout, often juggling a soccer ball (or at least giving it my best effort) while crying my eyes out. I knew if I disengaged from things I loved, I would completely spiral downwards and possibly never bounce back. I had a fantastic and supportive husband who was my rock. Thanks to my years of spiritual training under my wonderful teacher, Glenda Jeong, I had a lot of tools. I put these tools to good use to move my family and me to the other side of this awful nightmare.

The day I credit to truly finding my authentic spiritual healer voice was about ten months after Kat passed. She continued her visits to me on a fairly regular basis, but one visit was different. I was settled deep into a personal, healing meditation. I had an image of my emotional body up on a screen in my intuitive center, and Kat's spirit was suddenly right there. She was full of sparkly divine awesomeness and beauty! I felt a sense of peace I hadn't felt since she passed.

She let me know she wanted to support me in sharing my healing work with others and that we could do it together. She reminded me that *my spirit also had other plans*. This was one of the first times I smiled when I felt her presence instead of being angry or sad.

The next day, I woke up and decided to offer to teach those meditation classes I'd promised to my friends for years. Without thinking about it, I sent off an email to a group of people, hoping I wouldn't chicken out if I put it out there. Everyone said yes. It was both terrifying and exciting!

The classes were fantastic, and my sister was by my side through it all.

Before I lost my sister, I was fairly secretive about the fact I was a healer, even though I had been doing energy rebalancing healings and guided meditations for more than twenty years. I rarely talked about personal energy management, spirit guides, or Akashic Records outside of my closest friends and family. I wanted to avoid the judge-y comments or confused looks I received the few times I tried to strike up a conversation about chakras and auras outside of my inner circle of friends.

I offered healings only to those I felt sure would welcome it or to those who were referrals from my energy and intuition classmates. I also started teaching my children the basics of grounding and shielding when they were around two years old. As an aside, I'm a big believer that every preschooler should learn to be a strong and beautiful tree and put a colorful bubble around them to keep them safe and happy!

Over the years, I expanded outside of my inner circle with my spiritual healings and lessons. Still, I never fully committed to taking on the spiritual healer and teacher role until my sister's spirit gave me a push. It just never seemed like the right time. I think I wasn't ready before, as I hadn't gone through a truly transformational experience. Running a mental health employment agency, getting married, and having children were profound growth experiences, but they didn't trigger the extreme spiritual overhaul that losing my sister did. Losing someone this close to you changes you at the absolute deepest level possible.

As with most huge lessons and spiritual growth spurts, it took an incredibly tragic event in my life for me to decide to stop worrying about what people would think, embrace the real me, and start sharing my energy rebalancing tools with others.

I still often think, *could my sister have had a longer, healthier life if she had taken better care of herself?* Maybe. She always put everyone else's needs before hers and gave her energy away freely, often forgetting to nourish and replenish herself. She was an amazingly loving and giving person, and that may be what eventually wore her down. But perhaps that was her journey. To give and give until she had nothing left to give in human form, and then move on to her spirit form and continue to give.

This is where spirituality and healing can become complicated, confusing, and maddening. We're often told everything happens for a reason, and we want to be reassured that there is a damned good reason that we lose our loved ones. Unfortunately, sometimes we never get to see that reason. Or we see it but don't accept it.

Part of being a spiritual healer, and a human being, is accepting that you're not going to know all the answers. It means accepting that you're intended to support someone on their journey, but not to interfere with their journey. When I was discussing this with my 13-year-old son, he said, "That is a lot of accepting, and it sounds really hard." Truer words have never been spoken!

I don't know if I will ever be able to listen to *I Will Survive,* my sister's signature song, without getting angry and bursting into tears. That sadness and anger are still inside me and need to seep out in divine timing. I don't have my sister here in person to talk with every day. It still really pisses me off!

I'm still working on the acceptance part, but I trust I'll get there. I'm now able to see the gifts my sister left behind. Her spirit is always here with me, encouraging me to continue on this spiritual path, comforting me, and filling me with love. She reminds me that we're more than our physical bodies, and will reconnect in the spirit realm someday, and that this will all make sense in time.

Until then, I've embraced my heart and soul's path, using my spiritual healer voice to help others. My 14-year-old daughter always says, "We are all just trying to live our best lives, Mom." I love that expression! I believe that is my soul's purpose—to help people to live their best lives.

Before I end this story, I'd like to pass on a short exercise that can give you a peek into your spiritual path and help you live your best life.

Gaze softly at this passage and begin to take deep, calming breaths.
Let your breath relax every muscle in your body.
Imagine that you are breathing in divine truth, clarity, and unconditional love.
Breathe these harmonious energies into every cell of your body, from the top of your head to the bottoms of your feet.

Release anything that does not resonate with this peaceful vibration.
Sense the strong connection to the earth below and the equally strong connection to the spirit realm above.
Now, visualize a beautiful golden bridge in your mind.
As you cross the bridge, you are entering a peaceful, safe, healing place that is only for you.
This is your intuitive center.
Sit comfortably here and just be with this calm feeling for another few breaths.
Now, ask your intuitive self, "Am I following my spiritual path?"

The answer should be loud and clear, *yes* or *no*. If it is *a yes*, keep up the good work and keep listening to your inner guidance! If it is *a no*, then give yourself the time, space, and self-love to accept where you are. Remember that acceptance does not mean you give up and do nothing. It means you are ready to embrace your heart and soul's mission. You are ready to begin to heal and to move forward bravely. You are ready to jump out of your comfort zone and into the incredible journey your soul has planned for you. Once we embrace that our spirit may have other plans, and they may be awesome and amazing plans, our lives can shift and transform beyond what we could ever have envisioned as possible!

I wish you an extraordinary journey!

 **Michele Tatos** believes that understanding and accepting our spirit's journey is key to our healing and happiness. For over twenty years, she has been providing energy rebalancing consultations and guided meditations. These sessions focus on aligning and harmonizing the energy body and chakras. Chakras are energy centers that exist within each of us, transporting energy from the universe around you into your aura and body to assist with your spirit's lesson plan.

She spent the first 15 years of her adult life serving in the mental health field in San Francisco, including in the position of CEO of a mental health employment agency. Then, she embarked on another inspirational journey working for a nonprofit that served individuals with developmental disabilities for the next ten years.

Michele describes herself as an extremely social introvert whose core passions include spending time with her family, spoiling her miniature schnauzer and two bearded dragons, playing soccer and tennis (and someday golf if her husband has his way,) hiking, meditating and reading science fiction books. Her education includes an MBA, many Psychology courses, and various Energy and Intuition training certificates.

She has enjoyed various fun *mom roles* in her spare time, including Girl Scout troop leader, PTA president, and youth soccer and basketball coach.

Learn more about Michele's practice at <u>beatreewithme.com</u>

A Last Message to Readers
What Can You Do With
Your Spiritual Gifts?

Thank you for reading this book and allowing us to share our spiritual lives with you. You being here is a huge validation for the spiritual experiences and the work that all the authors did to reach out with their personal stories for those who need to read them.

I love the word sisterhood. It reflects a divine feminine connection that lives among us, even if we don't think we're spiritual. Together, we are part of a connection that supports, loves, and holds space for those who need it. You know our stories. Now you can use your own story to support yourself in this precious life and share it with another woman who can choose to do the same.

I hope you resonated with something you read here, many somethings actually. There is always more to experience, and connecting to Spirit is yet another way to be supported and loved. The guidance is clear. Be true to yourself, even through the hard stuff, and your life will change. And the world will change accordingly.

You are powerful, and perhaps one day will call yourself a healer too. Find me when that happens; I will celebrate you with my whole heart. And I will ask you to tell me about your higher self; you will know her well.

Please review this book on Amazon. You will help us give other women the awareness to investigate, embrace, and fucking rock their spiritual voices.

Whether or not you ever see yourself as a healer, see yourself as being able to heal you.

Spirit and your higher self are waiting.

Dianna xo

My Wholehearted Thanks

Readers, you are the reason we are here, and I am grateful. You bring yourself to these pages and match with the messages left by our authors. It's a gift that you consider those messages relative to your own life and an even greater gift that you take them out into the world. Thank you for being here, being open, and helping another woman find her spiritual voice. We could not get to my goal of empowering every woman to use her voice more and live out loud without you.

Authors, how do I thank you? You are so gifted. I still sit in awe as I read your spiritual experiences over and over again, learning something new each time. You showed up when and where you were needed, guided to be here by your version of Spirit. I love that about you. You used your connection to Spirit to understand that the world needed to hear what you have to say, what needed to be voiced. Talk about backup! As a community, I saw love, respect, and holding space for people and things that needed it. That's who you are, recognizing the beauty and healing that is accessible through Spirit, through you. I am forever indebted and am proud to be a tiny part of your world.

Laura Di Franco showed up again as not just a badass publisher but also the author of our foreword, setting the stage for readers to embrace what would come after it. Her contribution of chapter five shows not just the depth of Laura's commitment to living from a spiritual place but also the joy that living there has brought her. I thank you for being my soul sister on this path of helping women find their voices. This woman is committed to offering healers the support they need to share their brave words while healing throughout the process. My work, business, and understanding of myself have changed exponentially since Laura came into my life. I will be forever grateful for her teachings, her friendship, and her mentorship. Thank you, Laura; three books in a year feels like a record to me!

Leesa Ellis, as our book designer for *Find Your Voice, Save Your Life 3* and the two other FYV SYL books in the series, you have arrived ready to rock your job and make sure that we are completely happy and satisfied with the important part of the book...its design. Thank you for knowing your stuff and helping me become clearer about mine.

Almir Gusić, our front cover artist, we have three books and now three amazing covers! I love a book that pops. You have responded to both the need for consistency and the need for newness and individuality. Your talent is great, and I am grateful to have you on our team!

Family and friends, I love you, and I am so grateful to have your support on this journey. This book may be a topic that is new and different for some of you, but you embraced it and me, just as I expected you would. Special shout out to Glen, Paige, and Whitney, family we are and will always be. Thank you for being there for me; your love and support mean more to me than you know.

Launch team. Wow. You stepped up when we needed you, taking time from your busy lives, offering words of encouragement, giving praise for this book. I am honored you've been a part of its launch that will help so many women find their spiritual voices. We truly could not have done this without you! When you look in the mirror tonight, remind yourself that you have helped other women immensely. Thank you, thank you, thank you!

Dianna Leeder is a Canadian author, podcaster, and owner of Crave More Life Coaching. She is a Certified Professional Co-Active Coach and an American Confidence Institute Certified Confidence Coach.

She has dedicated the last four decades to helping women find and confidently use their voices. A self-professed life-hack, Dianna uses her spiritual intuition to help women understand their highest self and become her in all their relationships, including the one with themselves.

Dianna believes the time of women's voices being silenced is over and, through her Voices Project, gives women a platform for healing through writing while offering their stories to support other voice quieted women. The result has been the *Find Your Voice, Save Your Life* three-book series.

Dianna lives in the Toronto, Canada area and shares her life with her hubby, two daughters and their partners, her future dog, and three super fun grandkids that she intentionally creates her relationships with. She's into travel and designing aligned spaces for herself and others.

Learn more about Dianna and her coaching programs at:

https://cravemorelife.com

Follow Dianna on Social

https://www.facebook.com/CraveMoreLife/
https://twitter.com/cravemorelife
https://www.instagram.com/diannaleeder/
https://www.pinterest.ca/cravemorelife

For resources and bonus gifts from Dianna, go to:

https://cravemorelife.com/findyourvoice

Join Dianna's free Facebook group Find Your Voice Women, for tips and talk on finding your voice with our authors

www.facebook.com/groups/findyourvoicewomen

To hire Dianna to speak to your women's group about

**FINDING YOUR VOICE, KICKING YOUR OWN ASS
or DEEP CORE MAPPING**

contact her at:

dianna@cravemorelife.com

Books by Dianna Leeder

Find Your Voice, Save Your Life

Find Your Voice, Save Your Life 2

Find Your Voice, Save Your Life 3

All available on Amazon

Are you ready to share your story?

To be considered as an author for our next
Find Your Voice, Save Your Life book project,
email Dianna at:

dianna@cravemorelife.com

Made in the USA
Columbia, SC
13 November 2021

48830986R00135